RETHINKING DEVELOPMENT

In Search of Humane Alternatives

RETHINKING DEVELOPMENT

In Search of Humane Alternatives

Rajni Kothari

1989

New Horizons Press
New York

First published in India by

Ajanta Publications (India),
1 UB, Jawahar Nagar, Delhi-110 007

North American edition published in 1989 by

New Horizons Press,
New York

ISBN 0-945257-18-X

NEW HORIZONS PRESS is an imprint of the **Council on International and Public Affairs, Inc.,** 777 United Nations Plaza, New York, NY 10017 (212/953-6920)

Typeset by Computype (a division of Third World Publications Pvt. Ltd.) 61 Madhuvan, Shakarpur, Delhi 110 092

This book is a tribute to

**E.F. Schumacher, Jayaprakash Narayan, Ahmed Ben Salah,
Indubhai Yajnik, M. Idris, Meera Mahadevan, Edward Goldsmith,
Bimla Bahuguna, Marc Nerfin and J.P. Naik**

*who have, in their diverse ways, tried to build forums
and movements that have sustained the struggles
for humane alternatives*

Contents

Preface

Development - deliverer of the people from poverty and injustice or Reason of State providing structures of security, exploitation and exclusive lifestyles to the ruling elites of the world? The theory and 'paradigm' of development still keep repeating the former, the practice and politics of development keep moving towards the latter. As the gap between the two keep widening, new and unanticipated conflicts keep piling up for which the modern State finds itself wholly ill-equipped and, desperataly looking for some way out, finds refuge in Technology with a capital T. This only further widens the gap, produces new upsurges of resistance and confrontation from below and drives the elites into their narrow fortresses that become increasingly isolated and remote from the real drives and throbbings of civil society. These elites are compelled to build walls of security around them for sheer survival and safeguarding of structures of domination, exploitation and exclusion that define the new content of the development project.

Meanwhile, however, the *idea* of development has sunk deep in people's minds as have the concepts of democracy, socialism and secularism, while the *project* of development, backed by powerful global, national and local interests, has produced a growing divide between the elites and the people. It is a divide that has affected the intellectual community as well and there has developed a raging debate on what should constitute the *agenda* of development. It is from this debate that the search for "alternatives in development" emerges and, along with a wide range of political activists and social movements, produces new stirrings of both intellectual and popular consciousness. This debate is still in mid-course, has given rise to new definitions of the agenda of national strivings and has increasingly become political.

As one involved in this debate I have written fairly extensively on this subject over the last twenty years. Like many others involved in this debate, I have engaged in it at different thresholds of the emerging reality - from the local/national to the international/global. And I have done this both at the level of attempts at theoretical comprehension and at the level of concrete propositions, ideas and proposals for creating a more humane future.

This book brings together a select range of these writings. In large part this selection is of a conceptual and theoretical kind. This is deliberate. For I am convinced that the fundamental crisis we face in coming to grips with the present human condition, and the role of the modern development project in it, is intellectual and, within the intellectual domain, philosophical and conceptual. The other major aim of this selection is to examine various points of entry into defining and re-defining the development problematique and the search for alternatives to the prevailing conceptualisation of it. Papers dealing with the environment, communications, political economy, the prospects of human freedom, the search for an alternative process of knowledge and the question of 'management of change' provide such entry points. With this in view I have also included emerging controversies between Third World intellectuals and those in the dominant centres of the world. A major and fairly comprehensive 'state of the art' paper on the development problematique has also been included to provide a perspective on the international debate on development. Finally, I have included my recent work on ethnicity which is taking me beyond the debate on development and into the deeper issues of relationship between civil society and the State on the one hand and the spiritual domain and civil society on the other. Together, the selection seeks to make sense of the emerging debate on development from the perspective of one who, while highly critical of the exclusion through homogenisation thrust of the modern development project, still considers it worthwhile not to reject in any wholesale manner the idea of development as such but to seek alternative conceptions of it with a view to building a humane future for all.

There are a large number of individuals and institutions that have enabled me to contribute to the debate on development and 'after development what?' Of the large number of cognate fellow travellers in the search for a more just and humane world, all of whom it is difficult to name, I should mention in particular my colleagues in the World Order Models Project, the journal *Alternatives*, the International Foundation for Development Alternatives (IFDA), the United Nations University, the Dag Hammerskjold Foundation, the World Federation for the Study of Future (WFSF), and of course, the family of institutions through which my work has flourished, namely the Centre for the Study of Developing Societies (CSDS), Lokayan, the Committee for Cultural Choices and Alternative Futures, the Research Foundation for Science, Technology and Natural Resources and the journal *Seminar* in India. The Indian Council of Social Science Research allowed me to support my own and others' work in alternatives. So have UNESCO, ESCAP, UNEP, the Pugwash Conferences, the office of the Director-General for Development of the United Naitons, and the Society for International Development (SID). Of the several individuals that have contributed to this collective effort, I should in particular mention Schumacher, Soedjatmoko, Marc Nerfin, Ashis Nandy, D.L. Sheth, Giri Deshingkar, Ramashray Roy, Sven Hamrell, Satish Arora, Romesh Thapar, J.P. Naik, T.N. Madan, Shiv Visvanathan, Vijai Pillai, Claude Alvares, K.G. Kannabiran, Vandana Shiva, Veena Das, Ivan Illich, Paulo Freire, Raimundo Panikkar, Raja Rao, A.K. Ramanujan, T.G. Vaidyanathan, Mary Kaldor, Eleanora Masini, K. Mushakoji, Janusz Golebiowski, Tamas Szentes, Jimoh Omo - Fadaka, Ponna Wignaraja, Kumar David, Lawrence Surendra, Herbert Feith, Kenneth and Elise Boulding, Richard Falk, Johan Galtung, Saul Mendlovitz, Yoshikazu Sakamoto, Ali Mazrui, Fouad Ajami, Yash Tandon, Nathan Shamuyarira, Jose Augustine Silva Michelena, Carlos Mallman, Gustavo Esteva, Orlando Fals-Borda, Andre Gunder Frank, Samir Amin, Immanuel Wallerstein, Ravinder Kumar, VIjay Pratap, Suresh Sharma, Raman Srivastava, M.P. Sinha, Harsh Sethi and Smitu Kothari. I am sure, even after this formidable listing, I have left out many who have in diverse ways contributed to the collective effort of which I have been part. Above all, Hansa, my wife, has, through her untheoretical unravelling of reality, made me so often aware of the deeper springs of human striving and of the mute and modest yet persistent 'voices'. So have Smitu, Miloon and Ashish, my three constant companions.

ORIGINS

This volume brings together a very select cross-section of my writings on alternatives in development. Most of them were written as part of the global debate on development and in the form of various inputs to the debate rather than as academic writings of the usual type.

The first essay on "A Conceptual Framework" was first written as a dissenting viewpoint on development strategies for the 25th Pugwash Conference on Science and World Affairs held in Madras in January 1976 and subsequently rewritten for the Indian Council of Social Science Research. "Groping towards an Alternatives Process of Knowledge", originally subtitled 'Beyond Interdisciplinarity', was written for the Division of Philosophy of UNESCO in 1981 when I was asked to draw the broader issues and intellectual challenges thrown up by our effort in building an appraoch to interdisciplinarity at the Centre for the Study of Developing Societies in Delhi. (It has remained unpublished so far.) The third essay on environment as an issue in defining the crisis in development theory was written for an ESCAP/UNEP conference on alternative development strategies held in Bangkok in August 1979. It was subsequently published in *Alternatives*, 5 (4), January 1980 and a shorter version of it, "Cultural Roots of Another Development", in IFDA *Dossier* in October 1979. The fourth essay viewing communications in the same way, was written for a Dag Hammerskjold/IFDA seminar on that theme held in Upsàlla in 1982 and published in *Development Dialogue* in November 1983. "Political Economy of Development" was a Kale Memorial Lecture delivered at the Gokhale Institute of Politics and Economics in September 1971. "On Eco-Imperialism", a rebuttal of Garrett Hardin's perspective on ecology, was written for *Alternatives*, 8 (3), September 1981.

Included in the next section are "The Development Problematique" written as a conceptual input into UNESCO's research programme on World Problems, in association with Vijai Pillai, my valued colleague

at the CSDS (unpublished so far). "Development Viewed Internationally" was prepared as a Report in my capacity as Rapporteur on the
United Naitons Symposium on International Development Strategy held
in Scheveningen, Holland in 1979. "Development Theory and the Third
World" is my report on a UNESCO meeting on State and Nation Building held in France in 1970, once again in my capacity as Rapporteur-
Generale. "Development and Freedom in Asia" was a lecture I delivered under the joint auspices of the United Naitons University, Sophia
University and the Kanagawa Prefectural Government in Japan, since
published in Michio Nagia (ed.), *Development in the Non-Western World*,
UNU, Tokyo, 1984.

Finally, "Ethnicity" is a paper written by me in pursuit of a new thre-
shold in my thinking on the human condition, under the asupices of
Lokayan and Asian Regional Exchange for New Alternatives (ARENA),
Hongkong, presented at a meeting at Lokayan in Delhi in 1988. It is to
be published later this year in a forthcoming book edited by Kumar
David of Sri Lanka. It is being included here with apologies to ARENA.

ON
ALTERNATIVE DEVELOPMENT

Alternatives in Development: A Conceptual Framework

In July 1955 Bertrand Russell and Albert Einstein issued a 'Manifesto' which, besides urging renunciation of war as a means of settling human disputes, also said that "There lies before us, if we choose, continual progress in happiness, knowledge and wisdom". The appeal, addressed mainly to the scientists of the world, ended thus:

> We appeal, as human beings, to human beings: remember your humanity, and forget the rest. If you can do so, the way lies open to a new Paradise; if you cannot, there lies before you the risk of universal death.

Thirty-three years later, the promise of continual progress and the way to a new Paradise does not seem so clear. Indeed, it seems more and more remote and, short of some basic rethinking on the very premises on which the modern industrial civilisation has been based, it seems more impossible of realisation than ever.

This is not just because a number of wars have been waged since 1955, nor even because the stockpiling of deadly armaments has gone on unabated and has greatly proliferated. This is no doubt a very important reason why human progress has been held up or distorted and diverted into wrong channels. But I submit that there is another and perhaps more basic reason.

Diagnosis

This lies in modern man's approach to science and technology. The very technology that has produced more and more deadly armaments has also produced a more and more wasteful civilisation in the very centres where modern science and technology have flourished and has, in consequence of this, given rise to a world structure that has become increasingly inequitous and conflict-ridden, in the process rendering millions of human beings—including in the industrial centres—obsolescent and redundant.

The centres where modern science and technology have ushered in wasteful ways of human consumption are not limited to the rich, highly industrialised, 'developed' North; they are also to be found in the poorer, less industrialised, 'underdeveloped' South. Domination of the nations of the South by those of the North is accompanied by domination of large masses of the people by westernised elites which are more closely tied to the metropolitan centres of the world than to their own peoples.

The problem of persisting 'underdevelopment' and increasing gaps between the rich and the poor nations—and, as a reflection thereof, between the rich and the poor in the poorer nations—have been sought to be explained by reference to a number of misleading diagnoses—the increase in population size, lack of motivation among the people of backward lands, decline in 'aid' from the rich nations, transfer of resources from development to defence in the poor nations, regional, linguistic and ethnic divisions in the latter, and so forth. None of these, however, seem to us basic or even important. They are either (like population growth) symptoms of more basic causes or (like the alleged lack of motivation among the poor) wholly misleading and wrong, arising from the prejudices of scientists and social scientists and the search for alibis by people overcome by guilt but not willing to accept reponsibility for basic injustices in the world.

The result is that even the political and intellectual elites of the countries of the Third World remain divided, both within each of them and between them severally. These countries have failed to exert themselves at regional and world levels, and have also failed to pursue policies within their own countries that are called for by their socio-economic, demographic and cultural conditions which happen to be quite different from the conditions that obtained in the developed nations during their respective phase of development. Instead, they (or most of them) are found to indulge in a rhetoric of confrontation, both at global and at domestic levels, and to seek alibis for their failures to restructure a world in which they happen to be in a majority. Thanks largely to the inimical consequences of modern science and technology, the dominant economic model that has resulted from it and has been accepted almost universally, and the politico-philosophical underpinnings of this model by a 'theory of progress' that had stemmed from the presupposition of infinite progression of resources that could become universally and equitably available, the world is being ruled by elites that are incapable of handling the problems confronting it.

But the basic shortcoming underlying all this is intellectual: if the world is 'structured' in a certain way it is because the thinking that has dominated the world for the last hundred years—and more—has been faulty. These have been the years that have been dominated by the idea of a uniform end product to be achieved by all societies—a state of urban, industrial affluence, managed by experts at the top running secular affairs through a 'rational' bureaucracy, and backed by a capital intensive technology. Even today—despite decades of misery and exploitation engendered by this model—the notion of catching up with those who are seen to be more 'developed' and along the same course continues with uncommon persistence. To no small extent this persistence —which is based more on institutionalised interests of a few powerful people than on conscious deliberation by the large majority—accounts for the general scenario of inequity within societies and a state of myopic dependence between them.

Towards a Concept of Alternatives

It is the slow realisation of this larger context of growing misery and destitution in the world that provides the background and rationale for the concept of *alternatives*. Most ideas take time in fructifying as general concepts capable of attracting the minds of men. There has to be a certain threshold of collective awareness, normally of a deep sense of discontent with the prevailing state of affairs, before such fructification takes place. In the past few years this threshold has been reached for the concept of alternatives and the various associated thought processes and normative perspectives that go with it. And as with earlier conceptual breakthroughs, the idea of alternatives, implying 'alternatives to what is' signifies a major dissatisfaction with both the existing state of *affairs* and the existing state of *analytics*—in short, with the existing paradigms of both science and politics. A feeling of fundamental dissonance between not only what is and what ought to be but also between what is and and what can be (if only human agencies intervened decisively) underlies the recent interest in seeking out alternative ways of attending to human problems. It implies two considerations: that the world is becoming too uniform, too standardised, too dominated by a single conception of life and its meaning, with little scope for other available cultural and historical propensities and potentialities; and that such domination of a single conception has led to political and cultural domination by a single region of the world over all the others.

The problem posed by the concept of alternatives is at once philosophical in respect of the validity of diverse worldviews and theoretical paradigms, and practical in respect of the struggle for survival and development of literally billions of human beings. It questions both the claim to universality of a model of life by virtue of its sheer dominance and the notion of determinacy of the historical or evolutionary process for all time to come. Instead, it affirms the validity of human intervention in the historicial process, and of this intervention taking different forms based on different perspectives on both the ends of life and the problems that life poses when faced by different conditions.

Every few hundred years (in recent times, every few decades) man is faced by a changed reality when ealier models and institutional structures—as well as conceptual paradigms and their underlying metaphysics—which were evolved to meet a different kind of reality are found not to work any longer. The need is to seek for alternatives to meet new situations.

Methodological Issues

This implies two crucial considerations. First, if the search for alternatives is not to be an end in itself (fulfilling some aestheic desire for change) but related to real needs, it is necessary that the utility and worth of various alternatives be measured by reference to some criteria of values which provide a unifying scheme of human experience and which can judge between alternative perspectives, models and policies; and with the help of which it is possible to pronounce judgement on which alternative is better suited to which needs. Second, if this is the methodology of pursuing the choice of alternatives, then surely while at any point of time and space there can be only one alternative, it may still be possible to have different alternatives for different configurations of space at a single point of time or at different points of time and history in the same place. The two considerations—of choice and coherence—must be pursued together. To the extent that human experience is to be guided by some unity of meaning and purpose, this would entail that, depending upon agreement on value criteria, one alternative is to be preferred to many others, at any rate in the overall model of human arrangements. And yet there should be scope for diversities in the details of these arrangements.

Thus, for example, to the extent that the capitalist mode of production and the social system based on it were found to be unsatisfactory, the socialist alternative that was proposed in the last century and realised in this century represented a unified concept. Similarly, as the Third World emerged as a coherent human expeience for which neither capitalism nor State socialism were found satisfactory, a third alternative was called for and is currently being evolved through intense deliberation and debate—as a common alternative to both the first and the second worlds. Meanwhile, with the growing realisation of the homogenising tendency of the modern State and the elite that controls it, there has emerged the necessity of insisting on further differentiations within all these three worlds. Taken together, these represent a series of alternatives within the search for one major theoretical alternative to existing arrangements.

Pitfalls

It is necessary to stress this if one is not to be lost in two familiar pitfalls in recent thinking. One is the view that we must somehow find an alternative to the 'western model', expressed as a reaction to the excesses of the western model, at times borne out of animus towards it, often from within western academic and intellectual circles, and then echoed elsewhere. While such a reaction is understandable and constitutes an important step in the growth of consciousness and knowledge, it also tends to distort the response by making it largely negative and without any real direction towards a genuine alternative.

The second pitfall is much larger than the first and has an even greater intellectual pedigree. This is the view based on cultural relativism, namely, that each and every society must evolve its own alternative and that the alternatives before man in society are infinite. I believe that every major new human experience calls for a new theoretical response, different from all earlier ones: a new theoretical paradigm is not just a mental construct but a response to a new empirical reality. But while this is so—and all assertions of universality for one particular model of life must be resisted on grounds of their being both arrogant and obscurantist—it is also the case that there is some unity underlying diversities. This is so in two respects, especially in the modern age.

First, the different societies one talks of are interrelated and the causes underlying the problems they face are at least in part to be found in these interrelationships. Second, there is a unity in the flow of history which gives it some determinacy, no doubt with a lot of scope for intervention, for history is no more than a sum total of human interventions, but not without limits. To ask for a different alternative for each micro situation without reference to the basic unity provided by both the interrelations in which different units stand and the determinacies of the historical process would be to ask for infinite fragmentation (which will not stop at national frontiers and will be sought by regions, ethnic groups, and communities within each nation as well). Any search for alternatives that does not seek to foster a new and better unity for all is liable to lead to disintegration and chaos. I think it is necessary to reject chaos as a preferred alternative for civil society.

The Global Context

That brings me to my last theoretical point. The current search for alternatives is not, or ought not to be, simply because the techno-economic model that dominates current thinking in the other two worlds is inadequate for the Third World. It needs to be said that the model is also inadequate for the other two worlds. And it needs to be said that a crucial component of the model is provided by a certain structure of international relations and a set of global distributions and control mechanisms. It is true that the model that dominates the world today is far more inimical to the countries and human beings of the Third World (barring the upper classes everywhere) than to those in the other two worlds. But it is still a *world* model and has to be attacked as such. The importance of an alternative approach to technology, for instance, may be more immediate for the overpopulated and capital-scarce countries of the Third World but it has relevance for the overabundant and heavily polluted cities of the other two worlds as well, though clearly not in the same manner, for after all one is dealing with quite different situations. The same is true of alternatives in energy, education, public health, urbanisation, communication and so forth.

The notion of alternatives as a new intellectual endeavour, involving both theory and action necessitates that it presents not a tangential effort but one that is integral to the strivings of the human species as a whole—indeed to creation as a whole. We ought to value scope for diversity within such striving and respect the autonomy and dignity of diverse entities and to that extent stress the pluralist notion of *alternatives*. But it is at the same time necessary to realise that at any one point of major historical change one is seeking out a new *alternative* which gives unity to the plurality and enables comprehension of each as part of an overall scheme of things. Failure to bear the latter in mind would be both ahistorical and lead to an accent on reformism for its own sake without a sense of wider purpose that provides unity and meaning to individual efforts.

The concept of alternatives, then, is not to be limited just to development policies; it should entail visions about society and polity, and it should do this in the context of the evolution of the human community as a whole. When available models are found wanting and a new alternative is called forth, this applies not just to social and economic arrangements within a given society, but to the ordering of the world as a whole. Alternatives is a conception not just in the theory of development. It entails a model of (and a perspective for) world order and the transformations entailed for such a world order. It is an exercise in values and their realisation at various levels of reality, always taking account of cultural diversities but also of the unities that inform these diversities. It is not just a different kind of model for China or India or Tanzania (or Brazil or Chile) that one is seeking out though no doubt these and other models provide a very large scope for learning and criticism and action. One is also concerned about the making of a different kind of world conceived as a set of interrelationships. Without seeking to alter these interrelationships the effort to alter individual societies is not likely to get very far. China is a case in point.

The philosophical perspective that should guide us in such a setting should steer clear of both imperialist claims to universality and the normless striving for relativity: it should affirm both the principle of *autonomy* of each entity (human as well as social) to seek out its own path to self-realisation and the principle of *integration* of all such entities in a common framework of interrelationships based on agreed values. The world as it is at present constituted violates both autonomy and integration as principles informing human arrangements. It is a world based, instead, on a framework of dominance that works through endless fragmentation and tensions, one that relies heavily on instruments of violence and institutions of inequity. It is only by seeking a new structure of the world, and as a basis thereof, a new form of technology and a new ethic of individual and group behaviour that are in consonance with the changed conditions of our times, that we shall be able to perceive the true intertwining of happiness, knowledge and wisdom and to restrain man from overstretching his rationality and undermining his religiosity.

Perspective on Alternative Development Strategies

Having laid out a general theory of 'alternatives in development', I shall now try to spell out a broad framework of development strategies for our time, especially for a country like India, though large parts of the framework have relevance beyond India. Briefly, three major aspects of development strategy and the need for an optimal relationship between them, may be proposed. These are:

1. Lifestyles. While retaining a good deal of diversity of a cultural and individual kind, there is need to have a consensus on such matters as desirable and undesirable consumption standards, use and distribution of resources for the gratification of needs, and norms for minima and maxima in incomes and wealth.

2. Organisation of Space. There is a need to stop thinking of 'rural' and 'urban' as separate sets of entities and to think of them as a continuing structure of city, town and countryside, of agriculture and industry, of hinterland and metropolis. Countries like India have a unique

opportunity to develop a social continuum in which, while the romantic utopian dream of village self-sufficiency may be left behind (tnere should be no regret about this for such a system had many negative features), we may also be able to avoid the scenario of huge metropoles draining the resources of the countryside in a parasitic manner. The scenario best suited to us—and to civilised life—is one in which the country is studded by a few thousand localities (regions), each clustering around a medium-size town, sharing in its amenities and its economy in a relatively egalitarian manner, in which all strata of society gain from the benefits of entering the modern age but avoid the ills of post-modern consumer societies that are prisoners of highly concentrated production complexes.

3. Production System and Technology. Such a structuring of space will need to be supported by a corresponding continuum of productive orientations and technology relevant to each of them. The strategy that we shall have to evolve will need to be integral to the development of the country as a whole—where both production and administration are decentralised to medium-sized towns and their rural hinterlands, where city growth rates are arrested from becoming grotesque, where employment opportunities in agriculture (which have some natural limits) are supplemented by employment in small and widely diffused industries, where educational institutions are located close to jobs and restructured away from the present emphasis on university degrees, where health facilities are not limited to the privileged, and where the economy derives its strength from the purchasing power of the great numbers of the people and not from the expansion of middle-class consumer industries and their 'export orientation'. Implied in such a restructuring of rural-urban and agricultural-industrial relations is a new techno-economic model for our society which will enable us to reach the goals set out by us in the Directive Principles of the Constitution and often elaborated since. Rural development must be conceived as part and parcel of this model as a whole, a model in which we talk less of rural development in our usual segmental fashion and more of development of individuals and communities—of all of them, irrespective of distinctions of locale or class. It is only in this overall context that 'rural development' will make sense.

Scenario for the Future

It is from an optimal interrelationship of the above three parameters that our design for the future emerges. It has to be a comprehensive design, of which economic development becomes an integral and a crucial part. I give below the essential components of such a design.

Principal Focus

The prime concern of economic policy for a just social order ought to be to generate employment that is able to absorb at least the new additions to the adult population, and where there is a substantial backlog of unemployment and underemployment, to absorb that as well. The major source of injustice today is to be found not so much in a condition of general scarcity as in the fact of the diminishing marginal utility of men and women, in the fact that millions of people find themselves idle and useless, often in their very prime.

Social Continuum

The crux of such a combination of policies designed to raise employment and alleviate mass poverty is to put agricultural and rural development at the core of public policy. But there is a counterpart to this approach in the area of urban development and industrial policy as well. Apart from heavy industries, which require large capital inputs and centralised organisation, industrial development should be employment-oriented as much as possible, should produce goods that are needed by broad strata of the population rather than by a small middle class, and should be widely dispersed over the country so that the employment that it generates benefits all areas rather than a few cities or regions as is the case today. Regional disparities constitute a crucial—and visible—dimension of social injustice. Most of the favoured regions are those with large urban centres.

Socially, this means that the present duality of city and countryside must give place to a continuum in which agriculture regenerates the villages; small-scale and medium industries are located in the towns; and large-scale industries that necessitate heavy inputs of capital and high technical efficiency are located in the cites. As such a fusion between industry and agriculture takes place, further intermediate links in this continuum—rural social structures in towns, urban amenities in villages—will develop, thus combining the best traditions of both rural and urban life and producing a composite and integrated culture.

My preferred world should be not one made of millions of self-contained villages but, rather, one of thousands of small nucleating towns towards which the rural landscape gravitates, thus doing away with both the present duality of metropolitan and rural cultures, limiting the large size and concentrated location to just the industries that cannot do without them, while at the same time enlarging the size and horizon of rural communities, and providing them with the necessary infrastructure of welfare and communication facilities. Such a spatial structure—supported by a decentralised structure of community decision-making, as argued below—would provide the necessary framework for the techno-economic alternative to the present dualist model of city *versus* countryside.

Policy on Education

It is not simply by altering the economic basis of rural-urban relationships that a more just social order will be created. We also need to alter the cultural underpinnings of the present patterns of dominance and disparity. An important source of the sharp duality of lifestyles and living standards found in most poor countries is the educational system, the aim of which continues to be to produce colonial type gentlemen, disoriented from the large society and constituting a class apart.

In most ex-colonial countries, formal education was initially meant to produce an elite, mainly to fill the ranks of the bureaucracy, the law-and-order establishment, and the technical positions in public administration and private enterprise. This orientation still persists in spite of the achievement of independence and in spite of the political elite's commitment to democratic and socialistic ideals. Education, far more than property or income, is the basis of privilege in our society.

Meanwhile, a majority of the population continues to be illiterate and unskilled, while the ranks of the highly educated in the urban areas keep swelling. Studies in this area suggest that whereas expansion of literacy and primary education produces very rich and rapid dividends, after a point higher education turns out to be counterproductive. Acquisition of a minimum educational level greatly raises a person's skills and his capacity to enter the employment market; it also raises his sense of potential achievement and his ability to relate to the outside world, his sense of political efficacy, and his general self-confidence and sense of dignity. In contrast, an undiscriminating expansion of higher education beyond the absorptive capacity of the economy produces an alienated class that is unable to relate meaningfully to the rest of society,[1] that rapidly inhabits various levels of the bureaucracy, making it increasingly inefficient and insensitive to the needs of the people and, with growing

---

1. I do not share the diagnosis that the main fault in higher education in Third World countries is that universities are far too oriented to liberal arts and general science training and do not give adequate attention to technical education. In my view, the universities (perhaps everywhere) have gone too far in accommodating this view and have in the process lost their character. It is the function of a university to train the minds of its members and provide basic analytical skills for facing concrete problems in life. Rather, the fault lies in the fact that universities are churning out engineers and technicians, economists and social scientists who are basically illiterate and who are taught from obsolete texts dumped by transnational publishers on to the neo-colonial markets. Graduates come out of these mass factories wholly unprepared for dealing with the problems they are likely to encounter in their work.

unemployment in its ranks, loses self-respect and becomes aggressive.

This polarisation between a large mass of illiterate and totally uns-killed and hence unemployed people on the one hand, and a class of people who are overeducated and hence also unemployed on the other, is a natural result of the hiatus between the elite and the people—and between the parasitic cities and a depressed countryside—discussed ear-lier. We must alter this condition by a major allocation of resources to mass-literacy, by giving special attention to the economically weak and socially handicapped strata, whose major avenue of mobility seems to be education,[2] and by a re-orientation of the job market so that employment within a wide spectrum of non-technical jobs is available to those without college degrees, thus deflating the importance of higher education and the disparities that result from insistence on degrees.

It is necessary to emphasise strongly the importance of widespread literacy in generating massive social and economic transformation. Pov-erty is, more than anything else, a cultural condition and if poverty breeds poverty and perpetuates itself, it is because it is located in a par-ticular cultural milieu—a milieu of ignorance, isolation, segregation and an extremely low self-image of the poorer classes, who suffer exploi-tation without protest and indeed consider exploitation to be the nat-ural state of affairs. This situation cannot be changed except by a basic cultural attack. And the primary precondition for this is literacy and minimum education. This point cannot be over-emphasised and needs to be expressed continuously and loudly.

Finally, higher education itself needs to be reoriented, by restricting university education to its logical role—to provide basic grounding in the main sources of theoretical knowledge. Some commentators appear to dismiss higher education (and institutionalised education generally) as largely unnecessary. I do not share this view. There is urgent need for a very large number of doctors, engineers, geologists, architects, designers, managers, even economists and sociologists. What is at fault is not their availability but their placement, their location. Most of them are unwilling to go where the real jobs are, the institutions where they learn are unwilling to train them for employment in local conditions, and the leadership is unwilling to tell them candidly about their duties

---

2. One of the unfortunate consequences of the recent attack on schools and education in some Third World countries is that upper-class elites that have already cornered edu-cational resources and occupy bureaucratic and professional positions (and have sent their own children abroad for studies) have been busy pruning down educational programmes—just at a time when such programmes were beginning to spread to backward regions and lower classes. Though the motivation of its authors is clearly different, the 'de-schooling' thesis poses the same danger as the 'limits to growth' thesis.

and their responsibilities. There is need to look upon education as a political process, upon the attainment of a degree or diploma as a social good that must be capable of being socially used, and upon the relationship between educational output and available work as part of a conscious plan of development. Higher education, instead of becoming an instrument of class privilege and exploitation and a source of disparities, must be made an integrator of human resources and human needs.

There is also need to undertake a major review of the whole institutional approach that has accompanied the modern view of education: classroom-based, bookish, graded and located in large campuses in large cities. This approach needs to be replaced by a closer relationship between education and work—including intellectual work, where education is sought for scientific and literary pursuits—and by bridging the gap that divides the location of one from the location of the other. City-based education must be largely for city people. For others, schools and other institutions must go where the people are, not the other way around. Unless these various aspects of the educational scene are approached with some perspective on the changing social reality, it is difficult to see how the deep cultural barriers that divide different classes and accentuate economic disparities can be overcome. Education can be made to bridge these gaps or to accentuate them. The need is to move from the latter orientation to the former.[3]

There is need to give special attention to the education of women. In our country, as in most parts of the Third World, women are less educated than men and within the depressed social strata and ethnic minorities the gap is even more pronounced. Meanwhile, the daughters of the rich are flocking to the universities and some of them are leading women's liberation movements (imitating their conterparts in affluent countries), which in our country means the liberation of the privileged. These gaps in education among women and between them and men are an important source of the persisting duality of cultures, economic levels and consumption standards, the latter more often than not being a direct function of the perennial shopping to which the educated women are so addicted. These differences also account for the wide divergences in the way the children of the rich and the poor are brought up, thus perpetuating sharp disparities for generations to come.

---

3. There are practices outside the educational sphere that contribute to the inequitable role of education. One is the wage and salary structure that obtains in society: the enormous gap between the top and bottom salary scales, the wide disparity between payments in the private and public sectors (the former being very high), and similar gaps between urban and rural jobs, even of the same type (the rural being underpaid). These differences provide a powerful rationale for prescribing higher (and foreign) degrees for the better-paying jobs, something that the poor and the weak can never afford.

Lack of education of women is an important cause of the exploitation of women, which is a marked characteristic of our society (though in a way that is quite different from that in western countries). The main basis of this exploitation is economic and it is found at its worst in the lower classes and among the scheduled castes—but most of all for women. As a matter of social policy there is need to pay special attention to raising the educational levels of women and mothers from the poor, under-privileged and conservative[4] strata of society in order to achieve a major spin-off process of social reconstruction.

The Ethic of Consumption

Even more fundamental than the gaps in the literary culture are the gaps in the material culture that divide the urbanised upper and middle classes from the people. Perhaps the most important and glaring contrast of today is caused by the extraordinary consumption levels and material possessions of the richer and high-status groups, following almost *in toto* the standards set by the high-consumption societies. The lust for things and for more and more things has become so myopic that it has given rise to all kinds of unethical practices, chief among these being a great deal of corruption among public officials and a thriving black-money economy that is sustained by the availability of a large array of consumer goods.

Apart from the vulgarity of such ostentatious living in a society characterised by massive poverty and malnutrition and apart from the creeping corruption to which it gives rise, such standards of consumption also undermine the whole fabric of economic policy. If a massive programme of employment and social welfare is to be generated, a high rate of savings and capital accumulation will be necessary. This implies a high rate of savings among those with large incomes as well as restraint on salary and wage increases among the employed classes, so that resources can be transferred to employing the unemployed (in a poor country to be employed is itself a privilege) and raising income levels of the poorly employed and the underemployed.[5]

---

4. Apart from the poor and the underprivileged, there are specific ethnic groups in which women are assigned a subsidiary status, and this condition is perpetuated by wide gaps between men and women in their access to cultural institutions, economic opportunities and political movements. Educational deprivation contributes substantially to this condition. Thus, both the general standing of the Muslim masses (as distinct, of course, from the small urbanised and educated elite) and the status of women among the Muslims have suffered from the low educational standards of the women.

5. Underemployment is even more of a curse than unemployment. After all, the choice of remaining unemployed is not available to the really poor, who must take whatever comes, however little, intermittent or degrading. For a fuller discussion, see my 'Political Economy of Employment', *Social Change* (New Delhi), 3(3), September 1973.

All of this calls for an *ethic of consumption* that discourages ostentatious living, cuts down the production and consumption of non-essential items and shifts production priorities towards fulfilling the needs of the poor. It is, of course, necessary to encourage saving among the peasantry, the lower-middle classes and even the labouring classes as is often advocated. But this will be an impossible task unless the pace-setters of society themselves adopt a consumption ethic that encourages austerity and reduces the gap in material culture between the different classes. Gandhi put his finger on the most crucial dimension of moving towards a just social order when he called for a *limitaton of wants* and warned his countrymen against falling prey to an industrial machine that not only reduces a majority of men to labouring slaves but also dictates what and how they should eat, wear, dress, and house. Today his insights are even more relevant than when he lived. If there is to be an end to exploitation and inequity in our society, the present norm of a high-consumption ethic must give place to one that both meets the minimum needs of all men and limits the needless expansion of wants that have no relationship to the basic requirements of body and mind.

The Nature of Production

Built into such an ethic of consumption is also an ethic of production that is critical to the achievement of justice in society. The current notions of social justice derive from a concept of economic equality that is essentially distributive. It is not surprising, therefore, that both theoretical understanding and empirical evidence have underlined the need for first expanding the cake and then distributing it. Part of the problem is that both production and distribution are thought of in terms in which the mass of the people are reduced to a position of subjects and onlookers. An economic ethic that seeks to meet the consumption needs of all while limiting the flow of inessential commodities involves a simultaneous increase in the incomes of the poor and the output of goods that they will need to buy with those incomes. This means that instead of conceiving production and consumption as two separate activities, one aims at an economic system that (to echo Gandhi) not only produces for the mass of the people but one in which the mass of the people are also the producers.

As with all visions, perhaps this, too, is an ideal. All that one can hope to initiate is a movement towards such a state. In practical terms this calls for a location policy that, while permitting large-scale organisation where it is unavoidable, will encourage a small-scale, labour-intensive, decentralised pattern of industrial development. Similarly, the market economist's retrogressive concept of 'effective demand' (that only the needs that are backed by the existing distribution of purchasing power are worth producing for) will have to give place to a concept of *need-effectiveness,* so that the real needs of the people as a whole determine what goes into the package of production. A combination of such a production system and the consumption ethic outlined above will lead to a climate in which progress towards dispersal and decentralisation of economic power becomes possible. As this happens, the orientation to social justice will become less technocratic and become more political and thus capable of initiatives from below.

Social Minima

Major casualties of the present structure of consumption and production are the large numbers of people in poor countries who suffer from acute malnutrition and the resulting physical and mental deficiencies. Their numbers are likely to increase in the next few decades. While demographers and bureaucrats are busy propagating birth-control measures to ward off an 'explosion' some time in the next century, inadequate attention is being paid to the problem of enabling those who are already born and who will be born in the next two decades or so to live a normal life and put in sustained work for their livelihood.

The picture of the culture of poverty that emerges from various studies is highly depressing: it is a picture of large families exhibiting physical and psychic abnormality, incapacity for sustained work even for a few hours, a pronounced inferiority complex, a tendency to deal with patterns of exploitation and coercion by directing them inward and against their own dependants, and a vicious cycle of parents inducting children into these characteristics of deprivation and degradation, turning them into the same kind of adults when they grow up, and thus almost *ad infinitum.* We must give top priority to a programme providing basic health care (with more accent on preventive health services) and an adequate supply of protein and other nutrients to the poor and especially to their children, drawing especially on the accumulated wisdom of both traditional society but also on relevant segments of new researches in the bio-medical sciences.

Here it is essential to stress a special advantage that Third World countries like ours have in charting a distinctive course of development in which the human cost that has accompanied economic growth in other societies can be avoided. Given our advantage in the low cost of trained manpower and the considerable plurality of knowledge systems, it is possible to spread the basic essentials of education and health over the whole country, to all classes of people and in a short time through concentrated and devoted effort. This will lay a surer basis for all-round and countinuous development than all the investments made in high technology, urbanisation, mass media development and the other appendages of 'modernity'. Health and education are the essential pre-requisites of social and economic mobilisation for sustained develop-ment, for the so-called 'take-off'. Once such a basis is laid, nothing can prevent a society from moving forward. What is more, it will be a pro-cess of development that will produce far fewer disparities and less inequity than is the case when the sole emphasis is on economic growth in aggregate terms without regard to the cultural framework in which it takes place.

Minima and Maxima

The above analysis provides the elements of an alternative model. The objective of development, should be to achieve minimum condi-tions of material welfare for all the people, the *minima* to be defined according to local conditions and norms, but all of them providing at the least a package of minimum items of human necessity such as food, clothing, shelter and nutritional needs to children and mothers in par-ticular, and socially approved minima of health, education, drinking water and public transportation for all. The extent to which these minima should be translated into personal or family incomes or combined with social welfare programmes will depend on local conditions and the nature of the future political system. But it should not be difficult for any system to work out a policy on essential minima for all as a basic component of development planning.

A policy of minima entails a policy of *maxima*. Indeed, without the latter the former is, in practice, impossible to realise in reasonable time. Also, beyond a certain point, incomes ought not to be allowed to grow nor human wants allowed to be artifically stimulated by the aggressive salesmanship pf modern industry or the demonstration effects from the rich capitalist countries. There are two reasons for this limitation, one which is relative and the other absolute. No one has a right to amass more and more income and riches when large sections of population live below subsistence standards. Also, it is morally undesirable to go beyond a certain level of fulfilment of human needs. For an unlimited gratification of wants leads to individual decay and social disharmony, an unnecessary destruction of natural resources, a fouling of the human environment, and thus a bartering away of the health and happiness of future generations for the present pleasure and lust of a few. Hence my emphasis on 'limitation of wants' as a necessary principle of my preferred world.

There should be a reasonable *scale* connecting the minima and maxima, that is to say, an admissible ratio between the two, thus limiting disparities and enabling society to implement the principles of natural justice. Entailed in the norm of such a scale is the further norm of *transfer* of surplus incomes and wealth above the maximum to those who have not yet reached the minimum.

Participation

Implicit in my preferred model for social and economic justice are also a number of other issues. The norms of minima and maxima are not mere economic formulations; they are part of a certain conception of a good and desirable life. Not only should an individual be entitled to a minimum standard of living; he should also be able to participate actively (though he ought not to be forced to do so) in the way things are produced and decisions are made. It is not just a minimum wage that one thinks of here in some kind of contractual relationship, alienated from the work process and the total scheme of ownership, production and distribution of the means of livelihood. Rather, one thinks of an apparatus that men and women themselves control and find meaningful and from which they derive a sense of personal power and significance. Furthermore, to the extent that economic activity is managed and mediated by political and administrative agencies, the whole problem of effective participation in decision-making, at the desirable level and in optimum units, becomes real. Without such participation the economic aims may indeed be difficult to achieve.

There is also the need to prevent the economic process, and what is now sometimes tellingly called the 'industrial-bureaucratic complex' of modern society, from taking on a will of its own and destroying every other value in its inexorable march. In other words, as the values of a participatory democracy and of non-violence in man's relations to man and to the environment are joined with the values of individual autonomy and social justice, it may well be that we should ask ourselves equally basic questions about the kind of institutional superstructure that we want to build. Three major aspects of this issue are (a) the rural-urban structure of the economy, (b) the territorial structure of the State, and (c) the participatory structure of the polity. As we consider these aspects, it will become clear that the current model of modernisation is not conducive to our goals; that the norm of a necessary shift from a predominantly rural to a predominantly urban structure based on large-scale industrialisation may not be the best thing that human intelligence has devised; and that urban metropolitan life, far from being a 'civilising' instrument, may turn into a structure of manipulation, exploitation and destruction of the very properties of man's natural environment that are essential to human survival.

Similarly, we may also question the norms of centralised government, large-sized States and big bureaucracies as necessary instruments
of national integration and political accountability; and as we question
these, we may begin to answer with greater clarity the problems raised
about local autonomy, about decentralisation of functions, powers,
resources and talents, and about the optimum size for genuine participation of the people. Perhaps there is something to be gained in the
very short run from large-scale enterprises, modern communication
media and centrally planned initiatives, although the real issue here is
less of scale than of control. But it is also necessary not to close all options
for the generations to come concerning the quality of life they would
like to have. As the prospects of the future are vitally affected by what
is done in the present—it is no longer possible to think in terms of just
a few months or even a few years ahead—it is a matter of considerable
responsibility that these various consequences of the present are borne
in mind.

It is necessary to consider here a widespread belief that rapid development cannot be carried out in a participatory framework, that only
a determined and authoritarian elite can bring it about, that this indeed
is the lesson of contemporary history. My answer to such a position is
that it mistakes appearance for reality, that the issue is not one of choice
between liberal democracy dominated by machine politics and State
socialism in which a small bureaucratic elite seeks to perpetuate itself,
but that both these systems are authoritarian as far as the majority of
the people are concerned (there is far greater similarity between the two
than appears at first sight), and that the real issue relates to the classic
predicament of political life, namely, the relationship between those in
power and those out of power, between the government and the people.
Seen in this light it is not surprising that the demand for authoritarianism has normally come from members of the privileged classes (the
businessmen, the bureaucrats, the technocrats), often reinforced by the
analyses and prescriptions of foreigners.[6]

My model of a participatory system is not conceived in terms of simple
political reforms. Rather, it is expressed in a number of sectors: concerning economic organisation and its governance, the nature of education, location of work and enterprise, choice of technology, size of units
(economic, political, demographic, communications) and the nature of

---

6. For a detailed consideration of these somewhat basic issues on the relationship
between modes of governance and the condition of the people, see the first book in this
series, *State Against D mocracy· In Search of Humane Governance.*

work. Participation is not some process of involving everyone and reducing all to a common denominator. Rather, it consists in evolving institutional structures from which diverse individuals get a sense of dignity and self-respect, as beings that are able to determine their own destinies. (Poverty and inequality are themselves reflections not just of prevailing relations of production but rather of structures and values that deny dignity to the human being.)

Nor is my thinking on participation conceived in terms of establishing idyllic and isolated small communities. My conception (outlined above) of a social and spatial continuum goes against such a utopia. I am also convinced that, given the numbers of human beings we have to deal with, such a utopia is no longer feasible. My concern, rather, is that structures at various levels and of various sizes imbibe the value of participation as integral to my model of a just society and my conception of the autonomy and dignity of all human beings. It is only through such an integrated view of the various components of such a model that an alternative political perspective can emerge and that policy issues can be discussed in a meaningful manner.

It would be folly, however, to look upon such a perspective as in any way smooth sailing on some neat course. Nothing is more difficult to realise than change in the social framework of politics—except for the worse. Every move on such a course needs to be fought for, by organising for it and building sustained pressures from below in the form of social and intellectual movements. And it is, of course, clear that these will need to be conceived and carried out in not one but many spheres, at not one but many levels. But I am firmly convinced that it is only on the basis of a clear acceptance of a decentralised and highly participatory democratic structure that social justice can be realised.

These, then, are the issues that arise when specific problems of economic strategy, political structure, educational policy and the reconstruction of the human space are considered from the integrated perspective provided by a set of values and the criteria that follow from it. Involved in such an approach is what may be called a design for living in which reason, compassion and a regard for the equal worth of all men and women are joined in the cultivation of a truly civilised life. And as we do this, the distinctions between economic and political issues disappear and we begin to see the real linkages that underlie any effort to produce a better world. My conception of alternative strategies entails such a comprehensive perspective on the future.

2

Towards an Alternative Process of Knowledge

A Perspective On Interdisciplinarity

Interdisciplinarity is still a pious hope, one of those values that continues to elude scholarly endeavour. To say this is not to belittle the importance of debates or publications on this concept—some of the most important human values and concepts happen to elude scientific effort—as to indicate that there may be something wrong in the manner in which we have approached the problem so far.

The search for an interdisciplinary approach and methodology, now on for more than a quarter century and reiterated with greater force as the years have gone by, has to be understood in relation to the fundamental malaise in which the enterprise of human knowledge and its relationship to the human condition finds itself. There are two different but interrelated aspects of this malaise. One of this, which has often been stated by philosophers and social theorists, consists in the fragmentation and fractioning of the knowledge system consequent upon the emphasis in modern science on specialisation and expertise. The other aspect, which is only dimly realised so far but which is more fundamental, consists in the contemporary reality that while the stock of human knowledge has been expanding rapidly—so rapidly that it is difficult to keep pace with it—our capacity to deal with basic problems has, far from increasing correspondingly, been actually going down. This inverse correlation between the expansion of human knowledge and the decline in the capacity to deal with real problems poses perhaps the most basic *problematique* of our time, something that may underlie many other *problematiques* and predicaments.

The reason for this can be related to the first aspect mentioned above, to the fact that it is expansion of knowledge based on its fragmentation

and on fragmenting reality along lines defined by academic specialisations, not on the basis of identifying salient aspects or clusters of problems emanating from an evolving reality. So that while the data base
and even theoretical conceptualisation of different 'special' fields have
been accumulating, indeed exploding, both the comprehension of reality in 'general' and the identification and grasp of critical parameters
and cutting edges thereof—leading to choices in respect of action—
have not benefited from this expansion, at any rate not significantly and
in a manner that would respond to the human condition.

Crucial to the 'alienation' immanent in the contemporary human condition is this alienation of the knowledge system from the larger reality
and its mutations. The science of man is increasingly moving along a
trajectory and momentum of its own, more often than not unrelated to
the dilemmas and traumas of the object of that science—man. Men and
women of insight and concern for the human situation will always transcend this but they happen to be few and often outside the mainstream
of the scholarly world or, when arising from within it, it is not because
of but in spite of its logic and dynamics, either due to political involvement in other movements or due to a fundamentally dissenting tem-
perament. But by and large scholars tend to follow the trajectory laid
out by their specialisations.

At certain periods in history, thanks to the impress of a powerful mind
which alters the course of a discipline (Freud, Keynes) or injects a totally
new comprehension of reality as a whole (á la Marx) these trajectories
may begin to change course and respond to a new historical condition.
For the most part, however, and in 'normal' times,scholarly trajectories
seem to assume their own course which are defined more by technical
developments within a given discipline than by sensitivity to the historical context, including in disciplines that had undergone deep stirrings at one time, e.g. in psychology and economics (including political
economy). As these stirrings, usually caused by prophetic minds, recede
in the background, their teaching tends to be trivialised and frozen into
either technical or doctrinaire capsules and zealously protected against
any challenge or attempt to recast it in the light of new developments.
At best a few new specialisations emerge and new courses of study are
devised. But on the whole the great debates of a new historical epoch
—and these debates do take place at all times—seem to bypass much
of the scholarly world which continues to go on at its own pace and
within the confines of academic disciplines and sub-disciplines.

This unrelatedness of the realm of knowledge to reality seems to be
particularly true of the last few decades when the human condition
seems to have eluded intellectual effort and is crying out for a new

theory of history, a new paradigm of science and a new philosophy of action. It is as if the world, engulfed in an all-encompassing crisis that is affecting all segments of reality and all regions and classes, is crying out for a new philosopher or prophet to appear on the horizon but none is in sight. The vacuum seems to be dimly and haltingly filled by a host of dissident writing and a great deal of intellectual groping beyond the fetters and boundaries of both single disciplines and the dominant worldview that all but the most diehard agree to be at once obsolete and fraught with dangerous consequences.

It is in the unfolding and branching out of this dominant worldview that the clue to the present malaise in the sciences of man and the search for what is called 'interdisciplinarity' needs to be traced. There are many aspects of this worldview that have contributed to man's alienation[1] but two of them are relevant for the present theme. One is a narrowly utilitarian view of science based on a conception of knowledge as an instrument of power in man's search for control and domination, primarily over the 'sinister' forces of nature but secondarily also over the social terrain and over distant lands, all with a view to seeking security and predictability and 'order'. This issue has been so widely discussed in its various facets in the recent debate on modern science and technology that there is no need to elaborate it. Except to point to the fact that the idea of a law-governed nature which enjoined upon science to seek out these laws was subtly used by modern man's secular urge towards mastery and control to legitimise his dominion over nature[2] and over social and political relations both within and between societies. Given the cultural location of modern science and technology (Western Europe) as well as its temporal location (17th and 18th centuries when religion gave away to the onslaught of secular drives following the Protestant revolution and the rise of economic man), knowledge became an activity that was organised as a means to secular ends, and human arrangements were viewed through a calculus of pleasure and pain, devoid of any mystery and of any search for eternal ends.

The second and related aspect of the modernist worldview is to exaggerate the role of the intellect and to put knowledge on a pedestal with the result that men of science and more especially experts in technol-

---

1. I have elsewhere dealt with this worldview and its impact on the contemporary paradigm of science and technology in some detail. See *Footsteps into the Future*, Orient Longmans, Delhi, 1974 and Free Press, New York, 1974.

2. In course of time the 'laws of nature' were themselves violated. Much of the contemporary environmental crisis, whether in respect of soil conservation or deforestation or in respect of pollution and erosion of the biosphere, points to modern man's abrogation of basic laws of nature.

ogy and management sciences—the former gradually being overtaken by the latter[3]—have acquired a command over resources and decision-making that has affected the prospects of both present and future generations as well as of cultures and civilisations far outside the centres where crucial decisions are made in the name of science and technology (hence the description of the era of imperial expansion as the Age of Discovery, hence also the rather intellectual conception of the 'development' of developing areas with the help of experts and technocrats).[4]

Instead of thinking of knowledge as part of a larger process of self-realisation, self-awareness and self-transcendence (which was the case with all ancient civilisations), it has been perceived as a means of steam-rolling the entire world into a set of uniformities and has reduced the rich diversity of both nature and cultures to predictable and predetermined states. This has been the thrust of modern physical science which has also greatly influenced the biological and social sciences which too, like the natural sciences, went for a methodology of validation that was based on verifiability and predictability.

With this the efficiency of the machines became the model for social organisation and the aim of knowledge was to reduce reality to manipulable components. The roots of the modern structure of knowledge through a set of specialisations and expertise lie in this overarching worldview of modern secularism and the conception of knowledge as expertise that is inherent in it. In it also lie the roots of the unprecedented power and autonomy of the knowledge system with its own

---

3. The clubbing together of science and technology (which led in course of time to the subjugation of the former by the latter) is a characteristic only of recent times. Even in Europe for a long time, science was pursued as an academic discipline based on a holistic approach, as a branch of moral philosophy, technology being left to innovative men among artisans and craftsmen. It is only after modern secularism and its imperial drive converted the slow moving Industrial Revolution into a universalist drive for power and affluence that the two got wedded and we had the birth of what is known as 'science-based technology' or, to put it more aptly, a technology-oriented science. On this see Ashis Nandy, "Traditions of Technology", *Alternatives*, Vol, 371-385, Dec. 1978.

4. On this whole theme see the "Poona Indictment" on the *Perversion of Science and Technology* issued in July 1978, a year before the U.N. Conference of Science and Technology for Development, by an international group of scholars assembled at a meeting of the World Order Models Project held at Poona, India. The "Indictment" was since published in the *Bulletin of the Atomic Scientists, Development Forum* and other journals. It can be obtained from the Centre for the Study of Developing Societies, 29 Rajpur Road, Delhi 110054, India or the Institute for World Order, 777, U.N. Plaza, New York, N.Y. 10017, U.S.A.

momentum and trajectory, its own priesthood and organisation through a set of sects known as disciplines, and the dependence of all practical fields on experts, specialists and technocrats provided by this priesthood.

Towards An Alternative Process of Knowledge

If interdisciplinarity is not making much headway despite persistent advocacy of it by both men of science and men of affairs, it is because it is still being pursued within the framework of the dominant worldview and the role of technical expertise in it. It is imperative for us to come to grips with this particular tradition of science and technology informed by the homocentric worldview which put man at the centre of creation and exhorted him to use knowledge to enhance his power.[5] Influenced by this worldview (which gained in power and acceptance in Europe after the seventeenth century), science, which was originally conceived as a search for the 'laws of nature' and a search for truth (which it still is for the more creative among scientists), became an instrument of mastery over both nature and the social order, in course of time becoming an instrument of modern technology and militarism and from then on of imperial expansion, of the ravaging of resources and the environment, and unwittingly even of the creeds of racism, of fascism and of totalitarian socialism.

These consequences are not inherent in the concept of either science or technology. There are other traditions of knowledge that are at the moment submerged which still persist and provide an alternative basis for organising man's estate—in China, India, Persia, the Arab countries, Africa, even in ancient and mediaeval Europe. What is common to them all is a view of knowledge as, first, a search for truth and, beyond that, a basis for man's enlightenment and liberation. In all these traditions knowledge is conceived as at once a means and an end, not just a means

---

5. It is necessary to stress the particularity of this tradition and its location in space and time and to counter its claim to universality. This claim can only be understood by reference to the universalist design towards domination and hegemony of the modern West. As pointed out by Toynbee long ago, modern European imperialism represents the first major effort at unifying the entire globe under the dominion of a single regional centre. It is a conception of universalism that is based on the expansion of a local civilisation and on dominance over the rest of the world, legitmised by a belief in the manifest destiny that was peculiar to Judeo-Christian religiosity in the post-mediaeval age. For a fuller discussion of this theme, see my "Towards A Just World", *Alternatives*, Vol. V, No.1, June 1979. It has since been re-published as "Justice and World Order" in the second volume in this series, *Transformation and Survival; In Search of . Humane World Order*

of control and dominion as in the modern West.

A second characteristic that stands out in most of these traditions of knowledge is their holistic conception according to which science and culture are not discrete activities but are facets of the same phenomenon. Nor indeed are the world of intellect and the world of action, or both of them *vis-a-vis* philosophy and metaphysics. For the act of creation and the pursuit of truth are inseparable. The dissociation that has been introduced between science and philosophy in modern times is unfortunate. Equally unfortunate is the dichotomy between knowledge and action. There is need to restore the comprehensive and holistic perspective. It is a perspective that still survives in many cultures but is at the moment submerged under the dazzling presence of modern technology. Today we face a situation in which the Western world is uneasy with its own *weltanschauung* and its imitators are uneasy with their loss of anchorage and vision. This may be an opportune time to consider afresh the cultural and civilisational challenge of our time and to restore to both an integral view of knowledge and a modest view of what man can achieve through knowledge alone (by which I mean external knowledge). There is need to return to the tradition which sees knowledge as part of a larger process of self-awareness, self-realisation and liberation. The foundations and methodology of interdisciplinarity need also to be based on a such a tradition.

There is a third and what may at first sight appear to be a contradictory aspect of this alternative tradition, namely the view of knowledge systems as inherently plural. Plurality is inherent in a holistic view of knowledge. Holism is not to be confused with universalism. If knowledge is to be integral with life, and if life is pursued in diverse cultural and historical contexts, then surely systems of knowledge—in both theory and praxis—must vary too and in their totality provide alternative schools of thought and action. It is only with the universalist claims of modern science (in turn based on a conviction of its superiority) that this view of alternative paths to truth and enlightenment has gone under. Any attempt to move beyond narrow expertise and instrumentalist pedagogy must contend with the universalist creed inherent in the dominant worldview underlying the natural and human sciences today. Interdisciplinarity must also encompass interparadigmatic discourse as well as a 'dialogue of civilisations' implicit in each of which is the notion of alternatives. Any linear view of the development of paradigms, as is implicit in Thomas Kuhn's view of scientific revolutions, must be categorically rejected in such a perspective on interdisciplinarity. Equally categorically should be rejected a conception of civilisation as something that is all-encompassing which is inherent in the imperial and universalising thrust of the modern West.[6]

I have deliberately dwelt at some length on the philosophical and political issues involved in the concept of interdisciplinarity. What we face today is not just a fragmentation between disciplines and sectors of knowledge but also, partly as a consequence of the universalist claims of the modernist worldview, a growing conflict between paradigms of thought and a grim battle between ideological systems each with totalistic claims and struggling for world domination and, with the growing challenge to Western domination, also a clash between alternative civilisations.

It is necessary to view the current debate on interdisciplinarity and an integrated 'science of man' in a historical perspective. For, to be sure, to a considerable extent a system of knowledge based on specialised disciplines as well as the 'universalist' claims of modern science and technology did contribute to the revolutionary advances of industrial civilisation and its spread to almost the entire globe which for the first time must think together in handling the challenges of the last leg of the twentieth century. But today we face a different historical situation in which the dream of European Enlightenment and the Theory of Progress has gone awry and there is need to control and redirect science and technology by drawing on more fundamental creations of the human spirit as found in the great religious and philosophical traditions, by seeking a new unity that transcends not just disciplinary boundaries but also ideological and civilisational divisions.

The Meaning of Interdisciplinarity in Today's Context

How does one place the search for interdisciplinarity in this larger historical challenge? How does one proceed from where one finds one-

6. More recently, with the growing challenge to the West and growing recognition by men of science and culture of the distinctiveness of other civilisations, and attempt is being made to 'synthesise' them all into a common framework. The attempt represents the power of the idea of universalism and, underlying it, the search for order and uniformity and the fear of diversity and possible chaos. This seems to be a basic psychological urge and is not limited to Westerners. For a brilliant attempt at such a synthesis by one who challenges the universalist claims of Western civilisation but still belongs to the same methodological orientation, see Ali Mazrui, *A World Federation of Cultures: An African Perspective*, Free Press, New York, 1976.

self in the existing knowledge system and its institutionalisation in the great universities and research bodies? What could be the methodological foundations of such an endeavour? What precisely does one mean by interdisciplinary aproaches and methods in such a situation?

Answers to these questions will depend on one's conception of an alternative model and one's understanding on how to move towards it. Any changeover from the present pursuit and organisation of knowledge, bound also by constraints of institutional structure and philosophy of research and teaching, towards an alternative model based on the triple goals of interdisciplinary, interparadigmatic and inter-civilisational structure and style of knowledge has undoubtedly to be looked upon as a process that gradually unfolds in individual as well as institutional settings. This is crucial: to think of it in terms of a *process*, not merely in terms of some organisational innovations. There cannot be a complete changeover at one stroke and the model one wants to move towards cannot simply be ordained by admistrators or even educators. It is something that must evolve, *sui generis*, in different cultural and intellectual settings, with enough sensitivity to variations of both context and actual need. There is scope for diverse ways of initiating and pursuing such a process.

Yet it is necessary to be clear about the general nature of this process, to avoid *ad hoc* experimentation, and to develp certain norms and methods underlying such a process. In what follows I shall first identify the wrong and misleading and simple-minded approaches that are often mentioned in the name of interdisciplinarity, then move to a consideration of more plausible definitions of the concept and in doing so draw upon the concrete experience of the research group assembled at the Centre for the Study of Developing Societies (CSDS).

What Interdisciplinarity Is Not

It is necessary to reject certain commonplace interpretations of the concept of interdisciplinarity and its actual application. Lumping together more than one discipline under a single roof does not necessarily lead to interdisciplinarity. Quite often this only leads to further departmentalisation of institutions and may produce greater rigidities and distances and more jusrisdictional and political problems than even uni-disciplinary institutions which, however, permit of divergent perspectives and openness in academic experimentation. It may be argued, with some plausibility, that having scholars from different disciplines at the same place is a necessary though not a sufficient condition. This may well be so but only provided some more basic norms underlying interdisciplinary research (as conceived in the preceding section) are ful-filled and the necessary environment for it provided; it is by no means the most important condition of interdisciplinarity.[7]

Nor is interdisciplinarity to be interpreted as an aggregation of con-cepts drawn from various disciplines. Lacking a more basic orientation, this may in fact produce confusion and give rise to a jungle of cate-gories and a multiplicity of jargons which have however not been absorbed in a general framework with a clear focus.[8] A lot of Amer-ican social science is replete with this type of interdisciplinarity that defies comprehension.

Another approach that is close to concept aggregation but with some-what greater merit is borrowing from other disciplines. If this is done under the pressure of some fashionable trend towards innovation (inter-disciplinary research itself has often been looked upon as a fashion), the result can be as bad as in concept aggregation. Where it is adopted

---

7. A very good example from India of a major institution that started on the ideology of interdisciplinarity but proved a complete non-starter because of a merely additive con-ception of it is the Jawaharlal Nehru University in New Delhi. The University modelled itself after various 'Schools' and 'Centres' within Schools instead of the usual division between Faculties and Departments. This somewhat different nomenclature was applied in practice by appointing a few scholars belonging to 'other' disciplines, e.g. a sociologist or an economist in the Centre on history or the Centre on politics. In practice this has made little difference. The Centres operate very much like Departments and are in fact scenes of great tension arising out of disciplinary loyalties. Thus the attempt to make econ-omists work in the Centre for political studies misfired and pressure was built to set up a separate Centre for economics. In the field of science a truly interdisciplinary attempt at creating a Centre for Science Policy proved moribund and it has been suggested that it better be wound up.

8. The same concept carries quite different connotations in different disciplines. Take the concept of decentralisation which is currently very widely discussed and is based on a really felt concern in different parts of the world. In political science the concept of decen-tralisation has to do with the nature of the State and the location and distribution of power and authority in it. In economics, however, it has a completely different meaning, namely greater share for market forces and private initiative. In sociology it is related to anar-chist movements and in psychology to individual freedom. To simply lump these var-ious meanings together will create a great deal of confusion unless the whole problem of decentralisation is viewed holistically and as a historical challenge arising from exces-sive centralisation of secular affairs (both globally and within individual nation-states, within both public and private sectors, and more generally in respect of man and tech-nology) on which scholars from different disciplines work together.

as a result of one's recognition of the limitations of one's discipline which makes one look beyond and draw concepts, modes of investigation and analytical or methodological perspectives from other disciplines, *without ever losing the focus and sense of purpose*, the result may be more beneficial. But there are serious limits to any approach that is just aggregative.

Shining examples of this are to be found in the systems approach adopted in modern political science (which, in its bandwagon effect, relegated basic concerns of political philosophy and analysis to the background from where they are only now re-emerging), the motivational school in development theory (which for a whole decade went on a rampage questioning the capacity of traditional societies to change), the market school of social bargaining (which reduced the complicated web of social interactions to a mechanical calculus), and various measurement schools such as sociometrics and psychometrics following the dazzling success of mathematical economics. Apart from distracting attention towards new fads, such borrowing has often led to a gradual loss of perspective and has produced a whole plethora of empirical knowledge that has proved to be of little value when it comes to facing real issues. Among other things, such an approach has dehumanised social science, marginalised key concepts (e.g. the concept of man from social anthroplogy, the concept of good from philosophy, the concept of community from sociology, the concept of State from political science, the concept of value from economics and the concept of person from psychology) and trivialised major disciplines and scientific traditions that had for long been concerned with basic parameters of the human predicament.[9]

There is absolutely no reason why people should give up the basic theoretical concerns, and conceptual foci of their disciplines. Each major discipline has its own tradition and pedigree and it is important not to lose sight of it. The task is to enlarge upon it in the face of new challenges, deepen its scope and meaning, and sensitise the practitioners of given disciplines to the need to redefine

---

9. Perhaps the best example of this is to be found in the contemporary rendering of Marxist analysis. Whereas Marx's own critique of bourgeois thought and his revolutionary alternative to it through a completely new mode of analysis and vision for the future represented a totality of intellectual comprehension, his followers, the 'Marxists', have frozen this analysis in terms of a set of inflexible and unquestionable 'laws' which are 'scientific'. In the process, in the words of one of the most sensitive social theorists of our time, Ferdinand Braudel, "the creative power of the most powerful social analysis of the last century (has) been shackled". See Braudel, *The Mediterranean and the Mediterranean World in the Age of Philip II*, New York, Harper and Row, 1976.

and reformulate human concerns in the wake of a new historical consciousness. If interdisciplinarity leads to a diffusion of focus and concern it can only produce shallowness in the whole knowledge process, preoccupation with technical minutiae and a loss of vision. This should be avoided and fought against at all costs.

Steps Towards Interdisciplinarity

A more fruitful attitude to interdisciplinarity emerges when scholars from diverse disciplinary backgrounds work together around a clearly identified problem or problems, provided however such working together is not mechanically contrived (e.g. by hiring people from different specialisations on research projects) but grows out of collective deliberation on a whole range of issues over a period of time. Two other prerequisites of the success of such an approach are a temperamental openness of the participants and their capacity to tolerate ambiguities and seeming paradoxes, and a high level of intellectual comprehension and philosophical grounding on their part which enables them to transcend their specialised training, sharpen their academic sights and produce a new language of communication in the process of defining and elucidating a given problem. Usually (though not necessarily always) this seems to work better among those who did not go too far in their specialised training and who may appear to their conventional academic colleagues in the profession (e.g. people who sit on selection committees) as not fulfilling the usual criteria of formal degrees or length of teaching or research experience in a specialised area. Some of the best interdisciplinary and interparadigmatic work has come out of what I would call creative dropouts during the formal schooling or training programmes. At any rate this is our experience at the CSDS.

Such a knowledge process depends greatly on the chemistry of a multi-disciplinary group which liberates each participating individual from his disciplinary bondage while still retaining the richness and vision and intellectual search that had both drawn him to a discipline and subsequently drawn him beyond (though not necessarily out of) it. Such a chemistry leads to processes of self-definition and self-consciousness that chasten the disciplinary identities of individuals and open up for them new intellectual thresholds and vistas which respond less to the inner logic and momentum of a particular branch of knowledge and more to the logic of historical forces and their contemporary empirical manifestations. Once this happens, even the term interdisciplinarity proves inadequate to define the knowledge process. For inherent in the interdisciplinary format is a mechanistic and aggregative, at best integrative, process rather than a transformative process which is what really takes place. What actually happens can perhaps be better described as trans-disciplinary or extra-disciplinary knowledge rather than an interdisciplinary orientation (though this is less a matter of language and more of substance). But basic to the whole chemistry is the fact that the intellectual process is located in each individual and is not just a function of juxtaposition of people from different disciplines. For true interdisciplinarity to develop it is the individual that has to become interdisciplinary, not the group.

This of course is not enough. For crucial to the growth of 'interdisciplinarity' as part of an integrated approach to knowledge (and action) and the flowering and sustenance of individuals embodying it is the institutional dimension. It is here that the greatest challenge lies and little headway seems to have been made as yet. While there is no dearth of outstanding individuals who embody in their life and work the normative perspective laid out above (though their total number would still be small), the real growth of interdisciplinary, interparadigmatic and inter-civilisational processes of knowledge and social action will depend on the growth of institutions around the world that share, sustain and nurture such a perspective—and such individuals. My rejection of the aggregative conception of interdisciplinarity and emphasis on what I have called the 'chemistry of the group' underlines this point.

This 'chemistry' involves (a) an environment that provides intellectual stimulation, frank dialogue, a self-questioning search and a model of integration based on plurality and multiplicity of viewpoints that however interact and cohere in a mode that responds to a given historical situation. There cannot be one model of such a mode; cultural, political and individual specificities must necessarily shape it in a given socio-historical setting. In course of time it must also produce a specific *identity* which has both a cerebral and an affiliative mode—a model of creative conviviality that is relevant to the building of an intellectual community in the context of a specific historical and political setting. As stated in a recent publication of the CSDS,[10] the group at the Centre felt the need for

that imprecise but nonetheless significant requirement for sustained intellectual work; an appropriate environment

10. Centre for the Study of Developing Societies, *Research Report* 1980 (Delhi, 1980).

of fellowship in which independent thinking is encouraged and open controversy breaks down generational and hierarchical barriers—in sum, an atmosphere in which intellectual curiosity and creativity are stimulated and individual worth is recognised.

Such a model of interdisciplinarity emerges best when the intellectual striving moves beyond empirical and methodological issues and gets geared to aspects of the larger human *problematique*, or to a given crisis situation at a particular historical juncture at either the global or the national or local or individual level, or to the need for new and alternative social theory in the face of new civilisational challenges or simply the running out of old and accepted ideas and assumptions (e.g. in develoment theory). Perhaps the best example of this which is right now engaging the minds of many intellectuals from diverse disciplinary backgrounds is the end of the Keynesian model of economic management and the breakdown of the post-war consensus on the international economic order, as well as the sharp decline in consensus on the role of the State in the process of social transformation.

Such an intellectual striving, in respect both of theoretical challenges and the need for a new research agenda, calls for a process of knowledge that fulfils two other criteria: that it is historically sensitive—both in respect of a changing global context and in respect of its anchorage in given cultural and civilisational meaning systems and mutations thereof—and that it has implications for human choice and action, for *praxis*. The pedagogic model of such a knowledge process must partake simultaneously of two basic charateristics: that it is based on self-awareness of a changing world and that it is self-consciously seen to be an act of intervention. With this comes a break with the natural science tradition as also with the positivistic empiricism in the social sciences of the behavioural and other varieties. For crucial to such a view of social sciences is a simultaneous effort at explaining and understanding social phenomena and influencing them in respect of *praxis*.

Also, as the knowledge process moves to take on this role of participating in historical change, it has of necessity to be of a holistic type that takes a total view of the human condition. This has been so in the past, e.g. with the Marxist revolution in thought and *praxis*, and must be so now and in the future. With this apparently crude concepts like participatory research, action research and 'relevant' research acquire a proper intellectual framework and meaning. Above all, with it ends the dichotomy between theoretical and applied, between empirical and normative, between academic and activist, between holistic and molecular and indeed even between past-oriented and future-oriented research—dichotomies that have bedevilled the world of knowledge for several decades now under the impact of the age of positivism and some overly idealistic reactions to it.

Interdisciplinarity in Practice

In the end I shall illustrate the norms and criteria laid out above by reference to the evolution of this process at the CSDS. While the issues raised in this paper have in good part been drawn from my experience at the CSDS and from my own work—it has become increasingly difficult to dissociate the two aspects—I shall try to exemplify them by reference to the concrete intellectual process as it evolved in this institution. In doing so I shall draw upon the collective self-analysis of the Centre provided by the theoretical introductions of its research reports.[11]

First, a word on the motivation behind setting up the Centre. The CSDS was established in 1963

> by a small group of scholars who recognised the need for historically sensitive theoretical and empirical research in social and political processes, in the cultural and philosophical anchorage of these processes and in their implications for human choices. They believed that the global context of India and other Third World societies demanded analytical perspectives different from those provided by the dominant and increasingly stereo-typed schools of thought. Such new perspectives could not, they felt, emerge from within the organisational structure of the Indian universities, based as they were on single-discipline departments and on the idea of specialised expert knowledge, all of which appeared to them to be hostile to intellectual explorations at the frontiers of the various disciplines and outside the established models.

I have in this paper talked of interdisciplinarity as a process of knowledge that evolves *sui generis* rather than an organisational form that can be stipulated from the outside. At the CSDS this has indeed been a process with some recognisable vantage points when

11. *Op. cit.* and CSDS, *Research Report*, 1963-1988, published on the occasion of the Silver Jubilee of the Centre. (Delhi, 1988).

new perspectives emerged and produced a new synthesis. Thus during the first decade of its existence (roughly the sixties) the research at the CSDS was organised around large-scale empirical studies and empirical social theory. There was at that stage a great paucity of indigenously collected data in India which enabled one to interrelate historical, cultural, political, psychological, economic and technological changes. Though there were masses of empirical data for standard professional work in a few disciplines like economics, demography and psychology, they could hardly be considered adequate or satisfatory by anyone interested in alternative social theories and in civilisational choices. As a result, theoretical work in the social sciences often tended to be sterile, devoid of cultural meaning, and lacking in integrity. The CSDS therefore embarked on a large number of empirical studies, interdisciplinary in nature and cross-cultural and comparative in scope. This work ranged from studies of institutions, leadership and values in the context of an evolving democracy to inquiries into the ethnic, socio-historical and psychological contents of social change and State and nation building to inquiries into the cultural location of modern science and the consequences of the adoption of modern technology for human choices. In the course of this work apart from gaining insights into the structuring of social variables in the Indian setting (with comparative studies in other countries carried out through collaboration with scholars in those countries) masses of quantitative data also became available and led the Centre to build an infrastructure of data analysis facilities.

By the end of the sixties two things happened. A firm base in empirical data and empirical social theory allowed the CSDS to move into new areas of inquiry. At the same time many scholars at the Centre, responding to a changing national and international scene, were itching to move into research and writing that was more focussed, oriented to issues of public policy, normative and involving interaction between theory and praxis. The convergence of these two factors led many at the Centre to branch off into new and selected areas of both theoretical writing and empirical research. The earlier interests in the processes of political and social change were by no means given up and continue to be pursued even now though in a manner that is informed by a new theoretical perspective.

To illustrate the new synthesis, the Centre has built a large programme of research on rural development which however focusses on dimensions generally left out by such programmes such as exploring not just the needs and interests but also the perceptions and visions of a desirable society as expressed by the citizens themselves "who happen to be the targets as well as consumers of development efforts", their concepts of alternative lifestyles, and their preferences and priorities along the whole gamut of social transformation. Through dialogues, debates and focussed workshops involving diverse groups and different streams of experience and action, this research seeks to explore new modes of participation. The basic idea is to integrate the process of self-definition and goal-setting of the nation as a whole. By involving citizen groups and activists operating in rural areas and small urban clusters in the definition and planning of development, a basis is laid for exploring the institutional aspects of various models of decentralisation, particularly as they relate to the redistribution of resources and professional skills for a decentralised democratic order, and the role of non-governmental agencies and non-party groups in such designs of distributive justice. In this manner it becomes possible to bridge not just disciplinary boundaries but also micro and macro dimensions, as well as theory and *praxis*.

To illustrate further, the Centre has planned a major study of ethno-agriculture which will identify traditional Indian agricultural practices, systematise them in the form of an alternative indigenous agronomy, and then try to feed this alternative science back to the agriculturists through new organisational structures. The project rests on the assumption that the so-called folk sciences and folk-technologies bear a creative relationship with the ecosystem on the one hand and the lifestyles of the peasants on the other, particularly in a society where less than 20 per cent of the people have access to modern science and technology. The project sees agronomy as a social as well as a biological science which should ideally involve not a one-way flow of 'knowledge' from the laboratory to the field—as seems to be the case with the new 'high-tech' push of biotechnology and genetic engineering—but as a collaborative venture of the practising agriculturist and the researcher.

The same perspective informs the Centre's work on an alternative approach to science and technology for a sustainable and environmentally sensitive process of social development, and on alternative concepts of human needs emerging from the dialogues among citizens, activists and policy-makers. The study seeks to get a richer understanding of the process of development by concentrating on the felt needs of the people and their subjective ordering as opposed to the 'objective', bureaucratically determined needs of the people.

So much by way of illustrating the kind of research efforts that represent the Centre's model of interdisciplinarity. This is also reflected in its theoretical orientation as it has evolved over the years. Three broad areas of collective interest have emerged.

First, the Centre has a number of scholars interested in alternative institutional modes and philosophies of development and their civilisational implications. These scholars are interested in re-examining the fundamentals of the dominant thinking on development, and in seeing development as a participatory, plural and decentralised process linked to the cultural imperatives of a society, on the one hand, and to the global political economy, on the other.

Second, the Centre has a small group of scholars interested in the broad area of science, culture and consciousness. This group is interested not only in the politics and philosophy of technological choices and science policy, but also in science as social knowledge, criticism and intervention, and in a socio-cultural critique of social science itself that would lead to a more self-aware social research in the Centre itself.

Third, there are scholars interested in normative exercises involving the world political economy, human needs, utopias and visions of desirable societies, and ideas of alternative man-nature systems, ethnicity, ecology, and indigenous lifestyles. Work has already begun on religion and tradition as sources of social knowledge, philosophy of science, and the moral values informing the public realm.

Arising from all this has evolved the 'overall philosophy of the Centre':

> in all its empirical and theoretical concerns, the Centre has been problem-oriented, not only in terms of the short-range concerns of Indian society and polity, but also in respect of the continuing and long-range concerns of the social sciences, social philosophy and of knowledge oriented action.

> This problem-oriented approach has confronted the scholars at the Centre with the challenge of transcending the rigid, yet artificial, boundaries of the various social science disciplines, and with the need to avoid a fragmentary approach to knowledge. It has also confronted them with the problem of reconciling the perennial contradiction between knowledge and action, which they must do through epistemological and normative debates

and through active interest in the institutions which mediate between systems of knowledge and action. It is this larger challenge which is leading some of the scholars in the Centre to experiment with methods such as participatory research, with programmes in rural development, decentralisation and alternative technologies, with the evaluation of policies at national, regional and local levels, with new forums for communication among the policy-makers, field workers and academics in the various areas of planning and development and with on-the-spot studies of conflict situations.

The scholars involved in these exercises aim at breaking down the false dichotomy between 'theoretical' and 'applied' research that modern science has created. They are aware that in the name of applied research, studies are done which, at worst, document and state in unintelligible jargon what is obvious to policy-makers and, at best, treat every problem as unique and episodic, unrelated to even immediately higher level principles that order the observed reality. Most avowedly theoretical studies, on the other hand, express only pious hope or moral indignation, guided by the principles of framed or reductive logic, unable to confront the empirical reality of live contradictions and hard existential choices that individuals and groups face in real-life situations. The Centre believes that problem-oriented research could be made to serve as a bridge not just between the empirical and the normative, the quantitative and the qualitative, but also between the historical, the contemporary and the futuristic.

The Centre has tried to see its work in the context of national and global efforts to hitch social knowledge to concepts of a more humane social science on the one hand and a more humane society on the other. It has seen intellectual creativity both as a direct intervention in social consciousness and as a means of indirect intervention in social structures. Social knowledge as self-awareness and social knowledge as criticism are two planks of the Centre's work. This does not mean that the Centre has any clearly laid down ideology (although no individual, as scholar or citizen, is barred from having one of his choice). What it means is that the Centre, operating through a dynamic process of debate and controversy between the individual positions of its staff members, has certain values and operates within a certain normative framework. Such a concept of knowledge not only recognises a continuity between knowing and acting but also between acting and learning that derives from listening to the ground forces at work, and between all of this and the learning that grows out of encounters of values and ideological debates.[12]

Out of this interest in the interplay between learning and intervention at various levels of national and international reality has grown the abiding interest of the Centre's faculty in the theory and practice of democracy as it confronts the problems of social justice and human needs. Whether as an expression of human creativity and of man's continuous effort to protect his dignity and cultural integrity or as the concrete expression of authority and protest against authority in an open polity, democracy has been observed, interpreted, evaluated and discussed as a system of human arrangements in most of the Centre's work. That some among the Centre's faculty have also taken strong political positions on pressing issues is only incidental (though not necessarily to those individuals) to this collective intellectual concern with the problem of human freedom in the late twentieth century.

---

12. In moving towards this orientation, apart from individual writings by political analysts at the Centre, two important initiatives were undertaken. One was a study on dialogues on development undertaken under the auspices of the United Nations University, since published as *Development Dialogues*, Delhi, Sage Publications, 1986. The other was a major programme launched as a project of the Centre on "Democracy, Decentralisation and Rural Development" in 1980 which became known as *Lokayan* (meaning 'Dialogue of the People'). Lokayan continues to function, though as it grew in its scope and span of concerns and it needed involvement of a whole range of activists and intellectuals, it has been made into an autonomous institution with its own identity and constitution. It is located at 13, Alipur Road, Delhi 110-054. It brings out a regular journal known as *Lokayan Bulletin* which is published six times a year in English and Hindi. Many of the faculty members of the CSDS continue to be associated with Lokayan.

As already hinted earlier, there cannot be one model of interdisciplinarity. The one evolved at the CSDS is an outgrowth of an indigenous effort that has responded to intellectual challenges within India and in the world at large as perceived by the scholars at the Centre. An account of its experience can only serve a heuristic function, as a basis of generating a debate on general criteria and principles, but no more than that.

Before I end, let me say a few words on the problems faced in building such an institution. First, it is our experience that because of its continuously experimental nature and because of the inherently empirical grounding of its theoretical work, the work of the CSDS does not correspond to any of the prevailing ideological or cultural models (liberalism, Marxism, Gandhism and so on) and to that extent is always in danger of being suspect in the eyes of those belonging to established schools of thought.

Second, work of this kind does not also fit the immediate and pragmatic concerns of governments and funding institutions (with their project orientation), and is therefore continuously faced with scarcity of funds.

Third, the group at the CSDS has believed that the kind of environment it needs to nurture such work can only be provided if it remains relatively small, non-hierarchical and non-departmental in its organisation. This has, however, its costs. Over time we have found that this small core of individuals, who have to stretch themselves and the time at their disposal to deal with new intellectual challenges and demands, tend to be too busy with their academic work to be able to devote time to organisation-building. The result is a somewhat sloppy administration and lack of an adequate infrastructure. There is hardly any attention given to public relations, maintaining communication with the scholarly world at large and to physical and administrative aspects of institution-building.

Lastly, such an 'environment' entails a very large degree of informality which necessitates a high level of mutual trust and give-and-take, and this can sometimes be taxing, especially on temporary or visiting faculty.

These various problems have got highlighted in recent years with growing recognition and interest in the work of the people at the Centre and the demands this brings in its wake. But there is adamant opposition to any attempt at a more formal organisational structure which could conceivably increase 'efficiency'.

Intellectually speaking, there has taken place in recent years an even greater broadening of the disciplinary, philosophical and paradigmatic base of the Centre. Increasingly, the new additions to the staff are from more speculative and historical disciplines, representing interests that are even more outside the mainstream of the social sciences than was already the case in the sixties and the early seventies. This has been all to the good and has added to the richness of the pool of intellectual concerns and orientations. Generally speaking, such a development alongside the growing interest in *praxis* has meant that interdisciplinarity is being sought out not just between various social sciences and the theoretical and philosophical concerns they represent but also between the social sciences and the natural sciences on the one hand and between these and the more speculative and aesthetic disciplines and concerns on the other. If present trends continue, the future growth may well be in the direction of literature and the arts, though naturally only in terms of such people in these fields who share the wider concerns and grounding of the Centre. As all this happens, there may well develop a danger towards diffusion of interests and towards a loss of overall purpose and perspective. The group at the CSDS will need to watch out against these dangers which are inherent in an interdisciplinary perspective on knowledge.

Interdisciplinarity is full of pitfalls and there is need to guard against its excesses. It is not an end itself, only a means to a process of knowledge that is integral, sensitive to the intellectual challenge of a fast changing human condition, problem-oriented and capable of creative interaction with reality, and liberating. The perspective laid out in this paper suggests one way of evolving such a process of knowledge as found in the concrete experience of one institution.

3

Alternative Development and the Issue of Environment

Perspective

The concern with the environment in its renewed and more urgent form is now more than twenty years old. A series of major conferences, seminars and programmes and highly publicised reports[1] have sought to infuse the environmental dimension into the thinking on international and national strategies of development. Yet another major effort is now under way to build the environmental concern into the basic thinking on development strategies and policies. The current spate of discussions following the Brundtland Commission Report seems to have provided a fresh impetus to this effort. Yet, for all that, environmental consciousness has not been aroused widely enough to put the question beyond the realm of controversy.[2]

----

1. A major international conference under UN auspices was followed by the setting up of UNEP (United Nations Environment Programme) and the propagation of the concept of eco-development; a sustained programme in public education directed by the office of the Executive Director of UNEP, the Dag Hammerskjold Foundation and other prestigious bodies; a large number of expert meetings, inter-governmental consultations and UN General Assembly resolutions; provocative and highly publicised reports from the Club of Rome; the Cocoyoc Declaration, and reports of a series of international and national seminars, workshops, training programmes and research projects; as well as a large output of books and journals specially devoted to this cause which are too numerous to cite here.

2. As a matter of fact a whole new controversy has emerged following the charge that the Brundtland Commission Report and the publicity given to it by various governments and NGOs who are otherwise enmeshed in the conventional development model underscore the fact that 'environment protection' has only become a facade under which the old interests will continue to rule the roost and the more genuine people's movements (of tribals and other affected communities) will either be coopted or made illegitimate and crushed.

There must be some reason why this all-important matter that has such a vital bearing on the prospects of development, the well-being of future generations, and the quality of human life on this planet has to be still argued and 'sold' in an almost defensive manner. There is still a great deal of suspicion, especially in the Third World, of the motivations behind such movements. And there are still many influential circles in the industrialised countries themselves which regard the arguments for ecological balance and environmental preservation as well-meaning but ill informed and unduly pessimistic. Surely, there is something wrong somewhere. If the case for preservation and sustenance of the environment is so obvious, why this constant need for its repeated justification; why this unnecessary defensiveness?

This issue is being deliberately posed at the beginning of this essay. It is necessary to face up to it if the case for human environment is to make a breakthrough, and if its concerns are to inform the thinking and action in various parts of the world. The reason for the present state of affairs may be found in the very manner in which important issues are posed in international forums. This manner is characteristic of all knowledge that is generated and disseminated in the modern world, viz. in fragments and highly specialised capsules. Modern science, modern technology and modern communications are all subject to this fragmented approach to human problems. The dialogue on development itself is no exception; it is held in a fragmented universe of discourse. (I shall show later that this itself is part of the basic predicament facing mankind.)

Not until the view of development as a linear aggregation of a series of specialised inputs gives place to a comprehensive and holistic perspective will the case for environment be fully established. Not until the UN system and other international—as well as regional and national—agencies cease to operate in isolated and watertight compartments will the environmental concern be seen for what it really is. It is not one more variable, or dimension, or even perspective, but rather a new comprehension of the human *problematique*, which entails the evolving of an alternative method of scientific endeavour and an alternative design for development. The point at issue is not one of convincing policy-makers of the need to build the environmental concern into development policies; it is not even one of perceiving the intimate interrelationship between the environment and development. It is something far more fundamental; it involves a clear admission of the faulty and inappropriate, wasteful and irrational, inequitous and exploitative and, in the end, highly dangerous and possibly suicidal nature of the present model of development. It calls for nothing less than evolving a new concept of development to replace the one now commonly accepted. Indeed, the current conceptions of progress and human well-being and the definition of human needs underlying the present development model, the role assigned to science and technology in it, and the relationship between knowledge and human arrangements assumed by it—all are at fault and need to be redesigned.

Later in this essay I shall lay out in some detail the elements of an alternative design for development (which should by definition be 'environmentally sound', just as it should be economically and socially more just and politically more participatory and democratic). But we must first provide a diagnosis of the reasons why the present model of development, which once held such great promise and gave rise to the vision of 'continuous progress for all', has come to grief. I shall try to provide such a diagnosis in the context of a fast-changing process of history, the philosophical underpinnings of current notions of 'development' and the consequences for the politics of development.

A Historical Overview

We may begin with some of the fundamentals. One is that we live in a period of profound transformation. It is engulfing and interlocking diverse regions, cultures and ecosystems into a common enterprise, giving rise, in the process, to new conflicts waged on a scale unheard of in earlier times. Most of the thinkers and philosophers from time immemorial, who have tried to define the human predicament by reference to the need to overcome conflicts through some kind of a social order, have thought in terms of conflicts within a single society or, at most, of conflicts between two or more societies. For the first time in recent years we are realising that this predicament is now worldwide. All actors in it and, perhaps most of all, the weakest and the most deprived among them, need to think in terms that cover all men and all societies. The end of colonialism, the unprecedented increase in population, the urgency of the economic problem, the sudden sense of the bounties of nature drying up, and the feeling of scarcity of basic resources in place of the feeling of continuing abundance for all—all these point, on the one hand, to a scenario of growing conflict that will become worldwide in scope and, on the other hand, to the need to work out new solutions based on a new structure of human cooperation.

Need for a New Paradigm

The present-day human predicament includes all these issues—the rampage of technology, the severe dualism of the human species, the sacrifice of life chances of future generations, and the destruction of other species and other sources of life and sustenance. Therefore, the salvation that today's man has to work out for himself, and for the whole of nature along with his own, must address itself to all these issues together, for the crisis that he faces is total as it was never before.

It is a crisis that calls for crucial choices that span a wide range of structures and processes. They relate to the world political order, the techno-economic system in its twin aspects of the opportunities it offers and the kind of relationship it forges with nature, the development strategy, and the intellectual effort needed to cope with the situation. We can choose if we will, to move from the present structure of dominance, inequity, loss of autonomy and dignity for millions of human beings to a more just and humane world in which both human collectivities and individual human beings are able to work out their respective destinies in a framework of integrity, balance and harmony.

Philosophical Underpinnings

Behind these myriad divisions that seem to permeate modern civilisation lies a dominant philosophical doctrine that has had its greatest triumph in our own time with practically the whole world accepting it. It is necessary to come to grips with it; for, underlying the irrational sway of modern technology, is this philosophical doctrine which, emanating from European culture, has brought the whole world under its sweep.

The Doctrine of Modernity

This is the doctrine of modernity, according to which the end of life is narrowly defined so as to be within the grasp of all—progress based on economic prosperity. It is to be achieved by the application of inanimate power to the fulfilment of human needs. There is no mystery about it; it is all very 'scientific'. Indeed, there are no mysteries in life itself, since most of them have been uncovered by science, and the little that remains will soon be uncovered. All that men and societies have to do is to discard tradition and superstition and become rational and 'modern'. And all they need to learn are the essential *techniques* by which happiness can be had by one and all. For a whole generation after the collapse of colonial power, this doctrine held sway over the minds of men and so dazzled national elites that they practically surrendered their hard-won freedom at the altar of the new religion called modernity.

Today that doctrine is in a shambles. Not only has the 'developing' world discovered that all the enormous noise and fury of development projects (and the surrender of national and cultural autonomy in the process) has led them into a blind alley; the 'developed' world, too, has discovered that the path of its own progress is not limitless and that it is highly vulnerable to pressures emanating from the Third World. Hence the sudden splurge of talk about 'interdependence', of the need for cooperation instead of confrontation. Hence the show of great concern for the poor and the underprivileged of the world. Hence the growing criticism of the growth-oriented and centralised model of development, questioning not merely strategies but also the goals of development. Hence the growing stress on alternative paths to the future in place of a uniform course for all.

With such questioning and doubt, however, more fundamental questions have emerged. Is it just the limits imposed by conditions of scarcity that has made the paradigm of modernity unrealisable? Or is it, rather, that there is something fundamentally at fault with the paradigm itself? Isn't the theory of progress, as developed in the West, based on an anthropocentric view of nature and a positivist conception of knowledge and science, which are responsible for a model of development spelling domination and exploitation? And if these be the essence of the Occidental culture, and its contribution to human thought and values, shouldn't we discard large parts of it, and look for alternative modes of thought and values embedded in some other cultures?

We live in an unstable world. It is unstable not only because the period of Western domination is fast coming to an end and there is taking place a wide diffusion of political and economic power, the full implications of which are not yet clear. It is also, and more fundamentally, because the philosophical moorings of that period have proved shaky. Men of thought everywhere are engaged in a deep search for new systems of meaning and values, new approaches to power and authority, new conceptions of human identity and cohesion and new bases of containing sources of conflict and ensuring human survival.

Search for Alternatives

Increasingly, such a quest for alternative systems of thought and being is making intellectuals turn to non-Western cultures known for long-standing humanist traditions and for integrated perspectives on the human condition. What is the role of the Third World in such a quest? Here the picture is not too heartening. Barring a few isolated individuals and small centres of creative work, thinking in the Third World is bereft of systematic inquiry into the fundamentals of life. This needs to be quickly corrected. It would be a real tragedy if cultures strong in speculative thought and deductive logic were to fall prey to the lure of positivist science, imported from the West at a time when the world was in fact crying out for new worldviews and meaning and value systems. The religions and civilisations of India, of the Islamic world, of the complex web of humanist thought that has informed China, and of Buddhism provide major streams of thought that could substantially contribute to the present search for alternatives. But, as yet, there seems to be little stirring among the intellectuals of these regions along these lines. The fact that these regions also happen to be new centres of political and economic power is no guarantee that they will provide intellectual leadership. The intellectuals themselves have to strive to impress upon the elites of these societies the need for radical reorientation of the goals and strategies of development.

Such striving should be informed by two interrelated points. First, modernity is not something that can be wished away. Both as a doctrine of life and a guide to prudence, and as a framework for attending to the affairs of society, it has shaped our world in a fundamental manner, so fundamental, indeed, that we so often call it the 'modern world'. Modernity is not just Western or Occidental; it is part of us all. Indeed, the West itself is part of us all. It is more than a mere geographical category. It has become the dominant tendency and a major tradition for the contemporary world.

Secondly, it is incumbent upon us all—in the West and in other regions—to relate this presently dominant tradition to other civilisational traditions and meaning systems, and to evolve a process of critical interaction between them. We live in a time when what seemed a closed debate on a wide range of questions is being reopened, whether it is in respect of science and the philosophy of science, in respect of more basic relationships in society at the micro level, or in respect of family, ethnicity, sex roles and generational differences. On all these themes, the discussion displays a deep scepticism about earlier formulations and an earnest new search. The wide-ranging controversy, however, often results in considerable confusion. So it is only right that we provide ourselves with a wide and all-embracing framework for the discussions in various spheres—a framework that weaves together the concerns of science, philosophy, culture and religion from alternative civilisational perspectives.

Science and Technology

There have been, in human history, diverse visions and perspectives on the role of knowledge in society and its relationship with values and lifestyles. What concerns us at the present juncture is the impact of a particular vision that came out of the peculiar European experience following the Renaissance and was organised in a particular direction after

the seventeenth century, specially after the advent of the Industrial Revolution. What is peculiar about this vision is that the spur to it came
from technology; in course of time there emerged what is known as
science-based technology or, more correctly, a technology-directed
science. In the beginning, science and technology flowed in independent streams—one close to natural philosophy and the other to practical craftsmanship. Gradually, as technological breakthroughs began
to tantalise everyone, a myth was created that science and technology
were parts of the same enterprise, 'modern' and 'rational', which promised perpetual 'progress' for mankind. Thus took place what may be
called an unholy marriage between two traditions. Why did this happen?
Why did science take on an increasingly technological character? Why
did it begin to be judged more by its use-value than by its truth-value?

The Cultural Context

The answer is to be found in the cultural location from which both
modern science and modern technology emerged. It was a culture that
treated knowledge as an instrument of power, as an instrument of domination over the sinister and unpredictable forces of nature and, later,
over social forces and institutions and, ultimately, over relations between
societies and between cultures and races. It is only by reference to the
particular cultural context that this peculiar scientific worldview needs
to be understood and can be understood.

So it is not so much the running amuck of modern technology as a
historical process of a fundamental kind which has led to the domination of one particular culture over all others. It has been brought about
through the mechanism of science, and through the view that this particular science was 'universal' and hence at once valid and beneficial
for all. It is essential to come to grips with this particular worldview,
of which science and technology are but means, that stands for steam-
rolling almost the entire world into a uniformity, reducing its rich diversity to a predictable and predetermined state. As we come to grips with
it, we may be better able to seek to alter the course of modernity—not
necessarily rejecting everything, but rather changing the internal relationships that govern the field of knowledge as well as the interrelationship between knowledge and society. And as we do this, we may
be able to rediscover traditions of science and the pursuit of knowledge
that are at the moment submerged. And, similarly, we may rediscover
technological traditions from other parts of the world.

Other Traditions

These other traditions of science have had long centuries of history and development and are still available to draw on. In the countries of Asia there are very strong traditions of science as well as of technology, which at the moment are submerged under the dazzling impact of modern science, but which are gradually becoming highly relevant. China, India, Arabia, Persia, Indonesia—in all these major cultural regions there were important traditions of science and technology. What is common to all of them is the view of science as basically a search for truth, as a means of self-realisation and self-control, not as a means of bringing anything, least of all nature, under domination. Similarly, there are traditions of technology. A great deal of work has been going on in the last few years to rediscover these traditions which, because of their tenacity and continued utility, have survived in the folklore and in the folk pratices of our peoples. There is need to rediscover these in a spirit of intellectual inquiry.

Towards a Holistic Perspective

One other characteristic of these traditions of science, as compared to the latter-day western traditions of science, is the view that knowledge and the pursuit of truth are a holistic enterprise, not a specialised activity. It does not view science as a discrete activity and culture as another discrete activity, with further fragmentation and specialisation under each. It rather thinks of science and culture and various activities under each as facets of the same phenomenon. It is this all-inclusive view of creativity, thought, science, culture, philosophy, art, technology, economics and politics that intellectuals are seeking today in this world of extreme division of labour and in conditions of alienation and neurosis. The act of creation and the pursuit of truth are inseparable. The modernists have introduced a dichotomy between science and technology, on the one hand, and philosophy and art, on the other, which is most unfortunate. There is need to restore the comprehensive and holistic perspective that was there and still survives in many cultures, although at the moment it lies submerged.

Today the Western world is uneasy with its own traditions, some of its people looking for magic answers from the East. It is a very opportune time for us to reinvestigate and re-establish these traditions and to relocate the place of knowledge and action in them. In saying this, it is important to have a modest view of what man can do, and a modest view of rational knowledge. One of the biggest maladies that the modern age has brought in its wake is the putting of knowledge on a pedestal. Never before had men of knowledge (which in the modern age means men of science and technology) acquired such a command over resources and such a power for making decisions affecting other cultures and civilisations far removed from the places where decisions are made, as well as other species and, indeed, the whole of creation—all in the name of knowledge. It is necessary to return to the tradition of knowledge that conceives it as part of a larger process of self-realisation, a larger process of realising certain values.

In the West, too, this search is on—perhaps more there than elsewhere. There is evidence that at a time when some leading intellectuals and scientists in the West are raising the banner of revolt against the dominant perspective, the elites in the Third World are becoming extremely enthusiastic followers of it, succumbing to the mythology of modernity and becoming keen purchasers of the commodities called 'technology' and 'science'. An organised effort on the part of the custodians of social conscience all over the world is called for to persuade the decision-makers to move away from the suicidal path they are taking.

The Politics of Development

In this effort, particular attention should be drawn to the political repercussions of the western path of development. This kind of development has not only produced a more and more wasteful civilisation; it has also given rise to an increasingly inequitous and conflict-ridden global structure of political and economic power. It has led to a bottling up of world resources—the bulk of which comes from the Third World—in heavy concentrations of capital and machinery located in a few centres that bear no relation to the real needs of human beings in various parts of the world. It has given rise to a techno-economic process that has rendered millions of human beings—including those in the industrial centres—obsolescent and redundant, and has greatly eroded resources and opportunities that could have sustained productiveness in countless human settlements.

Permeation

The prevailing model of development has had two fearful consequences. One is that it has ushered in wasteful ways of human consumption, not only in the rich, highly industrialised, 'developed' North, but also in the poor, non-industrialised, 'underdeveloped' South. The second is that the pattern of domination of the North over the South has permeated the nations of the South. This is to be seen in the domination of large masses of the people by small privileged elites, westernised and more closely tied to the world metropolitan centres and to the experts and financiers of multinational corporations and lending agencies than to their own peoples. These elites are even more wasteful and given to consumerism than their Northern counterparts whom they seek to emulate. They are far more responsible for producing structures of inequity and exploitation in their societies than their counterparts in the North. This is not to underrate the importance of the fact that the roots of the contemporary patterns of inequality in the world are to be found in colonial and neo-colonial forms of dominance. But it is necessary to see that these forms have penetrated, or reinforced, the inequitous social structures of the colonised countries.

Misleading Diagnoses

A number of diagnoses of the problem of persisting underdevelopment and glaring dualism between the rich and the poor nations—and, as a reflection thereof, between the rich and the poor in the poorer nations—are misleading. The increasing population size of the poor, lack of motivation among the people of backward lands, decline in 'aid' from the rich nations, transfer of resources from development to defence in the developing nations, regional, linguistic and ethnic divisions in developing societies—are all examples of such diagnoses. Some of these (such as population growth) are mere symptoms of more basic causes. Some (such as the alleged lack of motivation among the poor) are entirely wrong. These diagnoses spring partly from the prejudices of scientists and social scientists and partly from the search for excuses by people seized by a feeling of guilt but unwilling to accept responsibility for basic injustices in the world and do something to redress them.

Basic Issue: Lifestyles

The primary cause for large areas of underdevelopment and inequity is to be found in the global structuring of man-resource relationship, in which a minority of nations have, in pursuit of a parasitic and wasteful style of life, shored up the large bulk of world resources. The spread of the same style of life among the elites of the countries of the Third World has meant that they remain divided, both individually and severally. These elites have failed to exert themselves at regional and global levels (except in endless rhetoric, mostly of confrontation). They have also failed to pursue within their own countries policies suited to their socio-economic, demographic and cultural conditions, which happen to be quite different from the conditions that obtained in the richer nations during their similar phase of development.

In spite of the rhetoric of confrontation a bond has been forged between the richer segments of both 'developed' and 'developing' nations, so that they continue to indulge in lifestyles that result in the perpetuation of global inequity, depletion of world resources and unsettling of nature's fine balance. Thanks largely to modern technology, the dominant economic model (that it has nurtured and made almost universally acceptable), and the model's politico-philosophical underpinnings (in a 'theory of progress' that had stemmed from the presupposition of infinite expansion of nature's bounties that were promised to become universally and equitably available), the world is being ruled by elites incapable of handling the problems confronting it.

Intellectual Brainwashing

The causes underlying all this are largely intellectual. If the world is 'structured' in a certain way politically, it is because the thinking that has dominated the world for the last hundred-odd years has been faulty. It has been centred on the idea of a uniform and homogeneous end product for all societies: a state of urban-industrial affluence, managed by experts at the top and backed by a capital-intensive technology—in short, the model of all-encompassing modernity. Even today, despite decades of misery and exploitation engendered by this model, the notion of catching up with those who are seen to be more 'developed', and along the same course, continues with uncommon persistence, not because it has the sanction of conscious deliberation by the large majority, but because it is sustained by the institutionalised interests of a small minority. In the process, a generalised erosion has taken place—of resources, of cultures, of equity. But the most appalling of all has been the erosion of the human mind in large parts of the world. Any attempt to undo the inequity and dualism of the present world must begin by undoing the intellectual brainwashing that has taken place under the impact of the modernist doctrine of development.

Significance of the Environmental Perspective

The concern with 'environment and development' is significant only in this larger political context and in the context of the intellectual necessity of redefining the whole purpose of development. It will entail the search for an alternative model of development based, not on specialised concerns of experts and aggregations thereof, but on something that is at once more comprehensive and more accessible to all human beings. It must promote a view of human welfare that does not assume some linear progression on some uniform pattern but, instead, allows for autonomy and self-reliance in a variety of local contexts so that everyone participates with a first-hand knowledge of actual conditions.

On environment there are many expert studies and, of course, there is still much to learn. But the more fundamental insight that has emerged from the more creative minds that are exercised on this issue combines four concerns: (i) a holistic view of development, (ii) a concern with a structure of equity that ensures autonomy and self-reliance of diverse entities in place of a structure of dependence that is sustained by the promise of aid and transfer of technology to enable others to 'catch up', (iii) an emphasis on participation, and (iv) an accent on the imporrtance of local conditions and the value of diversity. The import and implications of this perspective are just the opposite of those of the perspective of modernity as an inescapable panacea for all. Seen thus, the 'environmental perspective' is no more and no less than an alternative perspective on development. Specific aspects of the sustenance and improvement of the environment can, of course, be studied in specific contexts, and these may involve a series of technical tasks. But these are precisely the tasks that are involved in moving towards alternative patterns of development and lifestyle in tune with a conception of human needs and social and economic welfare to ensure a sustained improvement in the quality of life in all regions and a just and equitable international order.

It would be a gross mistake to think of environment outside of this larger global political context. This approach necessarily makes the environmentalist appear as anti-developmental to one set of people and the whole development enterprise as an encumbrance and nuisance to another. Such suspicions already exist. To treat different aspects of world development as discrete and independent dimensions has given rise to aggressive pessimism on the part of conservationists and an equally aggressive restlessness on the part of developmentalists. The problem is compounded by the fact that the conservationists are indentified with the North and the developmentalists with the South. So there is at the moment a virtual deadlock on this issue with little sign of its resolution.

The irony of it all is that the conservationists come from the region where the development dogma (based on the doctrine of modernity) originated and the developmentalists come from regions which have traditionally taken an integral view of man and nature and are even today better equipped to pursue an 'environmentally sound' development path. The irony is made only deeper by the fact that, although the incessant pursuit of modernist development by Northerners over centuries has had gruesome economic and political consequences for the Southerners, the Southerners are so possessed by the need to quickly undo global disparities that they fail to see that they would never realise their goal if they pursued the path laid out by the North. In their own interest, they must reject this path. Incidentally, they will then find some of their best friends among the environmentalists. The environmentalists, on their part, need to make common cause with the advocates of global equity and a new international order, and to conceive of environment as providing a series of opportunities for pursuing a new development path rather than a series of constraints on development as such. Conceived in this way, environment too becomes a resource—in fact, the most basic of all resources—for alternative development. With this will end the impression of an adversarial relationship between the two.

The Nature of the Present Crisis

A more concrete analysis will make these points abundantly clear. The basic cause of the present-day scenario of crisis can be stated quite simply. Arising out of massive poverty in large parts of the world, growing disparities between and within regions, worsening terms of trade for poor countries and for rural areas within them which further widen these disparities, and a corresponding increase in dependence and decline in real freedoms, there is rising discontent and restlessness among the poor of the world. These are manifested in political instability, growing incidence of tension and violence, and the consequent feeling of insecurity among powerful nations and among national elites. All this increasingly endangers peace at all levels, regional and international. While the real causes of the crisis remain unattended to, the symptoms are tackled with increasing repression, accelerating arms race of various kinds, and the conversion of the whole world into a garrison State. And yet, so grave is the crisis, and so interwoven are its various elements, that it is only by getting to the root of the problem and tackling it with a clear head that a major breakthrough can be achieved in the human condition. It is only thus that a steady and sustained process of realisation of values and aspirations in diverse regional and cultural contexts can be ensured, minimum levels of satisfaction and confidence attained in various centres of the world and, through all this, a more stable basis found for international peace and co-operation.

What, then, is the 'root of the problem'? Without going into remote historical and philosophical issues (some of which have been touched upon in other papers in this book, as well as in earlier books in this series),[3] we may say that underlying both the general historical process that engendered the phenomenon of 'underdevelopment' and the

---

3. See, in particular, the second volume in this series, *Transformation and Survival: In Search of Humane World Order.*

persisting—indeed, in some ways accentuating—state of inequity and poverty in our own time is the dominant model of development emanating from the West, a model based on the doctrine of modernity, the theory of progress, a manipulative view of science and a hedonistic view of human happiness.

The Crucial Aspect

There are many aspects (cultural, technological and political) of this historical process which cannot all be dealt with here. But the one that has proved crucial in bringing about the present state of affairs is the growing conflict over the access, distribution and direction of world resources for maintaining and raising standards of consumption and lifestyle achieved by the urban middle classes in the industrialised world and, through emulation or prompting, by the middle classes everywhere. This makes it necessary to spread the culture of consumerism globally and at the same time to contain and confine the capacities of newly industrialising countries within narrow technological limits. Hence the crucial role of the transnationals. Above all, there is the increasingly global sweep of economic diplomacy for ensuring enough surpluses from the world countryside to meet the growing demands for resources of the metropolitan centres in the face of fast-growing populations in the Third World, which is bound to put some brakes on the traditional export orientation of their economies. Similar pressures and distortions follow from the effort of the urban middle classes in the Third World to retain, and hopefully raise, their living standards.

All these concerted moves to preserve the economic advantages of the already advantaged generates an accelerating pressure on world resources and produces a structure of inequity and exploitation by eroding local autonomy and self-reliance and denying basic necessities to the large majority of the people of the world. So much for the present development model based on relentless consumerism.

It is the same ethic of consumerism that erodes environmental quality too. The present patterns of development are so wasteful and destructive of natural resources—land, water and entire ecosystems—that they are producing an increasing and exponential growth in desertification, deforestation and soil degradation, which together are leading to an overall erosion of the productive process itself, and most of this in the developing countries.

Relevance to Developing Countries

Those who think that environmental erosion is largely a problem for the industrialised countries are quite off the mark. For, increasingly, the reverse is taking place. Even pollution, which was supposed to be confined to industrialised countries, is increasingly being 'exported' to the countries of the Third World. And pollution is but a minor aspect of the environmental problems, the more important aspects being the depletion of renewable resources at a rate faster than their regeneration alongside the exhaustion of non-renewable resources, a rising rate of withdrawal of marginal land from productive use (thanks to biological degradation and desertification) and many other forms of decline in productivity, arising from the application of alien forms of technology and the systematic undermining of indigenous traditions and skills that were best suited to local conditions. Such intrusions into the local environments have not only increased disparities within and between regions but also increased dependency across the board all over (of the countryside on the cities and of entire countries on outside forces), undermining, in the process, local self-reliance and participation of local communities in making decisions that vitally affect them. Environmental erosion is, thus, no more than a physical and ecological expression of the overall erosion of societies wrought by development patterns fostered by consumerism.

Approach to Alternatives

It follows that the movement towards an alternative model of development should apply to all regions of the world, whether 'developing' or 'developed', and that it should combine in its framework both a sustainable process of development, through a continuous regeneration of renewable resources, and a reduction in resource and income disparities between and within regions. Such a symbiotic relationship between environmental and socio-political goals is inherent in the conception of an alternative pattern of development. In what follows I shall spell out a few basic postulates.

Removal of Poverty

The goal of development at the present time should be, first and foremost, the removal of poverty, not a mere increase in national product (which more often than not leads to wasteful consumption by elite strata with little or no benefit to the poor). Now, removal of poverty entails a series of sub-goals such as removal of disparities across regions, between cities and rural areas, and between the rich and the poor within each sector, as well as between the present and the future generations. Even this is not enough. There is need to categorically direct development to the benefit of the poorest strata, giving up the dictum that inequality and income differentials are inevitable in the process of growth.

This involves a different approach to technology, resources and environment. Removal of poverty is not possible under conditions that denude basic resources of nature to which the poor had always had access and for which they did not have to depend on institutionalised decisions. There is need, therefore, to move towards a model of development that has the potential of providing prosperity with utmost equity and in harmony with nature (i.e. by preserving its resource base for sustained development for all classes and for future generations).

Equity Through Local Self-Reliance

Development for equity entails the recognition of the primacy of local development and an end to external dependence. In the existing pattern of develoment, the villages are dominated from outside the local spaces, the society as a whole by a class of technocrats and entire nations by global purveyors of technology and power.

The goal of development should, instead, be actualisation of the potential of each locality. Such potential will be quite extensive, once the drain to the outside world dicated by the present patterns of development and decision-making is brought under control. This involves maximum reliance on renewable resources, regulation of the speed of such resource use, and recycling of resources within the locality. In point of fact, resources available within a local environment are more in tune with the requirements of the area, and most of these are nature's free gifts which do not lend themselves to outside controls except when a society surrenders its options under the hypnotic sway of imported models. This also implies that the conception of alternative development is itself not uniform, though it is certainly informed by certain norms and the historical context (on this more later). Plurality is in-built in this view. It is a conception of *alternatives*.

Self-Reliance and Decentralisation

The néed, then, is for greater self-reliance in every locale, maximum utilisation of nature's resources for productive use at decentralised levels, and the orientation of scientific effort to the problems of the common man. Only thus would Gandhi's vision of not only production for the masses but also by the masses be realised.

Development as Liberation

Such an approach to development, once implemented, can have far-reaching consequences. It would be the best insurance against the drain of resources to the affluent areas and against the shoring up of world resources by a minority of nations. Within each country, it will improve the terms of trade between agriculture and industry, and between rural and urban areas. And within the village society, too, once the drainage of resources and the perversion of institutional structures and information flows, due to rapacious technology, are brought under control and the traditional understanding of nature's life-support system allowed full scope, there will be less scope for exploitation and greater scope for equitable relations and broad-based participation of the people in the productive process. The new development pattern, in other words, involves a whole chain of liberating measures—from the country as a whole to the last man, woman and child in it—and makes it possible to tap the vast potential that nature can provide but is not allowed to. Environmentally, such a pattern of development opens many doors. By minimising the use of depletive assets, it preserves resources for under-privileged groups in the present (for the living generations) and in the future (for the generations to come). By promoting a use pattern that is in consonance with nature's principles (such as recycling and sym-biosis), it controls pollution and promotes health and well-being. By ena-bling a diffuse pattern of resource-flows, it enables man to escape centralised control over life's basic needs. In short, it becomes the cat-alyst of a genuine alternative to Western-style industrialisation and the harbinger of a non-elitist path of development for all.

Endogenous Science

Such a model of development (aimed at removal of poverty and dis-parities, ensuring of equity between and within regions and generations, encouraging autonomy, local self-reliance, decentralisation and people's participation) will necessitate a redirection of the scientific effort itself. It calls for not only the much-talked-of 'regeneration of villages' but also the regeneration of science. Under the present model of development, the main emphasis is on 'transfering technology' to the developing coun-tries and 'taking technology' to the villages. In both cases the pesumed beneficiaries are treated as passive recipients to whom a set of stand-ard techniques and practices, evolved in some advanced country or insti-tution, are to be doled out. The monstrous arrogance of this approach is obvious, but no less obvious are the deleterious consequences to both the autonomy and the well-being of millions of people. What is called for now is a radically different approach, which makes villages the bas-tions of scientific inquiry. There is a lot to learn about the mysteries underlying traditional practices of recycling and about the endless web of interrelationships between diverse land systems, water resources, plant physiologies, animal and bird species and other elements in the rural ecosystem.

New Road to Prosperity

Once such a spirit of learning develops, it will become possible to draw upon the rich potential of biotechniques based on nature's principles (as against the presently advocated universalist doctrine of biotechnology which will lead to a destruction of genetic diversity). It will then become possible to avoid rapacity and at the same time promote prosperity and well-being. This can be done by an in-depth study of each component of a specific environment—its air, water, soil, plants, animals and other living elements in it, and interrelationships between all these. A knowledge of these various processes will provide scope for not just an equitable and decentralised pattern of development but, through it, for continuous improvement in the quality of life of all strata of the people.

It is essential to restore the original symbiosis between science and nature which has been disturbed because science has become an instrument of exploitative technology (as was discussed earlier in this essay). The approach proposed here also corrects another mistaken notion, namely, a negative view of the environment as something that imposes constraints and 'limits'. While certain constraints must be respected, as they are based on sound reasoning, there are also immense opportunities for growth which are provided by the same environment. Gathering of such opportunities should be the task of science.

Approach to Nature

The new approach to science and to development suggested here is based on a certain perception of nature and man's relationship to it. The presumption that the role of science is to master nature and harness it in the service of man has turned out to be an illusion. This must give place to the essential purpose of science, namely, understanding the processes of nature—the opportunites it provides as well as the constraints it imposes. Planning the development of a given area becomes easier with this understanding.

Such an approach will make for a partnership between science and nature (in place of an adversary relationship, as at present) and—this is equally vital—between the scientist and the villager. There is a vast area of research and development that lies ahead in this field. But it will need to be based on a different philosophy from the one that usually informs R&D establishments. The scientist will have to take on a more modest role—as a participant in a total system of relationships. As was stressed earlier in this paper, one of the basic postulates of an alternative model and philosophy of development is to treat life as a whole and not in fragments. This calls for a perspective on science that is Oriental rather than Occidental.

Gandhi and Mao

This brings us to yet another point which is of the utmost importance. There is at present a virtual divorce between political philosophy and scientific striving. As a result, outstanding thought from the Third World—such as Gandhi's conception of self-rule for the poor and Mao's non-elitist path of development—has failed to gain long-term aceptance even where it originated. Where lip service is paid to their ideals, the State in both societies has placed overwhelming emphasis on central-ised control of the economy, in the process breeding a power elite. Simi-larly, Karl Marx, who is known as the prophet of equality and whose name moves millions in Third World regions, had dreamt of doing away with centralisation of power and eradicating the distinction between town and country and between manual and intellectual labour. Yet, he too had failed to question the technological centralisation involved in modern industrialisation; all he advocated was that the means of pro-duction should be owned and controlled by society. In both capitalist and socialist societies, the whole emphasis of scientific thought has been on social management, on more basic processes of nature. However, it has become abundantly clear in the thinking of leading scientists them-selves that social organisation must seek consonance with the process of nature, not abjuring intervention as such but making each interven-tion maximise nature's operating principles for the benefit of man. The most significant of these principles is diversity, which entails locale-specificity in resource management, and hence a diffuse and decentral-ised process of decision-making in the spheres of production and con-sumption as well as in the determination of surpluses and lifestyles.

It is not that Gandhi, Mao and Marx were wrong in their philosophy. It is rather that they or—in the case of Gandhi—their followers pressed a wrong and outmoded science in realising their ideals, a science that no honest scientist could accept as real. The task that faces these soci-eties now is to redirect scientific effort in the service of the ideals of Gandhi and Mao. This calls for a different conception of the purpose of science from that found in the West. To the western mind, science, like all knowledge, is an instrument of secular power for creating a good *social* order. We must reject this as at once inadequate and dangerous. It is dangerous because power as the end of knowledge usually degen-erates into power of the few over many. It is inadquate because crea-tion of a good social order can be no more than a means, the end being the liberation and self-realisation of each being. We come here to the

Oriental conception of knowledge as a means of seeking truth which, in turn, is a means of liberating the self. (In Oriental thought truth is not an end in itself.) This harmonises perfectly with the conceptions of diversity and decentralisation. But Gandhi's basic principle must be borne in mind, namely, that such liberation is to be of all individuals, not only of the educated and the better-off. Such a conception rejects the dualism inherent in the western paradigm and seeks the ends of individuals as well as of society in a composite philosophy of nature. With this also, incidentally, the discord between development and ecology disappears.

4

Communications for Alternative Development

Signposts of Our Time

I shall focus mainly on the crisis in the theory and practice of development in our times and consider the issue of communications in that larger context. I shall do this by (a) providing an overview of the kind of period we are moving into, and (b) considering what modes of intervention such a period calls for—through joint thinking and research, through new conceptualisation of the development *problematique* and, no less important, through active participation in the global process.

I shall first briefly outline the countervailing forces on both sides that are emerging in a period which I see as one of deepening dialectic of the forces of transformation and growing ability of the *status quo* to contain and defeat these forces.

To start with the positive developments, I think there is a continued assertion of the Third World in reshaping and restructuring the power relations of the world. Taking place simultaneously are the rise of the masses, their awakening and mobilisation at the grassroots level and the growing challenge to the authority of hegemonical structures by people's assertion of their democratic rights. So both at the level of the States and at the level of the peoples, there is a certain assertion against dominant structures.

As regards technology and the economic and political management of societies, some progress has been achieved towards the idea of indigenisation and rediscovery of rich and diverse traditions. There is a growing ecological consciousness, much greater than at the time of the Stockholm Conference, and there are larger and numerous groups working on this issue throughout the world. There is greater awareness of the importance of culture in the process of develoment.

There is a growing critique of the State and its role in human liberation. The assumption soon after the Second World War, by both elites and radicals, that the State would be a liberator and equaliser, is no longer avidly held and there is a creative reconsideration of the relationship between the State and civil society. There is a rediscovery of civil society as an autonomous expression of human and social will: the whole process of decentralisation and of rediscovery of identities.[1]

Within this larger process of transformation, there are certain other major assertions. One is the movement for women's rights. Although it has its own substance, I also consider this a very important symptom of what I would like to call a redefinition of the content of politics. Issues such as preservation of the environment, the relationship between the sexes, the question of public health and the whole area of education, which were hitherto considered outside the purview of politics, are now being brought into its framework. The women's movement underlines this more powerfully than any other movement that has emerged during the last decade.

More recently, people are attempting to find a more common base to these various movements: the ecological, the feminist, the movements for peace and for self-determination and democratisation. So far, this drawing together has happened more in the North than in the South given the urgency of the nuclear threat and the great salience of the peace movement. But some such common ground is being strived at even in the Third World. The human rights movement is getting increasingly radicalised, moving away from the old notion of providing safeguards to few intellectuals or journalists and political dissenters towards the whole range of civil and democratic rights: the landless, bonded labour, the miners, ethnic minorities, women, and increasingly children, especially of the poor.

These are all signposts of considerable creativity in our period. However, there are complementary moves to contain and defeat them and we should be fully aware of the mechanisms and strategies by which this is being done. There is a growing integration in the world economy of the First, the Second and the Third Worlds: as the whole development process is transnationalised, petro-dollars are recycled. Third World elites are incorporated and Third World nationalism is being rendered chauvinistic through militarisation and arms deals. At the same time there is a revival of the older paradigm of development: the free market economy, monetarism, export-oriented growth, free trade zones,

1. For an extensive analysis of the whole question of the role of the State, see the first volume in this series, *State Against Democracy: In Search of Humane Governance.*

etc. This is not just symbolised by leading examples in the North such as the US, but also by all kinds of Third World societies, for example, Sri Lanka, Singapore (which is being propagated as the model for Southeast Asia), and South Korea. We have seen the disastrous consequences of the same development in Nigeria and, of course, this influence has been at work in Latin America all along.

Technologically, while there is some progress towards rediscovering alternative processes, the dominant tendency is towards displacement of humans by machines. The obsolescence of human beings as productive forces is an inherent part of the new productive processes that are being designed, and the so-called new economic recovery in the North is planned on the basis of large lay-offs and robotisation. There is, despite a rise in ecological consciousness, increasing ecological destruction. This deeply affects the life chances of millions of marginal populations, particularly certain ethnic groups and the self-reliant rural poor who rely almost exclusively on the forests. There is evidence of growing ethnocide and threats to the survival of certain cultures in many areas of the world.

The issues of the pillage of natural resources, ecological destruction, and the threatened survival of traditional cultures are linked with probably the most ominous doctrine of our time; that entire social strata, such as the very poor, the disease-prone, the women of the tribals, are dispensable.

Every day, in Delhi alone, there are something like five brides burnt, for the simple reason that they fail to extract from their parents still more money and gifts so that the consumer standard of the family in which they are married can be continuously upgraded. And within the same middle-class society I have heard very respectable people say: If only we did not have the poor, the backwards, the tribals and so on, how much easier our progress would be, how quickly we could catch up with the West, how soon our nation would become strong and powerful. I am not exaggerating. And that attitude necessarily leads to a certain brutalisation of the human spirit. We all tend to preserve our sanity by immunising ourselves against the forces of destruction and destitution and ignoring their existence or passing them by —even as we read the daily newspaper or listen to the radio. And this process is by no means limited to India, nor even to the Third World.

The result of all this is the increasingly oppressive character of the State: the alienation of national elites from the civil society: and the rise not only of mafias, hoodlums and criminals but also of their use by party and political machines in many parts of the world.[2]

---

2. *op cit.*, especially the chapter on "Democracy and Fascism in India".

The international division of labour is changing fast. On the one hand, there is the larger transformation in the status of women brought about by the feminist movement. On the other hand, changes are taking place which are seriously affecting the poor by exploiting their women and children. Not only is rising unemployment affecting the prospects for work of the weak as a whole, and women in particular, but the unorganised sector of the economy which employs women and children at highly exploitative rates is growing rapaciously. All this is undermining the trade union movement, in country after country. And the State is becoming instrumental in all this, often under the impetus of global agencies, such as the IMF and its conditionalities.

The latest attack on human rights comes through yet another distortion of the State, namely the growth of national security States that are increasingly militarised and spurred by police and para-military establishments. All these developments are part of the larger integration and transnationalisation that I have been addressing myself to. But it would be wrong to blame exogenous factors alone. Indeed, a great deal of blame must go to the elites of the Third World.

Thus, while there is greater creativity and the opening up of new spaces on the one hand, there is perhaps a more determined and conscious process of co-optation, containment and defeat, on the other.

The Need for Alternatives

We have been looking at some of the signposts of our time. But they are not signposts for a new paradigm, just part of the reality in which we live. What would be their significance for alternative development thinking? I suggest that there is a need to go beyond the original conception of 'another development' and 'alternative development strategies', beyond the Brandt Commission and North-South dialogues, beyond Cancun and mini-summits convened by Third World leaders and appeals by heads of State. There is a need to rethink the basis of development cooperation and technology transfers, to recapture the real basis of self-reliance and the basic needs perspective—and to do this in the context of the rise of new movements and new actors on the scene.

Most earlier thought on alternatives was largely addressed to the State and the international order. It was based on the naive assumption that the political process took place in an arena of rationality, persuasion and changes of regime. We have discovered that there are much larger forces at work, and that mere changes in government do not take us much closer to an alternative world. We have to rethink the whole process of power and distribution beyond relations between States and see it primarily as relations between peoples. In so doing we should discover the new agents of change and the new catalysts of transformation, mobilisation and renewal, and we should think of both communication and cooperation in these terms. We have to think beyond dividing the world into North and South, East and West. Because basic to the whole undertaking is, as I mentioned earlier, a redefinition of politics. The question is, what we should include in politics. Because so far, I think politics has been underplayed in the enterprise called development. Indeed, in the minds of some, there has been an attempt to abolish politics altogether. This tendency towards depoliticisation has led to a bureaucratisation and technocratisation of the development process, handing it over to both well-meaning and ill-meaning technocrats, committees, UN conferences and so on. Even campaigns are coopted and depoliticised, as in the recent World Disarmament Campaign.

What then is the new, or emerging, conceptual basis of thinking towards an alternative platform? I do not think there is a ready-made theory at work. We are still groping towards one. Nor do I think that we will arrive at one, because I think the new actors on the scene will decide what their future will be. All we can do is to assist this process of reconceptualisation. What follows is a tentative outline of what I see as my contribution to it.

I shall again start by listing four or five major signposts, both conceptual and substantive, drawing in part on the analysis of global trends and counter-trends that I have already outlined. The first is the extremely serious conflict over both access to and control over natural resources. This conflict is between regions, North-South if your like, but also between classes, and within societies. Ecology has to be seen as a societal issue and not simply as a question of the relationship between man and nature. The connection has to be made with the availability of resources to which the poor had always had access and of which they are now continually being deprived. Not only are we making them poor and doing nothing to relieve their poverty, but we are also forcing destitution upon them by taking away from them the little that nature itself provides.

The second major factor we should take into account is the militarisation of the world, resulting in increasing vulnerability of nations and peoples everywhere. Militarisation and development have to be seen in a symbiotic relationship, one that is rendering the whole development process both unsafe and exploitative. Any thinking on alternatives will need to discover the sources of tension and inequity in the development paradigm as it currently exists, and the accentuation of the same under the impact of militarisation, and to counter both simultaneously.

The third major factor to be considered is that we are in the middle of what is likely to be a long drawn-out crisis in global economic relations. We have to rethink the whole basis of economic relations. I personally see a growing and identifiable weariness, cynicism and defensiveness coming over people who have been dealing with development cooperation and those who have been concerned with how to restructure or modify the present international economic framework. The larger reality of the global economic crisis, which informs international economic relations and percolates into national economies, has to provide the overall context of any thinking about development cooperation, whatever its shape or form. Personally I have very little faith in development cooperation that is based on aid from States to States.

The fourth major parameter or basis for the new conceptualisation of the global situation is the inclusion of human rights and the survival of cultures as intrinsic to the development process. To put political and economic issues into watertight compartments and write off the whole human rights issue as propaganda devised by Northerners—as elites from the South often do—is, if I may say so, pure deception and doubletalk. It is like saying that the environmental issue is a false one and is the result of propaganda devised by Northerners. This is precisely the way in which the elites and propagandists of the Third World have tried to undermine liberties there and have glossed over the pillage of the resources of their poor. Nor is this exclusive to the Third World. There are signs of growing repression of the poor and unemployed in the North also. We cannot separate the dimensions of conflict over resources, the militarisation of the world, the global economic crisis, or human rights and the survival of cultures. We have to see them as interrelated. This has been another fault of development thinking to see problems and their solutions in unidimensional terms. It is why the solutions have not worked.[3]

Items for Analysis

Within this conceptualisation, I see a need for four or five types of analysis. One is to recapture class analysis in a new and different perspective. There is, almost worldwide, the rise of a new social class. In traditional Marxist terms this should be called a class of 'declassed'

3. On these various dimensions and their *inter-relationships*, see the output from the United Nations University Programme on 'Peace and Global Transformation', Tokyo (UNU headquarters) and New Delhi (Office of the Programme Director). For the initial conceptual paper that started the programme off, see my "Survival in an Age of Transformation" in the second book in this series, *Transformation and Survival: In Search of Humane World Order*. For the first 'composite' statement on the various dimensions, see *Towards a Liberating Peace*, Lokvani, 1988.

people. From the peace and women's movements to the catalysts of the
human rights claims of the people and the oppressed, leadership has
come from a wide range of communities, castes and classes, which can
no longer be categorised in mere economic terms. A new social class
has arisen which wants to transform the world.

The second major dimension is the rise of women, which I believe
can not be handled within the traditional class analysis. It has to be seen
as a factor by itself, and as a social category and class of its own.

Thirdly, there is the position of the poor in the social structures of
our time. The new division of labour does not permit us to absorb the
category of the poor within that of the proletariat, not even in trans-
itional categories like the lumpen proletariat. The position of the poor,
the tribals, the forest people and many other indigenous societies and
cultures calls for a different categorisation and conceptualisation of the
poor. I think poverty, as a basic issue of human liberation, has to be
conceptually accepted on its own and not as a result of traditional economistic analysis. Equally, care should be taken not to throw out the baby
with the bath water. Class analysis must be recaptured but made relevant to contemporary reality.

The fourth issue I have already mentioned, but it is critical to any
re-examination of thinking. It is the role of State in the whole process
of development and liberation.

Fifthly, there is the long shadow of consumerism. Analysts of the
world system, political theorists, self-critical analysts of the socialist
world and Third World analysts are now all agreed that the demonstration effect of a particular style of consumption that originated in
Western industrial societies has undermined the autonomy of other societies, including the socialist ones (now including China). An increasing
number of writers from within the socialist countries are begining to
accept these theses. Consumerism is a force by itself. It is not generated
by this or that factor but is almost autonomous of human will. In India
there was one state which was always communist: Kerala. Now, because
of the Gulf economy, Kerala has been transformed. In five years its per
capita income has doubled, and in the process socialism has gone by
the board. In fact, prosperity in a number of Third World countries orig-
inates in oil revenues in other Third World countries. The remittances
coming from Gulf countries to some of the South Asian and Southeast
Asian countries are upsetting traditional balances. A Pakistani friend
of mine callls it 'the Dubai Factor' in his country, and asserts that the
movement for restoration of democratic rights in Pakistan is highly
unlikely to succeed in Punjab, the most populous core of the country,
because the Dubai factor has so transformed its economy and the mot-

ivational structure of practically every family in it. The democratic movement may be succeeding in Sind and Baluchistan and in the North-West frontier and elsewhere but not in Punjab. This is an important factor to bear in mind when we talk of rising standards of living. What actually happens to surplus economic wealth in intrinsically poor and backward societies must be carefully examined. Prosperity based on consumerism and the rise of a *nouveau riche* class may prove more destabilising than providing a more secure base for a traditionally poor society.

The Role of Communications

It is against such a changing perspective that the role of communications has to be perceived. It has to be thought of not as a specialised concern, but as part and parcel of the struggle for human liberation, freedom and justice, strengthening the struggles of communities and cultures, of national entities that are thought to be marginalised, and of already marginalised peoples within these and other societies. It should be communications that exposes the hypocrisy of the rhetoric in international forums, which is in direct contrast to the same elites' behaviour in their own societies. Communication should be a process that contains the forces of backlash and promotes the forces of transformation and survival. Even within the 'Third System', this will involve identifying new actors and constituencies and moving beyond the highly articulate and eloquent interpreters of the human condition to the real, unheard voices. Some of these are occasionally found in the *IFDA Dossier*[4] but much more of this is needed.

There is also need, as James Robertson has continuously reminded us, to move out of an overwhelmingly Third World oriented thinking and to include the deepening crisis within the West, and within the North-East: a crisis that can engulf the whole world, if it gets worse.[5] And it is already getting worse. In this context we need to examine the prospects of what some people call 'dealignment' within the present blocs: dealignment as an ally of non-alignment. The process has already started both within the Soviet bloc and within the Western bloc. But again there are two kinds of trends, for there are enormous pressures being brought to bear to keep the blocs intact. The question is what can

---

4. *IFDA Dossier* is published six times per year by the International Foundation for Development Alternatives, 4, Place du Marche, 1260 Nyon,   Switzerland.
5. James Robertson's latest book is *The Sane Alternative*. He is heavily involved in the alternative movement in the UK and one of the editors of *Turning Point*, a newsletter issued from The Old Bakehouse, Ilges Lane, Cholsey, Nr. Walling-ford Oxfordshire OX10 9NU.

be done to speed up certain trends and to slow down others? We have to develop means of communication that cut across the blocs, across North-South and across East-West. Indeed, across South-South as well, for very often South-South affairs degenerate into alliances of elites against the people. It is said of the ASEAN bloc that it is essentially an intelligence community; watchful of and operating against the dissidents. That also is a South-South problem.

An ominous global project seems to be taking shape, the aim of which is to put an end to humanity and civilisation. It is a very serious project. Hundreds of thousands of scientists are involved in it. The project may be a success even without a nuclear holocaust—through the destruction of resources and through the doctrine of dispensability of the poor, a kind of 'triage' on which I wrote earlier.[6] The fact that societies and economies are becoming increasingly militarised affects the entire resource base and so the availability of resources for development and for the eradication of poverty. Ultimately, each society may be forced to give up on its poor, its ethnics, and its minorities. This can hardly be a condition for survival of the species. It would only generate a climate of tension, confrontation and violence.

There is a very interesting thesis emerging from the work of some political ecologists. It is that, even if a nuclear war does not take place but only the preparations for it, these alone, along with other trends of the present capitalist economy, can still lead to the death of 250 to 300 million people—the expected casualty level of a nuclear war. It is vital for us to understand what this mindless global project is about and to call for a countervailing one which will be *our* project: for survival, for humane development and for redefining the agenda of politics, for human freedom and integrity of the environment, and for a basic commitment to values without which the human species cannot survive.

We should put an end to the dichotomy between economic and political dimensions as is, for example, exemplified in some of the current thinking that an emphasis on human rights will take attention away from economic problems. I suggest that the unidimensional and almost exclusively economic basis of the development paradigm has undermined the prospects for not just development, but for the sheer survival of large strata of the world's peoples.[7] Mere transfer of resources

6. *State Against Democracy, op. cit.* , especially the chapters "On Humane Governance" and "Democracy in the Third World" and ' *Transformation and Survival, op. cit.,* especially the chapter on Bridging Two Worlds".

7. For a detailed analysis of economism and its consequences for development theory, see the chapter on 'The Development *Problematique'*, in this book .

and technology does not necessarily bring us any closer to the realisation of a desired state. Unless one builds the human rights dimension into the development paradigm, this will not happen—human
rights as understood in the context of this essay, as rights of the people.
In short, if we are to intervene in this crucial struggle between the ominous forces of destruction and a still weak and vulnerable force for a
just, demilitarised and humane society, and between the fire that is
engulfing the world at the topmost levels and the myriad attempts to
extinguish it worldwide, we have to think of human survival as the main
aim of the development paradigm. We have also to see it as an essential condition of human creativity. And we must think of survival—
like a subsistence economy—as not a negative, minimal goal but as a
dynamic force projecting a positive alternative to the theory of progress
and the goal of affluence, one that finds dignity in genuine equity and
in diverse cultures working out their own strategies in local movements for democracy and autonomy. 'Global problems, local solutions'
is no longer a mere slogan. It is the very condition of human survival.[8] Hence the relevance of the people, of movements, of *politics*.

---

8. See the chapter on "Decline of Parties and Rise of Grassroots Movements" in *State Against Democracy, op. cit.*

5

Political Economy of Development

The highly specialised and fragmented character of social science disciplines has led to a system of higher education which has little relevance to the problems facing the people. There is need to break this isolation of academic disciplines both from each other and from the wider society and its needs and problems; even good theoretical work will not come forth so long as this isolation continues. This is especially true for the twin disciplines of economics and political science—although once the concerns of these two are joined, other areas of knowledge will have to be drawn in too. Let me say right away that when I speak of breaking this fragmentation and isolation, with some people working in economics and some in politics, I do not simply mean that they should be located in the same institution, with one or two sociologists and psychologists thrown in on the side. This is what is usually meant by the so-called 'interdisciplinary research'. My concern is rather with the development of composite perspectives and normative frameworks that combine the insights and tools of the different disciplines—in the work of individual scholars. We have in this respect an illustrious pedigree of rather powerful men of ideas and their application to real life situations. I refer to the pedigree of political economy. I am glad to see that there is of late some recognition of the need to revive and develop the tradition of 'political economy'.

At any rate, in this essay I want to focus attention on precisely this area of the relevant linkages between economic and political factors in contemporary society's pursuit of goals and values. The nature of this pursuit, and the intellectual climate in which it takes place, have changed quite considerably since the days of the pioneering exponents of political economy—from the standpoints of both classical liberalism and sci-

entific socialism. And the principal point of this difference is the change
in the political context of the world we live in. The role of the State and
of ideology, the growing process of 'democratisation' the world over,
the increasing accent on mass welfare and mass participation in
decision-making, and the effort everywhere to mobilise the wisdom and
techniques of economic science to the purposes of State and nation-
building—these are the factors that have changed the issues that the
new political economy must strive to deal with. To this must be added
the enormously difficult pressures that the short run brings on peoples
and governments in the wake of unprecedented demographic conditions and their economic and political consequences. There are many
who think that in the long run both modern technology and modern
technocracy will solve the basic problems of material human welfare.
I do not subscribe to this viewpoint but I do not wish to go into that
issue here; I have dealt with it elsewhere in this book. For what hangs
heavy on our conscience and on our ingenuity to meet our problems
is the short and the medium run. Keynes was never more right than
in the decades we live in. There is need to develop an adequate approach
to the issues of political economy in the new setting.

Historical Context

In our country this linkage has turned out to be of crucial relevance
to our performance as a people and as a nation. Economic development in India, while no doubt building on earlier processes, has been
consciously pursued as a State objective and not just left to a *sui generis*
process of growth. As time has gone by, economic development and
its objectives have grown in importance as a matter of vital concern to
the State. At the same time the adoption of a democratic political framework and the concomitant growth of new publics, new elites and new
pressures at various points in the social structure have meant that Indian
society must pursue various goals 'simultaneously' rather than 'sequen-
tially' as happened in most western democracies; and that continuous
pursuit of diverse goals has become a legitimate and demanding exercise of leadership and governmental institutions. Meanwhile, ideological debate has shifted from polemical warfare to more realistic
problems of choice, and the issues of growth and distribution, aggregate welfare and social justice, political stability and structural change
have increasingly come to the surface. It is being slowly realised
that these issues cannot be dealt with even modestly on the basis of
traditional models of long range, self-generative development which
claimed to provide an almost automatic take-off to sustained growth;
and that there is need to be sensitive to variables that were hitherto con-

sidered *ceteris paribus* and outside of neat mathematical frameworks. Similarly in politics the point has been increasingly brought home that the principal issue to tackle if democracy is to make a success is the issue of economic satisfaction of the people. A most critical election was fought and settled on the issue of *'garibi hatao'* and even since that the issue of poverty has dominated the national scene. Whether or not politicians at different levels take this seriously will in part depend on how far social scientists take it seriously and bend their energies to clarifying the issues involved in realising it and posing alternative policy scenarios.

Thus from different vantage points India's social problems call for an anaylsis of the interactional field in which economic and political factors operate. Historically, however, things have so developed that systematic attention to this very field has been lacking. There are many reasons for this. Firstly, there was a long period of relative autonomy of the two processes of economic planning on the one hand and the pursuit of political power on the other. For more than a decade after we initiated a conscious and directed effort at economic development, Indian planning was characterised by considerable insulation from political pressures for distribution and justice. Similarly, the political process tended to pursue its own logic for longer than a decade since we held our first general election. The process of politicisation that everyone now talks of was for long limited in respect of consolidation of the power elite, cooptation of restive elements into the existing structure, and gradual mobilisation of new social strata into the institutional framework of government and the party system. All this went on relatively free of any clear articulation of economic issues and transformation of people's material needs and discontents into political controversy.

Now it is necessary to say that such relative autonomy of the economic and the political spheres had its advantages. Thus, not pressed by distributive demands, the Planning Commission could concentrate on the accumulation of capital and its investment in both basic infrastructure and the towering heights of an industrial economy. While the full benefits of this was expected to be felt in the next phase through greater utilisation of capacity and reaping the fruits of import substitution, the country had without doubt moved significantly out of a colonial type economy and out of the kind of dependent relationship to the metropolitian areas of the world as was the case with large parts of Africa, Latin America and Southeast Asia. This may be changing of late. Similarly, the ability to consolidate the central political structure of the country and lay the basis of a considerable process of national integration through the operation of a democratic-federal structure, without premature pressures for economic performance, may have enabled India to lay the foundations of a stable political order and avoid the traumas through which various other countries in the 'Third World' have had to pass. And yet it is this cognitive gap between economic and political development that is responsible for our inability today to provide an adequate framework for thought and action when economic performance has become a major political issue and when, on the other hand, political and ideological pressures are calling for a fresh look at the whole planning model.

This is one reason for our neglect of relevant linkages in our approach to developmental policies. A second reason, which was partly related to this mutual autonomy of our political and economic spheres, derived from our adoption of borrowed models and misleading and often false criteria. In economics we took over lock stock and barrel linear models of growth aimed at pre-defined targets (which were by and large derived from the accomplishments of other countries) while in politics we tended to judge our performance in the light of models and standards derived from western parliamentary democracy based on a competitive party system and theories of interest representation. In both spheres for quite some time we failed to develop our own evaluative standards and failed even to understand the enormously innovative model of development that we had in practice given rise to. Wrong criteria both blinded us to our real accomplishments and made us insensitive to our real failures and problems. In the event aggregate statistics and abstract models of control and manipulation became a substitute for perceptions of the real processes at work—in both our political life and the structure of our economy.

Thirdly, reinforcing these trends was a singularly inept orientation and organisation of our social science disciplines. Economic science became a blackboard science with its elaborate boxes, arrows and 'functions'—lifeless, monotonous but compelling in its power to blind reason and understanding. Political science, on the other hand, became a bookish science, quoting from archaic histories of thought and burgeoning constitutional treatises—out of touch with the exciting realities that were unfolding right under the nose of distinguished professors in distinguished universities. Both these could have been avoided if economists and political scientists had tried to work together on common problems or, better still, if each of them had incorporated the concerns of the other in their own work. But this did not happen, partly due to the over-specialisation and the so-called 'rigour' of the economist and the under-specialisation and complacency of the political scientist. The arrogance of the economist confounded with the diffidence of the political scientist—with the real intellectual anchorage of both lying outside the country. There were no doubt some outstanding exceptions in both spheres but they were very few. Only after the Emergency did a general awareness of the linkages between the two grow.

Meanwhile a whole lot of trivial disciplines grew up under the impetus of foreign consultants and foreign trained persons—public administration, management, social work, area studies and so forth. These produced a whole lot of new 'methods' and large tomes of descriptive material—elaborate in their empirical pretension but empty in any real contribution to social understanding. Economists and political scientists began to be impressed by these so-called micro-disciplines—reading from uniformly boring and repetitive village monographs[1] and unending administrative 'case histories'—rather than from the different macro perspectives of each other. Perhaps such cooperation was not very easy, given the level of competence of a majority of political scientists in the country. But what was possible—and was not done—was a formulation of problems and issues on which the insights and analytical perspectives from different disciplines could be joined. That this was so despite the empirical reality of a distinctive pattern of development that had already taken place in the country is a sad reflection on the hiatus that divided the social sciences.

Significantly, the pressure for attending to the political-economic linkages and for a consequent modification of perspectives on both economic planning and the process of political power came not so much from academic social scientists—despite a few exceptions—but from the accumulating grievances generated by democratic politics raising doubts

---

1. There are, no doubt, major exceptions, especially in the work of some social anthropologists who have brought larger concerns of civilisation and polity to bear on their elaborate studies of micro communities. M. N. Srinivas researched his interest in the dynamic components of Hindu society in a pioneering study of the Coorgs in Mysore and, on the basis of that work, popularised the generic concepts of 'sanskritisation' and 'westernisation'. See his *Religion and Society among the Coorgs of South India*, Bombay, 1952. Later, through his study of Rampur village, he developed the concept of 'dominant caste'. See M. N. Srinivas, "The Dominant Caste in Rampura", *American Anthropologist*, February 1959. Andre Beteille, in his *Caste, Class and Power: Changing Patterns of Stratification in a Tanjore Village*, Berkeley and Los Angeles, 1965, showed how political power had begun to transform traditional caste loyalties. Both these authors were concerned with larger (macro) processes and chose to study them in depth. There are other similar studies, a few of them by foreigners. But the bulk of village studies lack this perspective and seem to be conceived as ends in themselves. Most of them are highly repetitious and oblivious of the larger forces at work in Indian society. S. C. Dube's earliest work, *Indian Village*, Ithaca, 1955, was a pathfinder for these studies. But was it necessary to repeat his research format *ad nauseum*?

on the credibility of a plan process which on the one hand failed to produce even minimum necessities for the mass of the people and on the other hand exposed the growing inequality of the economic process. There ensued a slow but definite response to these questions—despite elaborate theoretical defences of the so-called 'basic model' from academic pulpits—which finally led to a new approach to agriculture and its place in the economy and, somewhat later, to a gradual review of the whole policy process. Simultaneously, the issues of justice and inequity, highlighted by the poverty and deprivation of a large majority of the population, began to come to the fore with the spread of political awareness and became the basis of a more effective controversy than existed hitherto within the political and party forums in the country.

As all this happened, no doubt, sensitive social scientists began to articulate the main issues of public policy and governmental performance and similarly a new generation of national leadership began to see the problems facing the country in perspective. For almost imperceptibly, over just a couple of years (1967-69), the struggle for political power and the challenge of economic performance got closely interwined and its essential linkage was grasped. Mrs. Indira Gandhi came to symbolise this awareness through a fresh approach to power and proved to be a catalyst of a new phase in Indian democracy. To her must go the credit of reconstructing the *whole process of politics around* the crucial theme of economic performance while at the same time making the process of economic policy-making subject to the scrutiny of political and social aims. With this the isolation of economic and political spheres, and let us hope, of the economic and political sciences as well, is likely to come to an end.

Rise of Policy Sciences

There are grounds to believe that this need will be reflected in scholarly work. With the advance of empirical social sciences and their impact on government and industry, and the growth of economic controls and planning even in capitalist economies, a number of issues have already been formulated in regard to the scope, methodology and utilisation of the social sciences for the purposes of policy formulation and execution.[2] Many of these were recorded in a preliminary but nonetheless convincing manner in a major work edited by Daniel Lerner and Harold Lasswell, *The Policy Sciences* (Hoover Institute Studies, Stanford, 1951). Lasswell has been particularly influential, since the thirties, in

2. For a fuller review of these issues and a research design, see my "Policy Planning and Performance in India: An Empirical Inquiry", Centre for the Study of Developing Societies, mimeo.

orienting social sciences to the concerns of public policy, drawing for this purpose on the work of economists during the depression (Keynes, Hansen, Kuznets), sociologists and social psychologists during World War II (Lynd, Stouffer, Thurstone) and the earlier interdisciplinary work of psychiatrists, anthropologists and others (Sullivan, Benedict, Mead, Linton, Kluckhohn), and on the basis of this accumulating wisdom in the social sciences, formulating 'developmental constructs' for the study of social change and public policy in modern times and especially as related to the democracies.[3] Many others contributed to this manner of thinking, both raising the status and significance of the social sciences and in turn making social scientists more 'problem-oriented', in the process breaking down the barriers that divided different social science disciplines. As such a perspective developed, it also became clear that not only was there a need to shed disciplinary boundaries for a comprehensive attack on the problems of public policy, but there was also for the same reason a need to interact closely with men of experience in government, industry and politics, as well as with specialists from other sciences and technical disciplines.

Unfortunately for the growth of the 'policy sciences', other developments in the social sciences overtook the concern with issues of public performance as a way of organising research. Chief among these was the accent on statistical method, formal paradigms and models in the search for a value-free science, and the increasing use of mathematics in the social sciences—together holding the promise of taking the social scientist closer to the presumed methods of the more exact sciences. As governments, research bodies and fund-giving agencies became impressed by the seeming rigour and certainty of quantitative methods, systems analysis and cybernetic models borrowed uncritically from the mechanical and biological sciences, the concern for more significant and painstaking work in the field of human engineering and civil government receded in the background. The accent henceforth was on precision at the cost of significance. This happened primarily in the United States—from where many of the recent influences in the social sciences have come—but gradually in other countries as well, including India.

It is only very recently, with an increasing number of political systems facing crisis-like situations at home, with the younger generation of social

---

3. Harold Lasswell, "The Policy Orientation", in Lerner and Lasswell (eds.) *The Policy Sciences*, cited above in the text. See also the earlier collection of Lasswell's essays on this theme, *The Analysis of Political Bahaviour*, International Library of Sociology and Social Reconstruction, London, 1947. Lasswell continued to work for many years on this perspective of social science research. See his "Sharing the Experience of Permanent Reconstruction: A Policy Science Approach", in A.R. Desai (ed.), *Essays on Modernisation of Underdeveloped Society*, Bombay, 1971.

scientists clamouring for the human relevance of scientific knowledge, with growing recognition all over the world of the stupendous problems faced by the developing nations and their governments, and a realisation that the process of development cannot be reduced to a few simple 'functions', that a revival of interest in more enduring human concerns and thus in policy-relevant social science is taking place.[4] The point is of particular relevance to India where the need for combining the theoretical and scientific concerns of the social scientists with the practical and 'pragmatic' insights of the policy-makers and the people has become more urgent than ever.[5]

Normative Approach

This is a good time to begin work on some of these questions both theoretically and in terms of spelling out a pragmatic approach to national problems. Of course, a lot of work is needed before a clear framework—or various alternative frameworks—will emerge for handling the different relationships in a dynamic fashion.

---

4. See, for instance, Wassily Leontief's Presidential address delivered at the eighty-third meeting of the American Economic Association, reprinted in *American Economic Review*, 61 (1), March 1971. It is worth noting that Leontief has contributed quite considerably to the quantitative model-building trend in modern economic analysis. It is also interesting to note that a past President of the Econometric Society had written in the same vein, "... it cannot be denied that there is something scandalous in the spectacle of so many people refining the analysis of economic states which they give no reason to suppose will ever, or have ever, come about ... It is an unsatisfactory and slightly dishonest state of affairs." F. H. Hahn, "Some Adjustment Problems", *Econometrica*, January 1970 (quoted in Leontief's address). Leading exponents of other social sciences have also expressed themselves in a similar way on the 'relevance' of much recent work. See, for instance, the Presidential address of Reinhard Bendix to the American Sociological Association and the Presidential address of David Easton to the American Political Science Association.

5. Professor D. R. Gadgil took a similar position in his address to the inaugural function of the Indian Council of Social Science Research. "To understand the organisation and working of social institutions and the actions and reactions of individuals in and towards them, to identify the origins and drives of what may be termed social forces, the mechanics or the etiology of social change and to appreciate the possibilities and limitations of deliberately defining goals or directing change, become in this context, the obvious objectives of social studies ... This might seem to explain why the social sciences are often called the policy sciences ..." Professor Gadgil, in this very perceptive address (see ICSSR, General Information, 1969), also made a strong plea for an active acquaintance of the social scientist with actual experience and for a 'two-way exchange' between academicians and practical people. He observed that in taking this position he was perhaps treading on controversial ground. In fact, he was expressing an opinion that was very much in keeping with developments in the social sciences all over the world. But it is a point that needed to be made in India where we seem to have a habit of borrowing from others' models and techniques which they are themselves about to discard.

at this juncture is to provide heuristic perspectives on the relationship
between things like nation-building, economic development, and the
achievement of a just and humane society. In the rest of this lecture I
shall try to briefly outline one way of handling this intellectual task and
raise issues that will need to be handled if the new political environment in the country is to be fully utilised for dealing with a rather pressing agenda of problems. As I see it, one of the first needs in this respect
is for a statement of first principles against which both economic and
political performance can be measured in terms of operational standards and criteria that follow from such principles. Without this the mere
emphasis on either performance or the policy process or the relevance
of social sciences will not take us very far. The danger of getting lost
in the maze of practical tasks and the interstices of statecraft is as great
as that of abstracting away from them. This is not the first time that
one has to bear in mind the maxim that there is nothing more practical
than a sound philosophy of life.

As I see it, the need is to develop normative standards which transcend both political and economic considerations and provide criteria
against which performance in both these spheres can be judged and analysed. Too much stress on the analytical at the expense of the normative produces an intellectual environment in which it is difficult to relate
anything. The theory of 'development'—and especially of 'political
development'—has for far too long evaded the most logical question
of the theory: Development towards what ends? Development for what?
In the language of classical thought, the question is: what are the ends
of the State?—the State considered as the collective and institutionalised will of human beings living in a defined territory. What are the
values that the State ought to strive for?

Now despite all controversies in regard to both historical analysis and
contemporary challenges, there has taken place a great deal of convergence in thinking on the basic end of social arrangements—as between
Liberals, Marxists, social democrats and philosophical anarchists—and
our own philosophical inclination in India accepts the same basic premise. This is that the end of society and of the State is the individual
and his freedom to realise himself. To be sure, there are major philosophical controversies around the concepts of individual freedom and
self-realisation—controversies that range all the way from epistemolog-
ical to phenomenological considerations. I am also deeply aware of the
connotations that have surrounded the notion of individual freedom,
especially in western thought. This is no place to get into these controversies. What is more, it is not necessary to resolve them in order
to agree on the basic premise that the end of a collectivity is the well-

being and realisation of the individuals who constitute that collectivity. From our limited purpose of establishing a *norm* against which political and economic performance could be measured and evaluated, this
involves (i), the concept of individual freedom as the end of social and
political institutions; (ii), the idea that social organisation ought to provide adequate opportunities for the fulfilment of individual potentialities and propensities; and (iii), the proposition that the freedom and
self-realisation of one individual or class of individuals does not provide justification for preventing other individuals and classes from realising their freedom and potentiality. Conflicts of interest are bound to
be there: indeed *diversity* is an important component of the concept of
freedom itself. It is the function of institutions to manage these conflicts,
reconcile them and resolve them so that not exploitation and oppression but solidarity and a sense of community become the institutional
expressions of the basic drive towards freedom and happiness.

Once we accept such a conception of individual freedom, there are
a number of other value preferences that follow. Three of these are of
particular importance and need to be affirmed as values that ought to
be pursued by the State. The first is the value of *justice* based on an affirmation of the equality of all human beings. Freedom, unless it is
informed by the concept of justice, can degenerate into privilege of the
few and manipulation of the many. To what extent the value of justice
ought to be guided by the concept of equality—to what extent justice
ought to be 'distributive' justice—is in turn to be decided by reference
to whether one is seeking a mechanical or an organic solidarity. I shall
presently come to this problem.

The second inferential value is that of *participation*. Unless man is the
maker of his own destiny, there is no scope for real freedom and self-
realisation. The laws and institutions that govern him must be based
not on coercion or forced acceptance, nor even on simple and habitual
acquiescence, but on his active and willing participation in their formulation, application, criticism and modification. This means a number
of things—a process of decision-making that is amenable to peoples'
participation, criticism and dissent; a territorial and institutional structure in terms of units and size of units that makes participation effective; and provision of minimum opportunities of a social and economic
kind which translate formal rights into a real exercise of freedom and
democracy. To what extent a formal institutional structure of democracy provides such opportunities should determine our attitude to its
desirability and legitimacy, and provide grounds for its modification.

The third valued inference of freedom is a negative one but it is one
of those negatives without which the more positive values become dif-

ficult to pursue. For want of a better term it may be called the value of *non-violence*. If individuals are to realise their potentialities and political institutions are to provide optimal conditions for them, it is necessary that there is an environment of peace, stability and predictability—with a minimum of violence. The term 'violence' is used here in a rather inclusive sense. It includes as much the violence of the 'system' against persons and groups (exploitation, oppression and so forth) as the violence of persons and groups against a legitimised system in the name of social abstractions such as 'revolution'; it includes the violence of majorities against minorities and minorities against majorities; and, of course, it includes the more usual types of delinquency and crime. I would include a fourth type of violence that is increasingly threatening the quality and integrity of human life and that is violence against nature. The western notions of freedom and rationality, based essentially on the manipulative model of the positive sciences, have led to a pattern of social arrangements which is based on large-scale destruction of man's natural environment and which violates the basic conditions for human self-fulfilment. It needs to be subjected to the scrutiny of a different conception of man's worth—which also includes a conception of the man-nature relationship. In fact the 'violence of the system' that I talked of earlier—which in a way produces or at least aggravates all other kinds of violence—is really a product of this highly manipulative model of reason and human striving. And it is not accidental that this approach to man's natural environment produces hardship and suffering to the less privileged strata of society who cannot afford the synthetic comforts of suburban living. It follows that an essential condition of human happiness, and of a just and participatory society, is that the individual is provided with means to counter such sources of systemic violence which obstruct and distort the realisation of all other values. Perhaps India, with its culture of refined sensitivity and its non-dichotomous cognition of nature and intellect, has a great deal to contribute to this particular normative perspective. Let me also state that the accent on the individual and his welfare and self-realisation as the criterion of all progress has also a long and distinctive pedigree in Indian philosophy. That this later degenerated into a closed system where individuality came to be assigned to a privileged few—just as in practice Indians have shown themselves to be among the most violent people in the world—are only warnings that in the absence of the institutional dynamics of a just society, high ideals can quickly turn into an ideology of exploitation and decay. This is something we have particularly to bear in mind in the years ahead.

Practical Implications

It is necessary to move beyond such a statement of first principles and spell out their implications in the context of the particular time and space configuration that confronts one. For the 'hard' questions begin only after one's normative map is laid out. Unless these questions are raised and at least theoretically dealt with, the map itself is not worth much. While it is clearly not possible to deal with these questions in any great detail in the course of a single essay, I shall attempt to raise some of them.

The first question that I would like to pose is in regard to the end of economic activity in the light of our normative map of maximising human freedom through the principles of justice, participation and non-violence. It is astonishing how little clarity there is even in regard to this most elementary question: what are the aims of economic development? The broad aim that is usually mentioned is 'raising the standard of living' of the people. But conventional wisdom immediately transforms this in terms of a series of aggregates—raising the Gross National Product, assuring a certain rate of growth, and in turn fulfilling a series of production functions, consumption functions, utility functions and other 'principal components'. Imperceptibly, in the hands of a routinised bureaucracy and a narrowly professionalised academia, these aggregates cease to become means to more primary ends and become ends in themselves. Against this way of thinking are those who would attend straight-away to the welfare and distribution problems, promulgate absolute equality and demolish all obstacles to its realisation. At other times quite other formulations are advanced, such as to 'bridge the gap' between the 'developed' and the 'developing' nations, and within the country between the 'rich' and the 'poor'. Against this maze of formulations, and the complacency derived from a self-generative model of growth that was not obliged to answer awkward questions, it needed the sensitive sarcasm of a Ram Manohar Lohia and the muted reflections of a few 'less modern' economists (a Gadgil, a Dandekar, an Ashok Mitra) to make us realise that we were indeed developing, our GNP was rising, our rate of growth was not too bad given all constraints—but that we had also simultaneously grown more unequal as a society and as a people; and, what was much worse, we had hardly done anything for our vast periphery of poor and the destitute. Surely the fact that this revelation of growing inequality and continued depression of the poverty line came as a bit of a shock to our leaders more than a decade after we had initiated a programme of planned development is enough indication of the poverty of our thinking on the ends of economic development. Unless a clear approach is

developed in terms of properly spelt out goals, this situation is likely
to persist, as was rather sharply shown in the almost epoch-making
report on poverty in India put out by Dandekar and Rath.[6]

I suggest that as a first step towards such a clarification it is explic-
itly and unambiguously stated that the principal problem of economic
development in a poor country is quite simply the removal of
poverty—'garibi hatao' is no empty slogan in a land of abject poverty.
Once this is admitted as the main consideration, we have then to move
to four other formulations which necessarily follow from this basic
consideration—the concept of a *minimum* standard for all, the concept
of a *maximum* beyond which a person's economic welfare is not admissible, the concept of a *scale* connecting both minimum and maximum
(that is to say, an admissible ratio between the two), and the concept
of *transfers* of surplus above the maximum to those who have not yet
reached the minimum. There is need for a composite policy on each of
these goals. The concepts that lie behind them are by no means new,
though I must say that political scientists haven't even begun to work
on these formulations and it is perhaps necessary to reiterate them even
for economists as components of a single statement of interrelated goals
derived from basic normative commitments instead of disjointed principles of welfare. There is no time here to work out the various implications and possible consequences of such a formulation. But I think
I have indicated enough by way of a framework of normative intent
to enable us to think in terms of a corpus of policy priorities and their
translation into reality. For it is clear that, without this central focus on
poverty and the four corollaries of it as outlined above, it is not possible to assure minimum conditions for the realisation of the values outlined above—of individual freedom, social justice, political participation
and non-violence. Similarly, these values also suggest that economic
well-being is not an end in itself, that you can have too much of it, that
beyond a point it is highly corrupting and destructive of both the social
fabric and the environment, that the manipulative thrust of modern
'management' generates wants that are unrelated and in fact prejudi-
cial to basic values, and that it is necessary to reconsider and reinter-
pret the Indian norm of limitation of earthly wants. They suggest that
countries that have already achieved the prescribed level of material
well-being have no right to bottle up resources in the name of national
sovereignty and self-aggrandisement and that, on the other hand, as and

6. V.M. Dandekar and Nilakantha Rath, "Poverty in India" (in two parts), *Economic and Political Weekly* , 6 (1 & 2), January 2 and 9, 1971.

when we are able to clinch the basic problem of assuring a minimum standard for all—and this will perhaps take 50 to 100 years for the whole world—'economic development' may cease to be relevant as a concern for the State. Whether or not the State withers away, its economic content will most likely wither away. (I would not advise my grandson to specialise in economic science.)

Beyond Economics

So much by way of raising some questions in regard to the basic economic problem. Immediately, however, one needs to face other issues if economic activity is not to lose in meaning and perspective. At any rate as I look at the problem, it is necessary to say that the norms of a 'minimum' and a 'maximum' are not mere economic formulations; they are part of a certain conception of a good and desirable life. Not only should an individual be entitled to a minimum level of living; he should also be able to participate actively (though he ought not to be forced to do so) in the way things are produced and decisions are made. It is not just a 'minimum wage' that one thinks of here in some kind of a contractual relationship, alienated from the work process and the total scheme of ownership, production and distribution of the means of livelihood. One rather thinks of an apparatus that man himself controls, finds meaningful and derives a sense of personal power and manoeuverability from. Furthermore, to the extent that economic activity is managed and mediated by political and administrative agencies, the whole problem of effective participation in decision-making, at the desirable *level* and in optimum *units*, becomes real. Without such participation the economic aims may indeed be difficult to achieve.

On the other hand, there is also the question of not permitting the economic process, and what is now tellingly called the industrial-bureaucratic complex of modern society, to take on an automatism of its own, and destroy every other value in its inexorable march. In other words, as the values of a participatory democracy and non-violence to man's social and natural environment are joined with the values of social and economic justice, it may well be that we should ask ourselves equally basic questions in respect of the kind of institutional superstructure that we want to build. Two major dimensions of this issue, with particular reference to India, are (i) the rural-urban structure of our economy and (ii) the territorial structure of our polity. As we pose these questions, we may well decide that the available model of 'modernisation' or 'development' is not conducive to our goals, that the norm of a necessary shift from a predominantly rural to a predominantly urban structure based on large-scale industrialisation may not be the best thing that human intelligence has devised; that the notion that as national income grows the share of agriculture and small industries in it must necessarily fall drastically need not be taken as a law of economic development; and that urban metropolitan life, far from being a 'civilising' instrument, may turn into a structure of manipulation, exploitation and destruction of those properties of man's natural environment that are essential to human survival.[7]

Similarly, we may also question the norms of centralised government, large sized States and big bureaucracies as necessary instruments of national integration and political accountability; and as we question these, we may begin to answer with greater clarity the problems raised in respect of State autonomy, of decentralisation of functions, powers and resources, and of optimum size for genuine participation of the people. Perhaps there is something to be gained in the very short run from large scale enterprises, modern communications media and centralisation of planned initiative, although the real issue here is less of scale than of control. But it is also necessary not to close all options for the future generations to come in respect of the quality of life they would like to have. As the seeds of the future are sown in the present, it is a matter of considerable responsibility that these consequences of present actions are borne in mind.

At any rate, these are issues that arise naturally when specific problems of political engineering, economic strategy and choice of technology are analysed and evaluated in terms of normative standards and criteria. Involved in such an approach is what may be called a 'design for living' in which reason, compassion and a regard for the equal worth of all men are joined in the cultivation of a truly civilised life. And as we do this, the distinctions between economic and political issues disappear and we begin to see the real linkages through which a preferred world of our normative liking can be brought about. Here is to be found the terrain of the new political economy as found in the context of the unlimited possibilities yet simmering discontent of the last three decades of the twentieth century.

---

7. There are many other aspects of modern technology and human engineering which we need to examine more closely than we have been permitted to do so far under the impact of a homogeneous and presumably inescapable path to progress. To give only a small illustration of the massive impact of the uncritical acceptance of an instrument, is it necessary to accept the automobile as the best means of human transportation? Is it wise to go in for small and cheap (sic) cars? Couldn't we do better with a vastly improved public transportation system? For a broader critique of modern technology as part of the philosophical drive of the theory of modernisation, see the earlier book in this series, *Transformation and Survival: In Search of Humane World Order*. See also my *Footsteps Into The Future: Diagnosis of the Present World and a Design for an Alternative*, New Delhi, Orient Longman's and New York, The Free Press, 1974.

Specific Policy Issues

Let me add right away that to conceive of linkages and interrelationships between economic and political issues in the light of such *a priori* normative standards and goals is not necessarily to engage in high level abstraction. In point of fact, the issues become far more concrete when they are perceived in the context of values and goals than is the case when they are perceived in an *ad hoc* manner and as simply a response to immediate pressures. To conceptualise problems of development in light of the values we cherish and the goals we wish to attain immediately concretises a number of issue areas on which we in this country do not yet have a clearly laid down policy. Nor have we begun to spell out alternative strategies on them and weigh their respective costs and advantages in the light of our value commitments for a preferred future. Let me illustrate:

Demographic Policy

There is need to develop an approach to the demographic substructure of economic development. By this I do not just mean a population policy—on which I could add little to the various expert bodies that are possessed of the problem—but a policy on the rate and character of urbanisation, on the role of rural areas and settlements in national development as against urban settlements and, within the urban complex, on the importance of small and medium size towns as against metropolitan cities. By the sheer force of circumstances India has been able to maintain its economic development at a relatively steady and low overall *rate* of urbanisation—a rate that has been lately picking up somewhat but is still around 20 per cent of the population. This is in many ways a unique demographic setting for a fast modernising society and provides a basis for a genuinely pluralistic and decentralised social order. But there is need for a *policy* here lest the onslaughts of education, farm mechanisation and urban industrialisation put us also on the course that most other nations have gone through. This, in turn, involves a clear policy on the place of agriculture and allied occupations in the overall economy, the extent to which machines should be allowed to replace men and bullocks, and policies in regard to transformation of rural society itself thus reducing the seducing effect of urban life. If a strategy is to be evolved in terms of a vast dispersed population in rural and semi-rural settings, the industrial policy itself ought to be geared to the production of needs and consumer demands of the rural population, and policies in regard to scale and location of industries will have to be conceived in terms of regulating migration flows to large urban areas and providing employment opportunities in conurbations of rural, semi-urban and suburban areas connecting up to traditional and new metropolitan centres. All this is easier said than done and calls for a major shift in the whole planning model. It also seems quite clear—as shown in the analysis by Dandekar and Rath[8]— that existing land cannot sustain the rural population which is constantly rising. What then is to be done to prevent the inevitable 'push' into urban squalor and misery, and the inevitable escalation of violence that will follow? These are issues that demand policy considerations at the highest level. They are also issues on which there are no Anglo-Saxon models to fall back upon.

Regional Policy

Secondly, it follows from this that there is need for a comprehensive approach to regional planning, on location of industries, and on geographical and functional dispersal of economic units. Anyone who has worked even a little on our biggest 'megalopolis', namely Calcutta, cannot help being impressed by the need to view the problems of a particular unit in the context of a region: as is often said for Calcutta, the problems of Calcutta will have to be solved outside Calcutta. The point here is that the conditions that give rise to violence and disorganisation are spread over economic, political, regional and psychological variables. One's approach to their eradication will have to be informed by a clear sense of goals. Once this is done, specific problems fall in their place. Even as specific a problem as slum clearance falls in its place because it becomes clear that what Calcutta or Bombay need most and as a matter of priority is not some face-lifting operation as the simple creation of jobs for the people hustled into these miserable conditions. And this cannot be done except through a regional approach to the dispersal of crucial factors of production such as capital, entrepreneurship and technical manpower.

Territorial and Federal Policy

Thirdly, alongside a demographic policy and a regional policy there is also need for a policy on the territorial and governmental structure of the country, most importantly on the size of states, on *domestic geopolitics*, on optimising federal relations, on levels of institutional autonomy, on the place of municipal administration and *panchayati raj* and cooperative institutions in the nation's political and economic structure. I consider this issue of an optimal territorial and governmental frame-

8. *op. cit.*

work for the country crucial to the realisation of each of the values outlined earlier.

Ecological Policy

Fourthly, to repeat a point made earlier, as part of this approach to
optimum physical conditions for a good and just life for the people, there
is need to evolve a policy on the ecological environment. This will again,
no doubt, include a population policy but also, in terms of the short
run, a policy on human ecology, with a view to maximising human and
natural resources for a better life for the present and, more so, for the
coming generations. Unless we attend to these issues rather soon we
will face the prospects of destruction of the very life processes that can
assure survival and development of our children. It is well known that
Indians—vegetarian though many of their thinking sections may be—
can be quite callous in this regard.

Educational Policy

Fifthly, there is of course the pressing present. Our normative model
would immediately suggest that the most significant issues are providing employment to all and giving primacy in economic policy to the
lowest deciles of the population. As we assert this clearly and unequi-
vocally and move beyond the phase of slogan-mongering towards a process of concrete decision-making, many other puzzles will fall in place.
There are, of course, the more obvious questions like: how does one
pursue and translate an incomes policy of minima and maxima conceived in the abstract? How does one generate jobs and for which sections? But other policy issues will also follow and call for resolution.
To illustrate, there is urgent need for a policy on reorienting the whole
educational system from the fashioning of an elite to an active relationship between literacy, work and employment for the populace as a
whole; from the present pyramid of a vast mass of illiterates at the base
and a miserable and angry *lumpen proletariat* made up of millions of educated unemployed at the top. There is need for a total overhaul of the
educational sytem based on some fundamental questions about our
whole approach towards the class structure of our society.[9]

One can go on adding to this list of issues that call for concrete policies in the light of our preferred values. I have been working for some
time now on the details of such an approach to the performance of the

9. For a provocative and excellent treatment of this subject which continues to be a
classic, see the 1970 Sardar Patel Memorial Lectures of K. N. Raj, *Crisis in Higher Education*, Ministry of Information and Broadcasting, 1970, *mimeo*.

State and their implications for the policy process and the social sciences. There is no time here to spell this out and in any case I have no ready-made capsules to offer. But I can say this much. The more one elaborates the relationship between normative goals and political and economic problems, the more clear the relationship between these problems itself becomes. This is not to underrate the more simple analytical relationships, as for example, between rate of population growth, rate of economic growth, increase in unemployment, growth of urbanisation and education, and rates of violence and political stability. Such analytical models are useful guides to a consciousness of the multidimensionality of the problems of 'development'. The point, however, is that in the absence of normative standards that are clearly spelt out, such models stimulate our curiosity and range of perceptions more than our will and ability to deal with them. If social sciences are to be effective in enabling man to produce a better society, it is mandatory on us all to understand and spell out the values on which such a society is to be based and to inform both analysis and action on the basis of such an understanding. As we do this, the practical sense of the politician and the planner on the one hand and the theoretical sense of the social scientist on the other will need to be joined in a common endeavour.

The point in all this is to move gradually to the larger transition towards a more rational and just society as a model for civilisation. India has perhaps a historic opportunity in this respect for contributing to the universal fund of knowledge and understanding. With the vast experimental span of its long heritage as well as its somewhat distinctive approach to political and economic development in the last few decades, with its setting of a continental size and enormously heterogenous polity wrestling with the problems of one of the poorest societies in the world, and with its attempt to realise widely accepted humane values despite much provocation to the contrary, it provides us with a microcosm of the world where perhaps almost all the conceivable problems of humanity are found in one form or another. Its record so far has been one of a mixture of failures and successes, crises and breakthroughs, and large continuities through still larger discontinuities. As one looks towards the future and seeks to comprehend possible alternative scenarios of likely developments *at the present state of one's knowledge*, one tends to fall back to an almost primeval mood of either optimism or pessimism (or oscillations between the two moods)—without definite grounds for either. It is necessary to move beyond this and to develop a firmer grasp of the reality we are trying to mould—of the *future* we are trying to shape. As we do this, it will also be necessary to move beyond our professional models and par-

adigms of understanding a complex reality—and to inform ourselves
with a clear statement of first principles. Social sciences differ from the
more positive sciences precisely in respect of this constantly shifting
range of choice and determinacy, freedom and law-governness, the normative and the empirical.

I have tried to present in this essay, in a crude and tentative fashion,
an illustration of the relationships between the normative and the empirical based on my own understanding of human goals and values, conceived in the setting of our times and the emerging future, and informed
by both absolute principles and contingent standards. As I see it, the
principal goal is to provide to the individual conditions for his self-
realisation. In turn this means that when we speak of the 'individual'
we have in mind *all* individuals. In real terms, this involves the provision of an institutional order that assures a satisfactory system of participation and what the Greeks called 'natural justice' based on an
assertion of equality of all men. It also involves an atmosphere of non-
violence to both social and natural environments as a necessary condition of the individual's dignity and self-fulfilment as well as of the
principles of justice and equality. As these values are laid out in terms
of a design for society's pursuit of goals, a series of other normative
emphases follow—reason not manipulation, well-being not wealth, freedom not individualism. In the language of abstraction, the basic relationship that emerges is between the process of *reason* and the processes
of *freedom*. The policy process, the utilisation of knowledge and intelligence, and statecraft as a whole are embodiments of reason. Institutional structures of participation, justice and non-violence, on the other
hand, are conditions of man's realisation of his freedom. It is the function of economic science to mobilise the processes of reason for the realisation of freedom. And it is the function of the science of politics to
see that freedom does not degenerate into privilege of the few and
manipulation of the many. Political economy is the science that joins
these two perspectives.

6

Beyond Development:
A Question of Management?

Management of social change, especially in a period of rapid and far-reaching transformation, is something that can be perceived in extremely different and radical ways provided we keep in mind the fact that the concept of 'management' is being used here in the classical sense of managing the affairs of society and not in the more modern and narrower sense in which management science is viewed as a part of business management and technocratic controls. The latter sense is not what I have in mind. 'Beyond development' is something that I very much approve of, because it is my belief that development theory as it has been pursued ever since the end of Wold War II has led us into a blind alley. There is a necessity of rejecting the prevailing theory of development or at least overhauling the prevailing concept of development. It stands self-condemned because instead of bringing better 'standards of living' for the mass of the people, instead of reducing inequality, instead of leading to the autonomy and self-reliance of the people and nations, it has done exactly the opposite.

Nature of Social Change

In order to understand what is involved in the 'management' of social transformation, i.e. rapid and far-reaching change, we must have a perspective on what in fact is happening around us (i.e., the nature of social transformation that faces us).

In several regions there is an acutely felt scarcity of natural resources. In a world that is getting increasingly competitive and crowded and where the presumption of continuous availability of resources has suddenly disappeared, this has given rise to major conflicts. These relate to gaining access to more and more natural resources, to retaining control over resources no matter in which country or region they are located. At the same time the ethic of consumerism is taking hold of all classes and of all nations and is leading to relentless destruction of natural resources—forest lands, river beds, coastal terrain and reserves of soil, water, and jungles. This is seriously reducing production capacities on a sustained basis and making technological progress an enemy of the poor. The resource situation, which was dramatised by the OPEC challenge but which has not taken on a multidimensional character, has also to be kept in mind while discussing specific political and economic issues.

All over the world there is a slowing down of growth rates. Signs of a renewed global recession are very much in evidence. This recession, emanating mainly from the world capitalist system, is spreading both to the developing world and to the socialist world, supplemented, of course, by inherent weaknesses within both the developing world and the socialist world. In other words, while there are other sources of recession also, the fundamental source is the capitalist order and its ramifications. There is no doubt at all that there is a slowing down of growth rates: there are some exceptions here and there like Brazil and South Korea, but generally speaking there is an unmistakable slowing down of production and growth, and this is telling most heavily on the poorer parts of the world both regionally and socially. This trend results in conflicts and violence which arise out of the restlessness of the bottom and the backlash of the top. The top is keen to preserve its privileges, living standards, and lifestyle, and in consequence the bottom is being deprived of whatever resources it had at its disposal earlier.

More basic than all these is the psychological factor. There is a growing sense of insecurity at all levels, all the way down and all the way up. At the top governments all over are becoming unstable propositions. The most powerful among States, i.e., the superpowers, are reeling from a sense of insecurity both vis-a-vis each other and vis-a-vis the rest of the turbulent world that is beginning to assert itself and will not any longer accept a passive role. The superpowers are themselves very insecure. At the other extreme, at the bottom of society the poor and the oppressed are feeling insecure both because of their plight and because of the environment around them which is crumbling. Their economic condition is terrible. The authorities and symbols they relied on for so long to provide them with some opportunity for a better life are no longer able to do so and are failing them and leaving them in the lurch.

Contributing significantly to the resource scarcity and the world economic crisis that are much talked of, is the spectre of world militarisation. The point about insecurity that I make is not found only in psychological and attitudinal forms; it is found in the behaviour of nations, in their brutalisation, in their increasing reliance on force both internally and externally. Seriously contributing to this is the world power structure, partly because it cannot any longer manage the world along some *status quo* formula and partly because of the inherent logic of the latest stage of world capitalism, namely its increasing reliance on production, sales, and transfer of armaments industries at home and abroad. This is leading to a global arms race from which no one is free and for the sake of which the local resources and potential that are available in societies are being forsaken and conflicts are being exacerbated in the world market created not just for arms but for the latest arms. The military establishment that is backing up all this, and which is rooted in the economic structure of certain societies, sees to it that no nation is allowed to feel independent and autonomous about its own security. Because of the increasing and rapid obsolescence of armaments, nations are found to become increasingly dependent on the metropolitan centres. What is spreading, therefore, is a global culture of militarisation and militarism which is eating into the resource base of societies and depriving common people of whatever resources could be allocated to their betterment. The prospect that seems to be opening before us for the next ten to twenty years is one of declining living standards and growing inequality, and growing conflicts and violence, largely because of the very close connection between the military build-up on the one hand and economic decline on the other.

Prognosis

Along these various parameters the prognosis that I envision is one of a period of growing vulnerability and of increasing deprivation of the deprived. Traditional institutions of the modern State, as the modern State was conceived in Europe and everywhere else, seem to be unable to cope with this situation. This is creating pressures on the elite in most countries, especially pressures to hand over power to the technocrats and experts who too are however unable to deal with the crisis, a crisis that is fundamentally political in character. The technocrats and experts are hardly equipped to handle a situation of this nature. When this formula does not work, it produces a deep vacuum—a vacuum not only in the structure of the political elite and of the administrative, technocratic, and managerial elite, but one produced by the erosion of most of the basic institutions of society. This gives rise then to the need for overriding institutions by personalities and to the blowing up of the role of personalities in the process. Unfortunately this also does not work and it produces long term insecurity and uncertainties.

Internationally it is a period of growing pressures from the world power structure. The pressures are political and economic, strategic and technological. They result in a striking decline of the autonomy and self-reliance of developing countries. After a long period of striving by many developing countries for achieving their own autonomy and self-reliance, there is a dramatic turn about and there is unmistakable evidence of growing temptation to seek redress for the domestic situation in international cooptation of one kind or another. India is a striking case in this respect, but others are also not too far behind. In fact, many of them have been far ahead. In consequence, the so-called interdependence that is being talked of internationally is being turned into a process of recolonisation of former colonial countries.

This then is the scenario of the human condition. It is a scenario that would dishearten, depress, and disorient most people. However. it is precisely a scenario that should not be taken in a fatalistic manner for that would be its real fulfilment. It is a scenario that must be taken up as a challenge, as a gauntlet thrown down by the vested interests, the dishonest, and the corrupt that are in power. We have to pick up the gauntlet and respond to it in a creative, constructive, and critical spirit. We must meet the challenge and meet it head on.

This is a task that the traditional management sciences, or the administrative sciences, or even the economic planning discipline cannot handle by themselves. It calls for a totally different conception of the management of social transformation. That this transformation has to be mediated, triggered, and catalysed, I have no doubt. Here the elite has a definitive role. We cannot leave human affairs to the dynamics of disorder and instability for that would be playing into the hands of the world fascist forces. These forces play upon the tendency towards chaos and disorder both within countries and internationally. If we are to intervene in the process of history—a role that is designed for the elites, the intelligentsia, and the leaders of social movements—we must reflect and act. I have been spending a part of my time during the last several years interacting and mixing with grassroots groups and organisations in India, with activists working closely with the people especially the poor and the oppressed, the tribals, the women and the lower classes. I strongly feel that it is a different kind of leadership that a country like India needs, but it is leadership nonetheless. Those who happen to be privileged enough to be in positions of power and responsibility as well as those who can strive to acquire control over, or rather steer, social movements and thereby give rise to new and alternative leadership, cannot give up responsibility. To that extent, therefore, it may still be 'management of social change', but we must be clear that it is not an expert conception of management. It is very much in the spirit of things that people themselves should be permitted to manage their own affairs and, for that purpose, they throw up leaders from among themselves as well as accept catalytic agents from outside their immediate surroundings. I want to reject categorically and clearly the conception of management and administration that is based on superior expertise, one in which the managers and administrators are supposed to know better what is good for the people. I accept the validity of the need to steer and manage the process of transformation which is fundamentally an intellectual and a political task, but I refuse to accept the prevailing conception of management or administration or, for that matter, politics itself which is based on the premise that politicians are experts and professionals in human affairs being able to handle the various situations effectively.

The Tasks Ahead

Having established some terms of discourse let me lay out the tasks of the managers and mediators of social transformation in the period that lies ahead, with particular reference to 'developing societies'. I happen to think that they are also relevant for the 'developed' societies which face a very different kind of crisis, perhaps even more serious than we do in the Third World. Fundamentally these tasks consist in striving and struggling against the dominant conceptions of development, leading to the dependency of the Third World that the modern development theories have created. They consist in establishing the identity, autonomy and self-reliance of various entities in the struggle for justice. I am convinced that there is a large scope for such counter-action against the dominant tendency during the period of growing conflict over resources, increasing hegemony of the world capitalist system, and the declining autonomy in practice of various societies. I also see major assertion and re-assertion of the human spirit in the form of a challenge to western dominance, challenge to the dominance of national elites and challenge to established and entrenched structures of power at the regional and local levels. I consider the secular assertion of Islamic power, ranging from the OPEC challenge of 1973 to the Iranian revolution, as a fundamental challenge to western hegemony, even if in its immediate aftermath, it has run into deep waters. The issue is how does one manage the transition from an initial revolutionary upsurge, a rebel reaction, towards the ultimate fulfilment of the cause for which the revolution was meant.

The point I am making is of a global nature. I am not refering only

to Iran, although it is my view that after the French revolution the revolution in Iran had a fundamental import for it questioned the very conceptions of development and modernity that had ruled the roost and
had allowed the penetration of societies by the centres of power in the
world. The issue is how to join the various comparable processes which
are stirring at the bottom and have not led to the desired fulfilment.
The issue further is how to link the various civilisational challenges
mounted by the powerful thrusts of Afro-Asia and Latin America into
a major counterforce against the blacklash of the declining western civilisation. The key questions are: how to develop a set of alternatives that
take us beyond the managerial limits of both world capitalism and state
socialism? How to restrain the weaknesses and blunderings of the capitalist and socialist options that are already in evidence? How to recreate
an authentic alternative to the corrosive competitiveness and individualism of the modern world? It is a challenge that must be faced, mediated and 'managed', but done so from the bottom up in an authentic
form which would be a different conception of revolutionary transformation but would be revolutionary nonetheless.

Much depends on what one means by revolution, but I have no doubt
that any movement or any fundamental change which replaces the dominant culture or the dominant mode and paradigm of thought is revolutionary. Whether it takes the form of the French revolution, or the
Russian revolution, or the Chinese revolution, or any other revolution
is a different matter altogether. There are powerful cultural and civilisational issues involved in the nature of each. But today we face a
crisis—a fundamental crisis—generated by the modern world theory,
the modern development theory, and modern social science that nothing
short of the reassertion of the human spirit in a fundamental manner
from the bottom of society will find the way out from the growing par-
alysis of the modern State that I discussed earlier. The tasks that lie ahead
in such reconstruction and reassertion of power and our identity are
going to be full of risks and uncertainties, but these are challenges to
which we must respond creatively. In my own view the western model
of development has run its course, the western model of democracy—
parliamentary democracy in particular—also has run its course, and the
western model of order and stability has run its course. From now on
the managerial capacities of our creative elites will have to be geared
to a totally different context. The borrowed concepts of management
and governance as well as those of revolution will not do.

Three Levels

These tasks are at three different levels. There is first the level of the

nation-state itself. As I said earlier, except in a few highly industrialised countries—and even in them there are problems—the nation-state,
which is the basic unit for rectifying inequity, is being corroded from
within and without. Institutionally it is unable to cope with the challenges that surface, a serious vacuum gets created and matters tend to
be decided outside the institutional framework that the modern State
provides. What we get is, therefore, a ramshackle structure in most of
these societies, where the top elite may think that it is enjoying power
and control but where in fact it is losing its hold. Forces of a different
kind are taking over at the intermediate and lower levels and because
of them the State is unable to hold itself together. A redress is found
from international contacts and in becoming a part of international deals.
I think it is necessary that the security of the State in the Third World
is fully protected. But for this it will have to be restructured and provided with an institutional framework of a more democratic and decentralised type than that offered by the model of centralised governance
based on the Westminster conception of parliamentary democracy. This
effort should be aimed at providing confidence and credibility to the
rulers and legitimacy to the State system. This can be done by extending the participation of the peoples of the area in governance and development. It is necessary that we examine carefully the nature of the
modern State as it functions in the Third World. Also indicated is an
in-depth study of the crisis that the State faces and of the program-
matic perspectives or movements that may be needed for re-establishing
the credibility and security of the State in the Third World. In large parts
of the Third World we are witnessing the erosion and possible disso-
lution of the State.

The second major task concerns the enormous and increasing awareness of a sense of rights at the level of the ordinary people in most Third
World societies. This throws up completely different kinds of challenges
for the modern State to handle, and for which it was not conceived. When
we look at the structures both of the model of parliamentary democracy and the model of State socialism as well as at the experiments that
have been tried out by radical military groups in some parts of the Third
World, we find that the basic assumption has been one of managing
and transforming things by carrying the people along, without necessarily providing for the participation of the people as part of the structure itself. The result has been a massive alienation of the people from
the polity in all the systems and their assertion, therefore, from outside
the framework of the State in the form of ethnic, racial and class conflicts which turn violent and are difficult to handle. The assertion of the
sense of power by the lower classes is in fact leading to a difficult sit-

uation. When the deprived assert their rights, the privileged mount a major backlash against the new forces of change. As a consequence the disintegration of the State begins to take place, enormous gaps develop between the base and the managerial top of societies, and increasingly recourse is taken to repression in dealing with these challenges rather than to expanding the horizon of the democractic participation of the people. I do not have any particular democratic form in mind except a broad sense of values that should permeate the system. The second set of important issues thus involves the relationship between the centre and the periphery—the relationship between the national epicentre and the various sub-centres which are seething with revolt and are witnessing a lot of turmoil and torment from below. How does one 'manage' the federal component of every society? The managerial issues involved in relating the government and the people, the centre and the periphery, the administration and the political parties are of a type that will require handling in ways different from those provided by the Westminster model or, for that matter, the model of State socialism.

The third set of issues, of course, are at the very bottom of society, at the level of the poor and the oppressed. They are concerned with their sense of identity, with the sense of finding their own place under the sun. They constitute an effective challenge to the hegemonical structures of local power groups, which then leads to the entrenched castes, classes and races and also educated groups to come down heavily upon such people and those who organise them. This leads to an enormous increase in the repression at the lower levels of the society with which the so-called managers and leaders seem to be totally out of touch. We have recognised quite clearly that we are moving into a fundamentally new age—the age of the people and of those who organise them. It is also the age of populist leadership which adopts the rhetoric of equality, socialism, social justice and development for the poor, but which in fact is involving itself in deceitful politics by pursuing policies that retard social transformation rather than further it. The age we are moving into has these two contradictory forces: one highly democratic and egalitarian, representing the power that is being generated from the bottom, the other highly authoritarian, deceptive, deeply cunning and devastatingly debilitating. A strange combination, but very real nonetheless. The very process of democratisation of societies, irrespective of what constitutions these societies have, has also created the conditions for institutional erosion and heightened expectations from individual personalities. The whole problem of charisma, that is often talked of by social scientists, is in a fundamental sense a problem of uncertainty and insecurity among both the people and the leaders. They both resort to the gimmick of identifying the whole society with a person, and when that does not work they go through a process of chaos and then turn to another leader. Latin American countries provide many such case studies, but it is true also of some Asian countries.

Need for Alternatives

It is necessary, therefore, to mediate in this critical situation and to provide alternatives to the people so that democratic urges find new channels of crystallisation and fulfilment. If they are looking up to a supreme leader, and identifying themselves and merging their identities with his or her identity, it is because of the lack of intervention by the thinking sections, opinion-influencing intelligentsia and activists of these societies. The uneven growth generates processes that force people to succumb to the various mafias as well as the criminal and corrupt practices that appear to have taken hold over most of these societies. The youth, a very large and growing mass, is rootless. The rural middle classes and the educated unemployed lack a sense of direction. These are the forces that can be mobilsed towards a crystallisation from the bottom, towards an organisation for change, towards management of social transformation. But these are also the forces that can be mobilised for fascist regimes. Europe went through this process in the inter-war period; we in the Third World are going through the process now. The idealist schools failed to mobilise these elements to join against the forces of reaction. They failed to galvanise them into a powerful current of transformation and instead forced these elements—the youth and the unemployed—to become the targets and, ultimately, the allies of fascist forces. I cannot emphasise this point too strongly. The story of most of our societies is the story of lost opportunities and missed challenges, of an elite that ceased to be an elite in the natural sense of the word and succumbed to the exploiting and domineering stratum— a parasitic stratum that became parasitic because it was not inspired, directed, and steered. But this could still be done and I have no doubt that it will be done, for the forces that are being released at the bottom of the society are so powerful that it is going to be difficult to put them down, although in the intervening period there is bound to be considerable oppression and interference by both internal and external forces and the combined strength of the two. I do not want to get into the debate around the IMF 'conditionalities', but it certainly has brought up some very pertinent aspects of the linkages that I am talking of. How international forces want some of the national forces, especially of the authoritarian type, to put disorder down not allow mass movements to gain, suppress organisations of the workers and peasants, and put a lid on the processes of transformation can be witnessed in many parts of the Third World.

What I have said applies as much to the failure of national elites and the intelligentsia as to the forces from the outside. Given the insecurity at the international plane as well as at the plane of the governments, this joining together of local oppression and international strategies for holding in check the forces of transformation is something that must be taken very seriously. I am sure that in the long run the forces that are released from the bottom will re-mould our societies and restructure them. I think there is a critical role to be played by the interveners, by the mediators, by those who care, and by those who can transcend their immediate class interest, because without managing the transition to the ultimate transformation, we are bound to get into a period of growing oppression, fascism and militarism. Without such intervention the situation may get out of hand and put an end to all the noble ideals we have subscribed to in our societies. I have no doubt transformation will be brought about in society, but when and by whom are open questions. Several models are available—the Chinese model, the Iranian model, the Cuban model, and many others. But models from outside do not always work. At one time we even thought of an Indian model. But the message must come across that each society and each cultural zone has a distinctiveness, its own structures of diversity and its own problems. Thus how the forces that are released will be channelised and managed towards a desired transformation, which also ensures both stability and dynamism, is something that will have to be worked out by the new partnership between the alternative elite that is emerging in most of the societies and the people themselves. There cannot be any preemption of intellectual objectives by projecting a new model that should emerge. But I do not think that history has foreclosed all options; history does not foreclose options and possibilities. Indeed it throws up surprises; even when we think we are at the bottom and sinking, a major breakthrough comes about. Some people come on the horizon to provide a totally different kind of turn to the forces.

To conclude, I would like to identify three forms of mediation for management of social transformation. One is the re-building, re-structuring, and re-strengthening of our States. I am convinced that this cannot be done without the massive involvement of the people and restructuring of the constitutional framework. The second is rethinking our conception of economic development and moving towards a model of development that is not corrosive of the natural resources and does not produce the kind of deforestation, desertification and erosion of the potential wealth of societies that the present model of economic development does. And finally we have to evolve a strategy of aligning the forces from the bottom. Various groups working among the people are there, but they remain fragmented and isolated. Micro movements abound all over the place, but there is not enough of a dialogue between them. There is no leadership that can provide them with a sense that despite ideological differences, despite their being localised and essentially marginalised as far as the larger system is concerned, there is the need for them to come together. There also is a need to fashion some kind of a common front, not necessarily along party lines. I feel that the political party system, as it was evolved over the last thirty to thirty-five years has outlived its utility and what we need now is something radically different. I do not know what it will be, but I have a feeling it will arise from this process of bringing together the various social movements that are going on—the movements of the peasantry, the landless and the oppressed sections and the far-reaching tribal and ethnic movements that are taking place everywhere. That is the third major task—evolving a strategy of aligning a new coalition of power that can produce an alternative to the present system.

I wish to end by saying that though I have disputed the concept of management of social change in the sense in which it has been used so far, I must stress the point that no society can do without an elite. It would be wrong for us to jump on the populist bandwagon and start saying, parrot-like, 'power to the people'. To assert that ultimately power to the people will produce some kind of a revolution some day, and then we will all benefit from it, would be an irresponsible attitude to take. There is a role, a definite and clear role, for those who are placed in privileged positions and who happen not to worry about their daily bread and butter to provide that kind of leadership with a sense and perspective that is in full empathy with the forces of change. Though it is important above all not to be indifferent, I will end by quoting a small poem that a representative of the Soviet Union recited in a recent meeting at Hiroshima. He is a distinguished academician of the Soviet Academy of Sciences. The quotation is from a novelist who has just died and whose work they are likely to publish. It says, "do not be afraid of your enemy, the worst he can do is to kill you; do not be afraid of your friend, the worst that he can do is betray you; what you should be afraid of are the indifferent that promote the killing and the betraying".

7

On Eco-Imperialism

Critiques of modern development theory are not restricted to the still emerging broad platform of 'alternatives' based on a normative search for a more humane form of development than is provided by the dominant western paradigm. They are also found to arise from quite other vantage points of a rather fundamentalist kind. I shall take as my point of departure one of the more influential of such thinkers in the West, Garrett Hardin.[1] His "An Ecolate View of the Human Predicament" provides a fundamental critique of modern development theory. In recent years there has been a flood of such fundamental questioning. In the main the critiques are of three types: Marxist, theological and ecological or a combination of these. (Gandhian thought is on a different plane—not a critique within a paradigm of civilisation, but a total alternative thereto.) Hardin is not a Marxist. If he has an underlying theology or metaphysic, this is not clear from such writings of his as I have seen. He is basically of the ecological persuasion.

Two Schools of Thought

Now there are two types of ecologists. There is first the eco-development school of ecologists who are concerned with making development both environmentally viable and socially equitable. They believe in the possibility of a steady, sustainable process of development for all and, while recognising the outer as well as the inner limits of growth, are convinced that a properly conceived model of development can reverse the structural characteristics of the present distribution of resour-

---

1. *Alternatives*, VII:2, published by the Centre for the Study of Developing Societies from New Delhi and the World Order Models Project from New York.

ces and power that is responsible for both the maldevelopment of affluent societies and the underdevelopment of poverty-ridden societies.
There is another school of ecology which believes in conservation pure
and simple with little or no regard either for the causes underlying
today's runaway technology and its ravaging of the environment, or
for the need for planning for the future which, while providing for the
basic necessities of all, would also ensure an ecologically sustainable
strategy of growth. Nor is there much regard for issues of equity and
distribution. Indeed, they see in these concepts possibilities of further
spoilation of nature consequent upon new demands made by the
hitherto poor and underprivileged, encouraging the poor to multiply
themselves which can only result in disaster. For it such a growth in
population of the poor will so overload the 'carrying capacity' of the
earth that human survival itself will be at stake.

Hardin considers all demands for equitable distribution of resources
its foremost exponents. Actually, he is one up on the others in the school.
He is not just worried about the poor of the world multiplying too fast
for the carrying capacity of the earth. He is even more worried about
this resulting in demands on the affluent countries which may be asked
to contribute part of their wealth for removing inequity and injustice
from the world and changing their lifestyles which, according to the
other school of ecology, lies at the heart of both the ravaging of the environment and the population problem itself.

Hardin considers all demands for equitable distribution of resouces
or any assumption that the resources of the world are the common heritage of mankind as new versions of Proudhon's doctrine of 'property
is theft'. He in fact rejects the very concept of 'world resources' as an
echo of Proudhon. Reflecting the by now well-known western attitude
of having cornered the resources of the world (large parts of which are
in fact located in the developing world) to keep them at any cost and
to resist any demands for a more equitable distribution thereof—if need
be by resort to arms (which incidentally Hardin bluntly advocates),
Hardin rejects all arguments for sharing of resources as dangerous. The
only resource he says he is willing to share is information, acting on
the clear assumption that the rich know better and they pass on "all
the little pieces of information [they] possess" for the poor to pick and
choose from, by teaching them to behave responsibly, by advocating
the doctrine of 'de-development' and by insisting that food will be
exported only on condition that the recipient undertakes to limit population growth.

The logic of Hardin's arguments is based on his firm conviction of
his own brand of ecology, his key concept being the *sanctity of the car-*

rying capacity', his major concern being to expose the misleading sentimentalism of all redistributive arguments and to show how any redistributive strategy is (a) not realisable and (b) unworthy, for it would in fact lead to ecological suicide.

In fact Hardin is not interested in the other school of ecology which admits the claims of equity as part of an alternative development strategy. Thus he rejects outright any claim that a population increase in the rich countries like the United States represents a much larger demand on resources as compared to a similar increase in poor countries (the well-known argument of 'ecological equivalance'). He ridicules such statements with a thunderous quip: "So what?" He goes further in fact. If the rich were to stop reproducing, the "world resources [sic] that might be freed in this way would soon be completely absorbed by the multiplying poor". This would mean that "instead of a world divided between rich and poor we would soon have a world of poor people only". This will reduce the standard of living everywhere in the world, a prospect Hardin shudders at.

Two points need to be noted in understanding Hardin's position. Note first that for Hardin, standards of living are a zero-sum game—he says as much—so that any attempt at improving the standards of the poor can only be at the cost of the rich, by forcing the latter to redistribute and thus lower their standards. He does not believe, as do other ecologists, that there can be a strategy of development that can benefit all. Note secondly that if indeed improving standards of living of the poor calls for structural changes in the global distribution of resources and power, Hardin is against it.

Apology for the Status Quo

In effect, Hardin's attack is not just against current development theory and related notions of aid and transfer and pooling of world resources into a global 'commons'. His is a far more fundamental attack on the whole sweep of modern history, and the concepts of justice and equity and the view that the bounties of nature are a common heritage of mankind on which no class or nation can have a monopoly, on which it is based. Thus it is not an accident that among the few concrete instances of ecological deprivation that he cites (with some of which I agree) is the "galloping deforestation of Nepal" which, according to him, "dates from the 1950s when the government put an end to the feudal control of land, thus opening the forests to fuel-hungry people"!

Like many others of his kind in the West, Hardin's principal eyesores are people, especially the poor and the hungry. If only these can be removed, or at any rate their numbers held in check, there may be some hope for civilisation. This in fact is his definition of the 'human predicament'—the spectre of the hordes of the poor overtaking the rich and robbing the latter of their hard-earned standards of living!

In effect then, underlying all the hyperbole of an ecolate perspective, the persistent logic of the primacy and sanctity of the carrying capacity as against the old-fashioned concept of the 'sanctity of life' which he rejects as being counter productive, and the grand theory of the 'Tragedy of the Commons', Hardin throws his weight behind the aggressive apologists of the American lifestyle which they are determined to preserve at all costs. He may not wish to order the world about as they do and his motivations may be quite different from theirs; he does categorically reject the arrogant Americanism based on the doctrine of 'manifest destiny' and the new expressions of moral imperialism and 'white man's burden' though all this is in the context of his rejection of foreign aid (to which I shall turn presently). However, a sane moral position is not enough of an antidote when the political perspective leads to the same position as of the imperialists; indeed, it may give a new and much needed moral respectability to the hawks of the West. Hardin is as much a victim of unintended consequences of good intentions as the others he castigates.

Ecologists of Hardin's persuasion are in fact subtle propagandists of capitalism, 'privatism' and global dominance, perhaps even lending conceptual support (even though rejecting the policy itself) of the doctrine of *triage* based on liquidation of the 'excess population' of the world. We may draw upon his own preferred aphorism of August Comte of the superiority of the intellect over the heart. It is Hardin's heart that rejects such liquidation (for he is afraid of such action becoming a precedent and a habit), not his head, for he shares with the liquidationists the view that overpopulation is *the* cause of all ills, including poverty, pollution, inflation and unemployment which are all, according to him, 'population-related'.

Nor does Hardin merely share the dominant perspective of hard-nosed imperialists in respect of population only. He approvingly quotes the contemptuous caricaturing of Third World elites by Daniel Patrick Moynihan, the smug superstar of American extravaganza, who gleefully and mockingly reports some fantastic feast hosted by President Bongo of Gabor. (Reminds one of how western media projected Idi Amin as a representative sample of the Third World!) He agreed with those who would give food to the starving poor in Bangladesh only on condition that they undertake to restrict their population and rejects all political objections to such insistence as "despicable hypocrisy". He identifies terrorism as "a major threat from now on" and says that "*The* only rational response to terrorism is police action" (emphasis by Hardin).

In fact, Hardin goes much further and propounds yet another of his grand civilisational salvos on the human predicament in our time: "Survival is impossible without police action in times of crisis, and the tacit threat of it at all times. This is the price we pay for civilisation". Police action not just against terrorism but also against "tacit threat of it at all times". With this Hardin joins the grand strategists of the Rand Corporation who, in order to protect the American lifestyle, would undertake pre-emptive wars against Third World countries which may threaten that lifestyle.[2] Nor is Hardin's stouthearted defence of America (he castigates those who would seek negotiated settlements with demands for redistribution as 'fainthearted') limited to terrorism. He ends his article by making what reads like a clarion call to America to muster the will to protect itself against the "silent invasion" of immigrants from the Third World, to resist the "process of takeover by uninvited guests" which, according to him, has already started. "There is little sign—yet—that Americans are going to resist". He is worried over the moral ambivalence of many Americans and asks: "Will America, like invaded France in Raspail's novel,[3] continue to be immoblised by ambivalence in the face of a silent invasion? If we cannot muster the will to protect ourselves we will find that we have shared not wealth, but poverty with our invaders".

So to the question with which Hardin starts his paper, "How should rich nations respond to the demands of poor nations", his answer is: forget about the demands for redistribution, ignore the talk that the rich have gotten rich by exploiting the poor, give them information on the rich countries' experience, above all teach them how to control their population, and if they do not listen or try to compel us to redistribute, stand firm and they do not stand a ghost of a chance. In modern warfare the poor countries are bound to lose to the rich and in any case the wealthy rulers of the former would rather use their wealth to keep their poor down than to fight against us. As for the terrorists, gun them down. And as for the immigrants, do not permit them to come to our country and share in our wealth (for it will only end up in our sharing their poverty). For we must at all cost defend American riches and lifestyle and control of resources, if need be by resort to 'police action'.

2. Guy J. Pauker, *Military Implications of a Possible World Order Crisis in the 1980s:* A Project Air Force Report prepared for the United States Air Force, Santa Monica, The Rand Corporation, 1977

3. The reference is to J. Raspail's *The Camp of the Saints* (New York, Charles Scribners, 1975), translated from *Le Camp de Saints* by N. Shapiro.

These are the concrete *politics* that emerge from Hardin's analysis and prescriptions. It represents a combination of Malthusianism, militarism and both contempt for and fear of the poor of the world, masquerading under an 'ecolate view of the human predicament' which, however, is based on the author's sincere interest in the survival of civilisation (read 'carrying capacity').

It is not enough, however, to expose the politics to which such ecology leads. The threat posed by such an ecology must also be met on its own grounds, namely the theoretical foundations on which it is based. I agree with Hardin that "the most pressing problem for the social sciences is to create credible theory". In the case of Hardin, it is the theory of the 'Tragedy of the Commons'. In what follows I propose to show that not only is Hardin's politics perverted and ethnocentric; his basic theory is itself at fault and largely because it too is ethnocentric.

When 'The Tragedy of the Commons' first appeared in 1968 it made quite an impact, especially in western ecological circles. This was a time when the concern with the environmental consequences of human want, indulgence and waste had attracted much attention and the presumptions of endless progress for mankind were being seriously questioned. It is necessary to realise, though, that even then the impact was mainly in countries governed by capitalist rationality with its individualistic, competitive and personal greed-maximising (rather than community welfare-maximising) ethic of behaviour. It made a lot of sense that when "each pursue(s) his own best interest in a society that believes in the freedom of commons", such freedom "brings ruin to all". As for those who did not believe in capitalist rationality, Hardin's logic made even greater sense for they had all along argued against such unrestrained individualism and there was in fact nothing new in what Hardin was saying.

Begging the Question

Twelve or thirteen years later, with the much greater deepening of the environmental consciousness and its maturing into a total vision of the human *problematique*, combining in its sweep both the ecological and the developmental paradigms and correcting the apolitical perspectives of both conservative conservationists believing in stability for its own sake and growth-economists believing in growth for its own sake on the assumption that it would automatically lead to the welfare of all, the 'Tragedy of the Commons' argument appears inadequate and one that in fact begs the question. For the issue is not any longer that unmanaged commons lead to disaster—which is rather self-evident— but that of restraining individualistic rationality of capitalist societies by in fact managing them in the larger interests of both human survival and human welfare.

Hardin's arguments themselves lead to this conclusion. Both his abstract logic and his illustrations point to moving out of either privatism or what he calls 'commonism' (a "system in which the commons is *not* managed") into some variety of 'socialism' and social management. If unmanaged commons lead to tragedy, surely the answer is to manage the commons. But as this obvious solution to Hardin's restatement of the age-old predicament of man-in-society (stated best in Hobbes's *Leviathan* and after him by many a philosopher interested in civil society)[4] does not suit his intellectual polemic and much less his politics, he dismisses the whole issue in one sentence: "The comparative merits of privatism and socialism need not concern us here".

Somewhat later in his argument, while discussing the growing danger of the polluting effects of rapid industrialisation on the atmosphere, he in fact does say that "since privatism is hardly an option for the air and waters of the world, socialistic or semi-socialistic regulation is called for". But once again he withdraws into his own distaste for commons as such. "Within national boundaries we know something about the requirements of good management even though we are often unwilling to meet these requirements, but how we are to secure the international cooperation of many sovereign States is still a mystery". In point of fact, there is no mystery about it except that the capitalist nations are consistently opposing any proposals for global management, whether at the Law of the Sea negotiations or in the North-South dialogue or in the prolonged negotiations on controlling wasteful uses of energy, not to speak of their opposition to any international agreements on controlling private traffic in armaments and other hazardous technologies. Hardin not only fails to examine proposals for controlling the menace of unmanaged commons, he sees in them all a design for robbing the rich nations of their wealth.

The 'rational herdsman' of Hardin is a wholly capitalistic creature, his 'utilities' taken out of elementary textbooks of capitalist economics, his argument about the relentless logic of such herdsmen leading to ruin wholly based on the calculus of pleasure and pain of the English Utilitarians.

Obsessed by his logic of the tragedy of the commons, Hardin refuses to face the common tragedy that faces all of mankind if we refuse to evolve common solutions to common problems based on massive inequities co-existing with wasteful lifestyles, both leading to an impend-

---

4. They all point to the central political question of the relationship between man and the State.

ing ecological disaster (of which overpopulation is an important component but which is itself caused by a world of such massive inequity and economic insecurity for large numbers of the poor and the dispossessed).

In his wholesale rejection of all practices and proposals for global commons—all of which he presumes, without empirically examining them, to be as unmanaged as his prototype pastureland, Hardin overlooks the good that they have done. He is insensitive to the starvation deaths that have been avoided through the supply of food from international sources. Perhaps, as appears from his discussion of food aid to Bangladesh, he is at bottom against such prevention of starvation deaths as this would lead the survivors to reproduce themselves, thus adding to the burden on the 'carrying capacity' of the earth which, according to Hardin's basic thesis, must be accorded greater sanctity than the sanctity of life of such Bangladeshis and similar others. He seems equally insensitive to the fact that the proposal for global food reserves is meant to reduce the political arm-twisting that usually accompanies direct food aid by rich nations, especially the United States. Hardin's theoretical blindness is, however, more basic.

Ahistorical

The arguments advanced by him in support of his diatribe against redistributive policies go against the whole history of redistributive and democratic legislation through which civilised societies have prevented both misery and chaos. As an 'ecolate' thinker, he pooh-poohs the very idea of justice for, in a world of scarcity, it would lead to the establishment of commons. But surely there has to be ecological justice too: if the enjoyment of 'such natural amenities as wilderness and quiet countryside' must be preserved, should they be preserved only for the richer upper deciles of the human species? And isn't it a fact that a large part of the plunder and ravaging of the environment derives from the philistine lifestyles and corresponding technologies perpetrated by the governments and corporations of the rich countries like the US? How much of the deforestation and desertification that Hardin bemoans is due to the needs of 'fuel-hungry people' and how much due to the vulgar consumerism of both the rich of the world and the governments and corporations of these rich countries still continuing to colonise—with the help of collaborative local regimes—large parts of the poorer countries? Let Hardin employ his methodological positivism, his preference for 'numeracy' as against literacy, and find out. If he is not totally blind to any fact that militates against his deductive model, he will, I am sure, come across quite a few startling revelations.

Hardin traces the demands for redistributive justice to envy and traces its psychology to that of 'property is theft'. For Hardin, ownership through the cornering and monopolisation of property entails no responsibility. Instead, the poor who ask for a share of it appear to him like thieves (consider his virulent attack on immigrants in the US). He completely overlooks the massive thefts and plunder carried out by the West through siege of entire societies by force of armaments and superior technology. He labels the demands of the poor countries parasitic. But who are in fact the parasites of the world—the poor or the rich, the world's lower classes living austere and 'straitened' lives or the world's affluent middle classes ravaging and destroying the resources of the world for maintaining their lifestyles? To all this, I suppose, as in his dealing with Mahbub-ul-Haq's discussion of the pressure on world resources caused by the rich population of the world, Hardin would simply say, 'So what'?

The same would be his response if it was pointed out to him that the so-called "spottily distributed resources of the world" (by which he presumably means the rich countries having more of these resources than the poor countries) is largely a result more of control and ownership and often forceful physical occupation than of actual location, that a very large part of the resources on which the industries of the rich countries depend are actually located in the poorer countries, that trade in these is not based on 'quid pro quo' as Hardin would want it but on built-in monopolies and unequal exchange, and that quite central to the argument for structural changes in the international order advocated by people like Tinbergen is this fact of ownership as exploitation, if not as theft. Hardin would say, 'So what'? For if the undoing of such structural injustices would produce greater demands by the poor of the world, that would mean both a greater burden on the carrying capacity and a possible reduction of standards of living in the US. The first does not suit Hardin's ecology, the second does not suit his politics.

I am with Hardin in his critique of American foreign aid and like him consider it as another form of foreign intervention. But I agree with him on this not because the rich counries have contributed to improving conditions in the developing countries which in turn has raised the rate of growth of their populations—Hardin's principal obsession—but rather because foreign aid has contributed to further widening the gap between the rich and the poor and has in fact been yet another instrument of imperial domination, plunder and 'theft', distorting the economics of the poor countries and putting them under massive burdens of debt[5]

5. Hardin's jibe at the poor countries by assuming that the World Bank loans will ultimately go into default and will have to be covered by the rich governments, principally the US, has no basis in fact and only reflects his strong imperial bias).

which in turn force them to remain colonial economies exporting their best agricultural commodities to balance their external trade. Hardin's censure of American moral arrogance is well-placed but he ignores the fact that the commercial and industrial interests in his country have consistently exploited the moralism of a Kennedy or a Carter for further tightening their hold on the poor countries. It is 'foreign intervention' in this sense.

Unfortunately, Hardin too, by supporting arguments like Jan Narveson's on giving food on condition of restricting population, is in fact advocating newer forms of intervention. He does not seem to realise to what grotesque uses such conditions will be put by aid bureaucracies and their political and military allies. It would be a small step from this to ask for physical supervisions and inspections by foreign 'advisors' who would then descend in the form of a new breed of colonisers which in turn will make the world distribution of resources even more skewed and 'spotty' and 'discontinuous' and imperceptibly lead ecologists like Hardin to support police actions and armed interventions. Strange bedfellows? But then that is what the ecology of Hardin's variety leads to.

The same is the case with Hardin's view of the elites and spokesmen of poor countries. I happen to agree that many of these elites, including some who are proponents of a new international order in international forums, are basically self-seekers and pursue policies at home that are anti-people. I also agree that international aid-givers have often bolstered up such elites and their unpopular regimes. Yet I think that both Moynihan's vulgarisation of the phenomenon and Hardin's absolutist denunciation of it—and using that as an argument against redistribution of global power—are misplaced. Hardin seems to be totally unaware of the growing revolt of the masses in these societies, the pressure this is generating on the elites often leading to their overthrow, and the more pertinent fact that as this pressure grows, the pressure for global redistribution of power and resources will grow also and more stridently and in a more compelling way than the present pressure of 'self-appointed spokesmen'. The pressure of the latter is largely rhetorical; in point of fact they are collaborationist elites whose rhetoric is phoney and meant for the record only. Hence the interest of the United States— or the Soviet Union for that matter—in bolstering these regimes. But there is a powerful democratic revolution overtaking these societies and once that happens, both the politics of American aid-givers and the politics of Garett Hardin will go under. And with that Hardin's brand of ecology as well.

Apologist

Basically, Hardin's is a critique of American policy by an American who however shares with the American elites their view of American national interest. For he seems to share the parochial, nationalistic, 'save the standard of living of Americans at all cost' ethos of the American establishment. Hence his support of the Moynihans and Narvesons. Hence also his failure to understand the more subtle and civilised European mind as represented by Tinbergen, Willy Brandt, the late Olaf Palme and their type. The latter may be naive and even mistaken in thinking that a smooth 'transfer' of resources between North and South is possible or that, even if carried out, would lead to any improvement in the condition of the poor of the world. But nonetheless they are far better possessed of the sense of tragedy that faces humanity if it refuses to deal with the sharp divisions that face it than are American nationalists like Hardin for whom the only tragedy that exists is the one posed by the multiplication of the poor.

It is ecologists like Hardin that have discredited the environmental movement in the eyes of so many and made it appear like a rich man's bogey, a view that I do not share.[6]

The ecology of Hardin's variety, namely an ecology for American national interest, should make him an attractive advisor to President Reagan who would find his views on terrorism, immigration, population and advocacy of mustering the will to protect American interests most hospitable. Hardin would sell Reaganism with a Reagan-like punch too!

---

6. I have discussed at some length the persisting dichotomy of 'environment' and 'development' and the ideological reasons for the same despite the great necessity of ending this dichotomy essentially by transcending both the paradigm and the mystique surrounding the concept of development. See "Alternative Development and the Issue of Environment" in this book.

ON DEVELOPMENT ALTERNATIVES

8

The Development *Problematique*

Developmental theory emerged as an important concern after World War II with the beginning of the era of de-colonisation and under the shadow of the Cold War. Its general ethos was one of inevitable progress definable broadly as a movement from tradition to modernity, status to contract, ascription to achievement. Such a dynamic, whether for the liberal or Marxist theorists, was seen as intrinsic to all societies. Where backwardness existed, therefore, this natural movement had been obstructed and the need was to identify and remove the pertinent barriers. The heuristic tool used for such identification was the historical experience of the West which was understood as the quintessence and embodiment of 'progress'. The liberal solution, reflecting Britain's experience in the industrial revolution, stressed free labour, reliance on market forces, a gradual process of industrialisation, adequate levels of investment generated by net profits and technological innovation. As part of the market strategy it also stood for exploiting comparative costs as central to the international division of labour and espoused free trade.

The Initial Construct

This was an idealistic construct in two ways: it attempted to derive an abstract and universal formula for growth from a very specific historical experience and it also, to some extent, distorted that experience. Britain was not, after all, entirely faithful to the principle of free trade. What is more important, the countries which followed Britain on the path of industrialisation did not initially follow the logic of the market but sought the shelter of protectionist policies and State intervention till such time as they felt themselves to be strong enough to face international competition. This was true, amongst others, for Germany,

Russia and Japan. The ahistoricism of developmental thinking in this
period is all-pervasive and will be met with again and again. Thus what
was seen as the stagnation of traditional economies was equated with
Keynesian low-level equilibrium and the appropriate Keynesian short-
term solutions were suggested. A strategy developed to overcome the
under-utilisation of the productive forces of a developed economy
through stimulating aggregate demand via increased expenditure was
applied to situations where, instead, the limitation of productive capacities was the main problem. In such a context the result combined inflation with continuing unemployment.

Similarly, identifying the needs of 'underdeveloped' economies in
terms of what they lacked in comparison with the West, Schumpeter's
theory was used to stress the importance of creating infrastructures adequate to modern industry, engendering the entrepreneurial spirit and
setting up poles of growth which would attract private enterprise. As
a planning instrument for long term strategy, the Harrod-Domar model
enjoyed great popularity. This established a circular linkage between
savings, investment, output and growth. Each increase in output
increased the investible surplus and thus laid the basis for increased
growth in a widening spiral. With increased growth, income levels will
rise and with it the capacity to save. Thus growth, once initiated, was
seen as having an inherent, self-propelling logic. Postulating that the
capital-output ratio is the crux of the analysis determining as it does
the investible surplus, this scheme, which remained the classic growth
model till recently (and persists to this day with a lot of economists),
implied capital-intensive industrialisation.

The orthodox Marxist line, enjoying the enormous prestige consequent upon the rapid industrialisation of the Soviet Union and its planning strategies, was equally prone to universalising the particular
experience of the USSR. The basic prerequisite for development was the
socialist revolution. This achieved, the Soviet strategy of heavy
industry—subsidised by agriculture—and the utilisation of modern
technology was the answer. Despite the rigidity of its logic, however,
this model did have the merit of drawing attention to the political and
social dimensions of development. At the same time, while there were
major theoretical differences regarding the choice of instrumentalities,
there was a basic agreement between the Marxist and liberal schools
regarding the fundamental importance of capital accumulation, industrialisation, growth and technology. By the early sixties, the Soviet
model of non-capitalist development stressed these techno-economic factors more than the necessity of a socialist revolution.

This basic unity of approach is reflected in the fact that, in practice,

there was an eclectic mix of strategies. Substitution policies were insti-
tuted whereby the State was called upon to make good the absence of
entrepreneurship, adequate levels of capitalisation and infrastructure.
In terms of using trade as a developmental tool, while the general temper
was neo-classical and stressed the theory of comparative costs—whereby
each country should produce what it could produce most cheaply and
thus capitalise on its comparative advantages—there was fairly early
recognition of the fact that the actual structure of trade militated against
the poorer countries which were primarily producers of raw materials.[1] A more profitable strategy would therefore be selective participation in world trade to the degree required to stimulate internal
industrial growth. The issue of participation in international trade also
involved the question of dual economies which became highly controversial in the new left critiques of conventional development.

It was noticed that in underdeveloped economies there existed a
divide between a small, highly paid, capital-intensive, 'modern' sector
and a large, subsistence level, labour-intensive, 'traditional' one. The
historical roots of such a gulf mostly lay in the colonial period with the
small, 'modern', sector being the part which was integrated most
strongly with the colonising country and oriented towards production
for the world market, an extreme example of this sector being found
in the extractive industries. Where development was defined as the
move from the 'traditional' to the 'modern' sector, this would imply,
in the absence of sufficiently high levels of internal demand, a closer
linkage with the international economy. The dual economy debate and
its ramifications are of particular importance because it is a *portman-
teau* phase which contains the major themes of development as conceived from a techno-economic viewpoint: the role of trade in
development and the structural implications of the use of diversified
productive modalities within countries. Whether, for example, the
modern sector was complementary to, or parasitic upon, the traditional
sector, and the reasons and conditions for either (or both). These issues
will surface again in the discussion of dependency theory later on.

Growing Discomfort

By the late sixties and early seventies the initial certainties and optimism of developmental theory began to fade in the light of experience.
The growing evidence of marginalisation and mass unemployment

---

1. Among those who brought this out the most articulate were Hans Singer, Francois
Perrous and Gunnar Myrdal. For a very well documented review of these and other authors,
see Bjorn Hettne, *Development Theory and the Third World*, SAAREC, Helsingborg, 1962.

revealed that economic growth by itself was profoundly inadequate. Chenery, writing in 1974, pointed out that while the per capita income of the Third World had gone up by 50% since 1960, the growth had been extremely unequally divided between countries, groups and classes.[2] What this called into question were the growth models of the Harrod-Domar type—not on the grounds of their productive inefficiency but rather because of the partiality of their logic which segregated the field of production from that of employment and distribution. The assumption had been that increased productivity itself would cause the benefits of growth to percolate through every level of society—an assumption that experience falsified. Instead, relatively high levels of growth could co-exist with mass poverty and, indeed, could accentuate it.

The earlier developmental strategies had not only stressed production as the main model of development but they had also assumed that economic factors existed unconditioned by social and political contexts so that the debate had largely centred on the issue of the substitutability of these factors which, in themselves, were seen to be imbued with an infallible and intrinsic potency. Gunnar Myrdal's work offers, perhaps, one of the earliest and most stringent critiques of this economistic bias.[3] He pointed out the crucial importance of recognising the non-economic determinants of economic behaviour as causal agents in their own right rather than as incidental elements which were simply added on to purely economic models. Thus the specific institutional and social climate of the developing areas, both as regards countries and regions and within individual countries themselves, needed to be taken into account. The increased sensitivity to the particular characteristics of specific societies meant a loss of confidence in the simple, linear, universal model of progress which had been trumpeted by Marx and whose distorted formulation, on the liberal-capitalist side, found expression in Rostow's theory of the stages of growth.

In both substantive and methodological terms, the problem was no longer one of overcoming obstacles which stood in the path of a progress understood as natural and automatic, a path in which underdevelopment was only a necessary phase which preceded development and maturity, an awkward and painful phase of economic adolescence. It was, rather, one of understanding underdevelopment as a concrete structural configuration with determinants peculiar to itself. Under-

2. Hettne, *op. cit.*.

3. See his *Asian Drama*, New York, 1968 and The Challenge of World Poverty , New York, 1970.

development was thus shorn of its teleological dimension and called for a 'structural' approach.

The Dependency Critique

The most articulate advocacy of the structural analysis of underdevelopment came from the dependency school which challenged some of the basic categories and assumptions of conventional development theory. The familiar distinguishing features of developing societies—marginalisation, unemployment, inequality, low wages, etc.—had been regarded by traditional developmental theorists as distortions or transitory phenomena. In the view of the dependency theorists, however, these were the natural features of underdevelopment and the surface manifestations of its underlying structure. In giving a summary of the views of the dependency theorists, it is necessary to keep in mind that they do not constitute an entirely homogenous group; nonetheless, there are some key tenets which are commonly shared. The fundamental premise of the analysis is that underdevelopment is a function of capitalist penetration. In this sense, the theory can be seen as a continuation of the imperialist drain theory outlined by Gokhale and Dutt and elaborated by Naoroji, leaders of India's independence movement, several decades ago.[4] Hettne summarises the main features of this analysis in terms of the following four points:

1. The most important obstacles to development were to be not lack of capital or entrepreneurial skills, but were to be found in the international division of labour. In short, they were external to the underdeveloped economy, not internal.

2. The international division of labour was analysed in terms of relations between regions of which two kinds—centre and periphery—assumed particular importance, since a transfer of surplus took place from the latter to the former regions.

3. Due to the fact that the periphery was deprived of its surplus, which the centre instead could utilise for development purposes, development in the centre somehow implied underdevelopment in the periphery. Thus development and underdevelopment could be described as two aspects of a single global process. All regions participating in this process were consequently considered as capitalist, although a distinction was made between central and peripheral capitalism.

4. Since the periphery was doomed to underdevelopment because of its linkage to the centre it was considered necessary for a country to

4. See B.N. Ganguli, *Dada Bhai Nauroji and the drain theory*. Asia Publishing House, Bombay, 1965. See also Ignacy Sachs, *The Discovery of the Third World*, MIT Press, 1976.

dissociate itself from the world market and strive for self-reliance. To make this possible a more or less revolutionary political transformation was necessary. As soon as the external obstacles had been removed, development as a more or less automatic and inherent process was taken for granted.[5]

The core areas of mature capitalism no longer stood outside the development issue as merely models to be emulated and sources of aid, themselves not being part of the strife of the developmental struggle. They are structurally implicated in it and, to paraphrase the famous phrase of Andre Gunder Frank, are seen as the developers of underdevelopment. Dependency exists as an articulated system and successful development involves a transformation of these relations. The core-periphery understanding of underdevelopment sought to expose the historical falsity of conventional development theory by showing that the major industrialised countries had never had the experience of facing the structural constraints of underdevelopment which were, in fact, their creation. The present condition of much of Asia, Africa and, in a modified way, of Latin America, was not comparable to Britain in the early 19th century but had been profoundly conditioned by the colonial experience. They could not, therefore, be simply located behind the core areas on the same evolutionary track. The growth models which assumed this were thus completely out of touch with prevailing realities.

The vector of research and analysis, under the impact of dependency analysis, was thereby shifted away from the traditional preoccupations with growth and capital accumulation *per se* to the linkages which conditioned the actual results of development.

The Centre and the Periphery

The debate within the dependency school was focused on attempting to precisely define the nature of central and peripheral capitalism and their mutual interactions. This proved to be an extremely elusive task. Should, for instance, the line of cleavage be between regions or between classes? Are the interests of the 'modern' sector of a developing economy—including the working class of that sector—essentially at one with the core economies as a whole or do they remain tied, at some level, with the 'traditional economy' sector of their country? Is the capitalistic core a homogeneous entity or does it offer contradictions which can be exploited by the periphery to effect a structural transformation? Can this disjunction be designated as a dual economy or is it more accurately described as structurally connected aspects of the same

---

5. Hettne, *op. cit.*.

economy? Does dependency completely preclude the possibility of development or can the two go hand in hand? What are the conditions for
this kind of dependent development?

While dependency theory saw underdevelopment as tied to capitalist penetration, the structure of core or metropolitan capitalism was
not understood as being isomorphic with that of peripheral capitalism.
Capitalist development at the centre, according to Hamza Alavi, is a
comprehensive movement which encompasses industry and agriculture,
capital goods and consumer goods. In peripheral capitalism, only dis-
articulated commodity production exists with extended reproduction
of capital only taking place through linkage to the metropolitan centres
and to their advantages. In other words, metropolitan economies are
sufficiently integrated internally to absorb their surplus for the purposes of further economic growth while peripheral economies are too
discrete to do so. Arguing, as it does, within the broad framework of
Marxist analysis, dependency theory faced the question: can peripheral capitalism be called capitalism at all when it contains a bewild-
ering array of modes of production? The answer it threw up was that
"social and economic relations arise not merely within social formations
but also *between* them, such as the relationships established by colonial
capital. As a concept of structures of relationship, the concept of 'mode
of production' does not—and in the case of peripheral social formations
cannot—exclude such relationships".[6] Thus where the linkage between
centre and periphery is the determining relation, this relationship conditions the essential nature of all subordinate economic relations, however diverse they may be. Structural dependency on the capitalist
economies justifies the characterisation of the peripheral economies as
capitalist.

It is, of course, true that the entire underdeveloped world, including
the oil producing nations, accounted for only 25% of total world exports
and that this share has fallen steadily since the fifties.[7] The question is
whether an unfavourable position in world trade is sufficient in itself
to explain underdevelopment. None of the metropolitan capitalisms,
with the exception of Britain, escaped this dependency in their forma-
tive stages nor are any of them entirely self-sufficient at the present time
engaging as they do in the exchange of goods and technologies. The

6. Hamza Alavi, "The Structure of Peripheral Capitalism" in *Introduction to the Sociology of 'Development Societies'*, ed. by Hamza Alavi and Teodor Shanin, Macmillan, 1982,
p. 1980-181.
7. Several Statistical Year books of the United Nations. See also Sachs, *op. cit.*, p. 280,
note 5.

understanding of underdevelopment exclusively in terms of centre-periphery external relations therefore seems partial. The problem should perhaps be posed differently—as an attempt at understanding why external trade has the effect of creating a dependency which thwarts internal development. This would reverse the analytical search to the extent that it would situate the issue of international trade within the nexus of internal conditions instead of concentrating exclusively on the external dimension. It would also lead to a re-consideration of the dubious assumption—and one that the dependency school shares with conventional theory—that development as an automatic process would assert itself in the simple absence of external obstacles. To some extent these shadowy areas have already received some attention as the questions provoked by the need to clarify centre and peripheral capitalisms testify

The Rise of MNCs

Cardoso's writing spells out most clearly the dangers and inadequacies of a simplistic understanding of dependency and underdevelopment. He points out that Lenin's theory of imperialistic penetration as capital accumulation in metropolitan centres, requiring peripheral areas both as markets and as sources of raw materials, with external ownership of the dependent areas' means of production is, in the face of the growth of multinational corporations, no longer an adequate description. Multinational corporations invest directly in local ventures and local markets do matter, not merely the metropolitan ones. This strategy requires a degree of local prosperity. While, therefore, there is still dependency in terms of capital-goods and technology, there is also development in dependency. This rather more complex analysis takes into account the fact that some developing countries are industrialising rapidly. Thus while the total share of world exports of the developing countries is declining, the share of their exports accounted for by manufactured goods rose from 10% to 40%. If value-added exports are seen as an important part of development, this is not insignificant. His analysis also points out the importance of internal fragmentation within the dependency situation in that there is a tension between those national groups which benefit from their incorporation into the international economy—both as employers of the foreign subsidiaries and those spheres which profit from their presence—and those who do not. The basic logic remains that of capitalist penetration, but its operation is less monolithic and more diversified. The battle lines now being drawn are not between nation-states but rather within them. Such conflicts of interest do not, in his view, constitute absolute obstacles to capitalistic advancement but are, rather, characteristic of it.[8]

The Issue of Energy

The oil crisis of the early seventies made glaringly manifest the uncertainties of many of the trends which had gained momentum after the Second World War. The most obvious, of course, was the cheap availability of energy on which the prospect of industrialisation was premised, and drew attention generally to the finitude of raw materials and to models of growth which were incognizant of these limits. It also exposed the growing power of the multinational corporations at the expense of the economic sovereignty of nation-states. The enormous flow of funds to the OPEC countries produced fiscal uncertainty and fluctuating exchange rates; technological innovations in micro-electronics, communications and transport enabled the relocation of industries and major industrialised countries found themselves gripped by stagflation—a combination of under-utilisation of productive capacity with inflation. This conjunction of events has been understood as indicating a structural transformation in the international economy.[9]

The crux of the argument is as follows: stagflation and currency crises are indications of a structural crisis in capital accumulation, of the relative decline of production, profits and investments. Restoration of adequate levels of profitability requires (a) a struggle for markets, (b) intensified technological innovations—particularly in such fields as alternative sources of energy, ocean-bed exploitation, biochemistry and genetics, (c) lowering of the wage-rate. The costs of these strategies are likely to be shifted to the working classes of the developed world and to the Third World. The impact on the latter, however, will be differentiated. The relatively developed countries within it, Brazil, South Africa, India, will be able, as 'sub-imperialist' powers and exporters of second level technologies, to exploit the situation. But even within these, the development of their capitalist potential through those national groups with international alliances will depend on capital-goods production and production for export ignoring the needs of the lower income groups—thus increasing disparity of income and deepening social strife. Both in the developed and the favoured nations of the underdeveloped world, therefore, there will be an accentuation of class

8. Fernando Henrique Cardoso, "Dependency and Development in Latin America" in Sachs, *op. cit.*, p. 112-118.

9. Andre Gunder Frank, *Reflections on the World Economic Order* , **Monthly Review Press, New York, 1981.**

conflict and a trend towards authoritarian government. For the rest, there is the promise of deepening dependence.[10]

The global dimensions of such a structural transformation of the capitalist economy signals, for Gunder Frank for instance, the end of the significance of the dependency model. "At the same time, though structural impediments to development and dependence certainly remain real in the Third World, the usefulness of structuralist, dependence and new dependence theories of underdevelopment as guides to policy seem to have been undermined by the world crises of the 1970s. The Achilles heel of these conceptions of dependence has always been the implicit, and sometimes explicit, notion of some sort of 'independent' alternative for the Third World. This theoretical alternative never existed, in fact—certainly not on the non-capitalist path and now apparently not even through the so-called socialist revolutions. The new crisis of real world development now renders such partial development and parochial dependence theories and policy solutions invalid and inapplicable".[11]

This is so because the crisis signifies unmistakably, in his view, the existence of the Third World as an integral part of the world capitalist order which in turn was an order represented less by the nation-states of the developed world than by multinational corporations—whether as sources for raw materials, markets or as areas for direct investment and location of industry.

Frank's concept of the globe as an entity integrated by capitalism represents a shift from dependency theory into the notion of the world capitalist system associated with Immanuel Wallerstein. The latter distinguishes between 'world-empires', such as the historic ones of Egypt and Rome—in which the controlling principle is political and cultural—and 'world-economies' "in which a great diversity of political and cultural forms can be accommodated and in which the governing principle is economic". The capitalist world-system is that system of "production for sale in a market in which the object is to realise the maximum profit".[12]

The 'World System' Thesis

The crucial factors are not modes of production *per se*, whether artisanal, feudal, share-cropping, etc., nor the role of the State, nor cultural

---

10. *Ibid.*, p. 18-22.

11. *Ibid.*, p. 127.

12. Immanuel Wallerstein, "The Rise and Future Demise of the World Capitalist System: Concepts for Comparative Analysis" in *Introduction to the Sociology of "Development Societies"*, op. cit., p. 370.

identity, but rather all of these as mediated by the world-system. A true appreciation of political and social events is only possible when viewed in the light of its position in the world-system as a whole. "Both classes and ethnic groups, or status groups, or ethno-nations are phenomena of world-economies and much of the enormous confusion that has surrounded the concrete analysis of their functioning can be attributed quite simply to the fact that they have been analysed as though they existed within the nation-states of this world-economy, instead of within the world-economy as a whole".[13]

The world system is not, of course, geographically equal in its operations. There are core, semi-peripheral and peripheral areas but no area, however dominant, completely controls the world-market and owes its pre-eminence, essentially provisional, to a world-system of relations that it does not control. After his exposition of the evolution of the world-capitalist system, Wallerstein identifies the present as the stage of the consolidation of capitalism. But this does not ensure the continuation of the system in the long-term and this for two reasons:

(1) For immediate purposes the maximisation of profits requires conservation of the surplus consumption, but in the long run the creation of surplus demands redistribution to create broad-based demand. The tension that results creates periodic crises which weaken the structure of the system.

(2) The co-optation of opposition groups is subject to the law of diminishing returns.

As with Frank, though, till such time as these contradictions take their full toll of the system and precipitate the socialist revolution, there is little prospect for those at the receiving end of the world-capitalist system but of increasing underdevelopment.

NIEO and the Brandt Report

World-system approaches are not limited, however, to Marxist critics. It finds a place in the pleas for a new international economic order supported by groups in both the developed and underdeveloped worlds and expressed most cogently in the Brandt report. This represents a North beset with unfamiliar problems of unemployment, economic stagnation and inflation seeking the grounds for a rapproachment with a South growing ever more frustrated and bitter. It is posited on the belief that famine, unemployment, impoverishment of natural resources and the imminent risk of nuclear war are issues sufficiently broad to unite the nations of both the North and the South in a desperately needed attempt to overcome them.

---

13. *Ibid.*, p.43

The Brandt Report argues that it is in the mutual interest of the rich and poor nations alike to address themselves to the needs of the poor and that this can best be done by a massive transfer of resources from the rich to the poor countries for the adequate development of the latter's agriculture and industry and the satisfaction of their essential requirements. Unlike the Declaration on the Establishment of a New International Economic Order (NIEO) made during the Sixth Special session of the U.N. General Assembly in 1974 which can be seen as a set of demands—increased grants of aid, technology transfer, stabilisation of the monetary system and of prices—made by the South upon the North, the Brandt report stresses a fundamental mutuality of interest and the need for acting together.

The mechanism for this concerted action is Keynesianism at an international level: increasing the demand capacity of the South through the massive transfer of resources and thus taking up the productive slack of the North and lifting it out of its stagflationary slump. The main vulnerability of this strategy is the same as that pointed out by Alavi in his criticism of Wallerstein[14] in that the emphasis is on trade; the main actors are seen as States when, instead, centrality should be accorded to the social relations of production, that is, to the structural and class character of capitalism as it operates in different regions. "The difficulty in achieving such international economic expansion has indeed always been that international agreements are made not between the peoples of each nation but between leaders representing classes whose interests may well be at stake in making any change in the *status quo*".[15]

Left Critique

Thus, from the perspective of the Left, the Brandt proposals, in so far as they require greater participation in the world economy by the poorer nations, are caught up in the same complexities that surround development in a dependency context. Finally, on the Right, they were opposed on the grounds that the underdeveloped countries should rather "balance their budgets, liberalise their economies and find their comparative advantages".[16]

Thus, both lines of classical development theory, liberal and Marxist, rest today with the understanding of the world as an interdependent entity though the nature of the interdependence is subject to diverse

---

14. Hamza Alavi, "The Structrue of Peripheral Capitalism", *op. cit.*,

15. Michael Barratt Brown, "Development Societies as Part of an International Political Economy" in *Introduction to the Sociology of 'Development Societies'*, *op. cit.*.

16. Hettne, *op.cit.*, p. 73.

and, indeed, conflicting interpretations. The Brandt report posits a human commonwealth—in the literal sense of the term—and its globality derives its sense from the mutuality of interests that this implies. The various members of the commonwealth still retain their individuality while being engaged in a shared endeavour.

Critique of World-System Analysis

In the Wallersteinian view, on the other hand, the international stage is peopled with puppets, some losing and some winning, but all governed by a power that transcends each and all of them. This power is, of course, that of global capitalism, at once everywhere and nowhere, and best manifest by the global corporations which, evading specific national anchorage, are ubiquitous and without particular affiliation. The planetary search for profit becomes a kind of *weltgeist* escaping all structures since all these—States, groups, classes, modes of production, cultures, etc.—yield their true significance only through its mediation. The world-spirit of profit is the only true actor in the global arena. In that this actor works through an enormous heterogeneity of existing concrete structural relations without being exhausted by or consequent upon them, Wallerstein's theory is an interesting instance of a materialist analysis without a materialist causality. It remains silent on the issue as to what concrete structure or relations need to be altered in order to reverse capitalism. In brief, it offers no clues as to the needed instrumentalities for socialist transformation.

Similarly, Frank's analysis of the world capitalist crisis in the seventies links together a vast array of phenomena—scientific research and development, technological evolution, relocation of industries, banking strategies, political movements, class-conflicts, ideological formulations, export policies, new geo-political formations (as in the case of 'sub-imperialism' identified with those developing countries with a substantial industrial base), etc., without indicating where the pressure points are through which change may be effected. Everything is implicated laterally with everything else through the crisis of capitalism, but capitalism itself lacks any vital, specific structure although it uses—and internally transforms—all existing ones. In so far as its extent is universal, every relation that is expressed by its operation is, actually or potentially, a world problem. In the face of such imputed globality, there would seem to be little place for local or regional initiatives. The rationalist voluntarism of the Brandt report may appear more promising and better tuned to current actualities in as much as the globality it posits is based on a common enterprise and not on any organic or systemic unity as such. Its pitfalls may be the very voluntarism it relies on but it at least does not suffer from the preconceived theory of inherent unity and interdependence of the world we live in.

Economism and the Role of Technology

The brief and partial review of the history of developmental theory given above is intended to show that the 'global' perspective of recent vintage has evolved from earlier and more discrete ones. Stages of development as described by Marx or Rostow were certainly intended as typologies of growth of universal validity, but this did not imply that the constituent entities of the globe were closely interpenetrated. The destinies of Africa, Asia and Latin America were not seen as belonging to the same framework as that of the developed, capitalist core. These had, so to say, 'arrived' and their relation to the Third World was fundamentally one of guidance, assistance and aid. If there was nevertheless an implicit notion of a unified world in their theorising, it consisted in the conviction that the evolutionary path to progress and growth was common to all nations and groups. It was precisely because of this assumed commonality that their reading of their own historical experience could be offered as pertinent models.

This, however, did not mean that their actual historical situation was intrinsically linked to the poorer countries struggling to emulate them; on the contrary, their higher stage of development insulated them from being so constrained. The role of the dependency theorists was to assault the empyrean heights by arguing that these were attained and held by structural coercion. Development at the centre was the simple obverse of underdevelopment at the periphery—both were opposed consequences of the same logic. The radical asymmetry of benefits led them to demand a cessation of the relationship and to turn, instead, to self-reliance in the concrete form of import-substitution strategies. In that the possibility of true development was thus seen to lie in national or regional dimensions, however, the crux of the development problem was still not conceived as world-systemic in nature. The latter came to the fore only with the economic perturbations of the seventies and found its most dramatic utterance in the quotation from Frank cited earlier: the overwhelming conviction that the crisis of the world economic system renders all notions of 'another development' or 'alternative development' meaningless. The world needs to be understood as a systemic whole; the operation of the forces of systemic integration is what is decisive for any developmental initiative; these forces are those of international capitalism.

Now, at first sight, the idea of a uniform and all-pervasive world-system is a perplexing proposition in the face of the extraordinary diversity of the globe in economic, cultural, political and organisational terms. What then are the underlying common denominators which can be defined as global in operation? Unless these can be located, not only do global analyses remain abstract, the possibilities for 'alternative' development remain inchoate too. This question can perhaps be approached by pointing out that both the Left and Right wing theories of development are convergent on the crucial importance of the economic factor as the motor which drives development. At the risk of some simplification it can be said that little differentiates them at the level of micro-economics. The mechanics of capital accumulation, investment and growth as the essential parameters are common to both although the instrumentalities differ. Even dependency theory does not question this model as such but rather the conditions which hamper its smooth operation. It seeks to remove the external constraints—in this case dependency on the centre—which impede the otherwise automatic process of growth guaranteed by the mechanism. What needs to be done is to permit the reproduction of capital within the periphery itself instead of forfeiting this crucial developmental function of the centre.

While the predominance of economism in developmental thinking may be beyond dispute the question remains as to what specific feature of economism renders it capable of being a globalising force. It is clearly not simply a universal and legitimate concern with building a humane and equitable social order in a direct and pragmatic sense. This would seem to be best served by the kind of economics associated with Gandhi and the alternative technology movement. Gandhi is opposed to economism to the precise degree that for him the nature of a society defines its economic form and not *vice versa*. There is thus no ideal economic form any more than there is a notion of society being geared to a primarily economic causal mechanism. Economics is not the analytical tool *par excellence* for disclosing the heart of a society; it is simply that ordering of productive forces which the nature of any given social entity demands and can sustain. It was this clear perception of existing social reality that led Gandhi to argue that the path of the West was unsuitable for India for the twin reasons of a surplus of population and paucity of investible resources.

The employment in industry of the bulk of the Indian population was simply beyond Indian means. The size of the population and the immediacy of its needs made it obvious to him that the distinction drawn in economic theory between growth and employment was both vicious and irrelevant in the Indian context. Employment needed to be at the centre of the economic process and fused integrally with growth. A viable economic policy necessarily involved the full utilisation of labour

power. This in turn imposed certain constraints in terms of technological choice.

The prime consideration determining technological choice was that
structural unemployment deepens to the extent that the capital-intensity
of production was raised. This, and not simply some pastoral nostal-
gia, was the rationale behind the advocacy of rejuvenating labour-
intensive occupations of the traditional sector. The argument that the
lower per unit costs of capital-intensive production would create a large
market ran the risk that spiralling unemployment at the mass level
would drastically limit the demand base. As this would adversely affect
the re-investible surplus rates, the burden of unemployment would have
to be borne by the shrinking number of the employed.

The Idea of Alternative Technology

The same result would occur, however, if an excessively labour-
intensive strategy were followed; the low productivity per work-place
would also reduce the increment of reinvestible surplus. The basic need
in such a perspective was therefore to increase the productivity of the
labour-intensive sector with the most marginal possible increase in capital costs—a task which, at the technical level, is one of the main concerns of the alternative technology movement. This endeavour has, in
the main, proved successful: "... a plea for more careful technical choice
would not be very sensible if viable alternative technologies do not exist,
as has been the accepted view at times in the past. Research and technical cooperation projects carried out within the World Employment
Programme of the ILO and also to a more limited extent by the international organisations and universities have, however ... conclusively
demonstrated that in virtually all sectors effective alternative technologies do exist".[17]

Alternative technology stresses the pragmatic options open to the poor
countries in the context of their most glaring disabilities. Thus it emphasises the necessity of lessening external dependence through seeking
recourse to local materials and tackling the ever-growing employment
slack by the utilisation of labour-intensive technologies which are thrifty
with regard to capital and complicated infrastructural prerequisites. This,
in turn, would enable decentralisation of production which, given the
fact that unemployment increases with urban scale, would itself lessen
employment pressures. Such policies simultaneously reject the notion
that the road taken by the core countries was the only possible one and
holds that the truly viable course for the peripheral countries is to

17. *Technology, Employment and Basic Needs*, ILO Overviews Paper, ILO, Geneva 1977,
p. 6.

address themselves rigorously to the specificities of their own condition. If adopted consistently, it questions import-substitution policies which duplicate the North-South dichotomy within national frontiers, let alone the idea of technology-transfer across a wide spectrum of sectors. It stresses the particularity of the technological needs of the peripheral countries and doubts whether the core countries have much to offer. Thus, as Hans Singer puts it, "assuming that the country's development policy is firmly oriented towards the reduction of poverty, technology can be directed towards those goods and services which form part of the basic needs of the community. These 'appropriate products' are likely to be different from the products developed in the rich countries. Where this is the case, no process of selection of existing technology, however careful, will serve the poorer countries".[18]

This conclusion is buttressed by the exorbitant costs of technology-transfer. Singer estimates that, by the end of the sixties, the cost to the developing countries for patents, licenses, knowhow, trade-marks, management and other technical services came to US$ 1,500 million. This figure could be double were it to include the cost of imported equipment, over-priced intermediate goods and transfer-pricing. Technology-transfer is not only exceedingly expensive but it is also highly conducive to increasing dependency in that 98% of all R&D is concentrated in the developed world, which is thus in a position to control all major initiatives. As it also dominates the current patterns of international trade, the strategy of export-oriented developmental programmes also suffers from similar drawbacks from this point of view. The main commodity the developing countries have to offer on the international market is cheap labour, but the dramatic new technological innovations in electronics and micro-processors promise automation possibilities which are substantially cheaper than the cheapest manual competitors.

The basic argument for a primarily self-reliant strategy tailored specifically to one's needs and freed from the dogma of universal indicators is simply that development along the lines of the dominant countries reduces autonomy to dangerously vulnerable levels as one has no say in the framing of the rules of the game. While the theoretical possibility of joining the winners always exists—hence the irresistibility of the temptation—the logic of the situation as a whole is consistently against the weaker 'partners'.

Wages of Integration

This emerges most clearly in the field of current technological developments. Such changes are strikingly manifest in the field of informa-

---

18. Hans Singer, *Technologies for Basic Needs* ILO, Geneva, 1977, p. 20.

tion technology, a term which refers to the unification of the hitherto separate industrial and service sectors on the basis of electronics technology and which thus covers electronic components, computers, telecommunications, consumer and professional electronics. Information technology is based simply on the fact that all acts involve a degree of information transfer—a transfer which, in electronics, is effected by the language of the digital signal. Information technology has, therefore, an enormous span and bears directly on industrial products and processes as also white-collar work and services. Products are changed primarily in that, by virtue of the 'intelligence' embedded in the 'chips' they are capable of qualitatively enhanced ranges of functions.

Secondly, there is a dramatic increase in the speed of the product cycle. In the case of office equipment it is cut down to 3-4 years from 13-14. This demands manufacturing systems flexible enough to amortise the capital costs over a wide range of products instead of just one. Finally, electronic products cannot be treated as simple incremental additions to just any system; they need to become part of a larger system and internally compatible with other parts of it. These features of increased material costs, faster obsolescence and greater need for integration mean comprehensively greater capital intensity and more complex and concentrated forms of industrial production in which R&D plays a progressively important role.

'New Technologies'

Theoretically, the new technology appears to offer certain advantages to developing countries in the sense that information regarding markets is now more easily accessible. Similarly, ease of transportability makes it easier to offer services without the cost of actual physical presence. The cost of entry into the international marketplace has thus been lowered. In fact, however. due to the enormous lag between the developing and developed worlds in terms of informatic capacity, these capital-saving features will only be beneficial to the latter who alone are sufficiently well-equipped to exploit them. Rada, therefore, asserts that: "Notwithstanding the inroads that some developing countries might make in one field or another (e.g. India in software), the overall situation is one of a growing gap *vis-a-vis* the developed countries in terms of the material base and infrastructure necessary to support 'information-intensive', value-added services and industries".[19]

This bleak forecast returns us to the consideration of the possibility

19. Juan Rada, "Information Technology and Developing Countries", International Management Institute, Geneva, 1983, p. 30.

of a self-reliant strategy for developing countries. National frontiers, however regrettably, are highly porous to changes in production systems. No country, however it might so wish, can remain impervious to technological changes of such range, power and dynamism. The pertinent point is not whether they are suitable or congruous with the needs of development as perceived from different horizons of concern; it is simply that they disclose possibilities which most leaders of the developing world find hard to ignore. It may be that in terms of 'basic needs', modernising China will do less well than it did under Mao, but few in China contest the inevitability of modernisation. The new technologies, both in terms of destroying the comparative advantages of low labour costs and in terms of the conditions they demand for optimisation (capital-intensive R&D, very high levels of systemic development and integration, extensive and sophisticated infrastructures of computers and telecommunications (*telematique*) etc.) can hardly be considered as ideal for developmental purposes within the existing circumstances of the Third World.

The assimilation of advanced technologies by the developing world in a disaggregated and naunced way is certainly a point to consider. But it nonetheless remains true that on the whole such innovations aggravate the disadvantages under which it already labours. This intense constraint of being compelled to absorb developments which are likely to be deleterious in their comprehensive impact on one's fundamental condition deserves closer attention.

If the justification is the need to maximise economic performance to the virtual exclusion of everything else or as the virtual pre-condition for any kind of development, we must accept the inexorable logic of economism. This idea stresses the determining role of economics in society but does not accept that economics itself is socially conditioned. Thus, while being omnipotent, it is in itself an autonomous realm subject solely to its own laws. Its concepts of profitability and productivity are founded in the disciplinary definition of these terms and not in empirical social reality. To this extent they are non-empirical and self-referential notions, closed-system definitions. This disjunction is what permits the seemingly strange anomaly of a booming economy with little general socially ameliorative impact. Such an understanding of economics is very different from one which comprehends it simply as the materially productive expression of the values that animate any given society and which thus ,accepts that varying societies have varying economies. Economics thus remains subsumed within the social rubric as such. Economic rationalism, on the other hand, is located in an abstract universe shorn of specific contextual definition and historical experience. It is an ideal construct, a mental structure maintained and extended by the laws of logical consistency and coherence.

The crux of the problem now reveals itself as the relationship between such an ideal construct and tangible socio-economic reality. It would be erroneous in the light of historical experience to regard these simply as dichotomous categories. Wherever economic rationalism has come, it has conquered. No localised, traditional economy has been able to withstand the dynamic vigour of its generalising, homogenising force. Economics as a concrete, material ordering of a specific society has steadily given way to the socially abstract profitability calculations of economism. It is indeed true that society resents this usurpation and often agitates violently against it in a variety of ways—political rebellion, psychological alienation, ethnic revulsion, etc.—but it is equally true that none of these have proved capable of halting or even slowing its progress. The essential independence of economic rationalism from social concerns is often illustrated with reference to profitability: anything which creates a demand is profitable—war for the armaments industry, pollution for the pollution control industry and so on.

The Market As Integrator

The abstractions of societies which have become economic structures *par excellence* derives simply from the nature of a market which ideally presupposes an infinite exchangeability and commensurately flexible media of exchange. All qualitative differentiation between things is abolished by necessary reduction to the common medium of exchange so that only price differences remain. Even these do not always mimic qualitative differences but merely reflect further quantitative variations in demand and supply. Thus primary and secondary goods are equally treated as commodities—that is, viewed fundamentally from the perspective of marketability—and hitherto non-economic factors are brought within the same sphere through devices like cost-benefit analysis. The idea of unlimited exchangeability is patently antipathetic by nature to all specifically local forms of material organisation, all forms of particularistic productive enterprise. This, of course, does not mean that the diversity of the production range is adversely affected—on the contrary it is mostly increased—but it does mean an increase in homogenisation, in qualitative improvements.

The aspiration of market forces towards universality, the mobility of exchange that it encourages and affords, is one of the main reasons why alternative technology approaches stressing utilisation of local materials and production for local markets have failed to have the ameliorative impact on poverty that was expected of them. They have largely resulted in the creation of a new entrepreneurial class. The assumption, unwarranted in the event, was the existence of more or less self-enclosed communities. For such groups, the notion of local materials and local markets has obvious pertinence, but the very meaning of local is lost when, as in fact, one is dealing with an economy based on a pervasive cash nexus and generalised commodity exchange.

Cooptation

Thus, when alternative technology develops a cheap substitute for an expensive raw material, or a relatively inexpensive tool with enhanced productive capacity, it will gravitate, not to where it is needed most but to where it fetches the highest price. In this way, in the present economic context, alternative technology is not an alternative at all but simply another modality of conventional technology, which caters to niches in the market which the mainstream of the latter has left unexplored. The absence of local circuits of production and consumptin also has a negative bearing on the multiplier effects of public works undertaken for the purpose of creating employment. These are maximised when the demand for wage goods that this generates can be catered to by local production. If this, instead, drains away to distant parts of the economy, the local employment picture will not be greatly altered.

Linear Drive

The logic of alternative technology as a developmental mode presupposes an essential constancy of social forms. Its notion of resources is based on what currently exists and its endeavours are limited by the horizon of the tangibly available. It works, thus, to improve the lot of people with the least possible disruption of their diverse natural and cultural rhythms, indeed with maximum conservation of these diversities. Its thinking assumes, and seeks, a stable world. Economic rationalism which forms the basis of technology and its constant mutations, on the other hand, is primarily concerned with the world as raw material, as potential for dynamic transformation. It assumes a world in constant flux and seeks to transform all existing structures, including their enduring and lasting aspects. Its fundamental drive is towards changeability as it seeks to shape and reshape all diversities and differentiations towards one homogeneous and malleable mass—the ultimate in the vision of modern science. This is obviously an entirely different perspective from that of alternative technology as a basis of an alternative development strategy that is ecologically sustainable and respectful of inner balance and harmony in both man and nature.

Deeper Issues

There is as yet an inadequate understanding of the deeper intellectual basis of this drive towards transforming world reality and inccr-
porating it into the world centre, namely the economistic thrust of
modern development theory, its exclusive reliance on technology and
its undermining of cultural diversity and political choice. The result is
that even major critiques of mainstream development theory have continued to assign predominance to the economic factor. Common to both
the conventional and the critical schools has been a largely apolitical
approach to development. Of course, part of the critique has been mot-
ivated by political considerations, as for example that aspect of the self-
reliance and NIEO schools which aim at building sufficient power of
the State in the Third World countries. But almost all these attempts
at theory share a conception of development as bundles of goods and
services—through trickle down approach for some as against an egalitarian approach for others, a rate of growth approach as against a basic
needs approach—with little systematic thought given to the need to
build into the model structural properties that were based on a conception of a just and participant society. Even the dependency critique,
while orienting itself to an important international dimension, tended
to focus on economic and technological factors and concomitant structures of exploitation and dependence within and between societies.
Though often prompted by a basically political concern, the analysis
of historical processes that in fact emerged generally failed to relate itself
to the nature of regimes, forms of participation and a clear view of the
political prerequisites of achieving desirable states of socio-economic
development.

During this whole period, however, there also slowly emerged another
comprehensive critique of developmental thinking which, while drawing upon the dependency, ecological, basic needs, self-reliance and NIEO
streams in a more holistic framework, has focussed on the need to perceive poverty, inequality and oppression as essentially political and cultural tasks. This larger critique has not taken the form of a very
specialised school like the others mentioned above. It has emerged from
a variety of vantage points and is, of late, receiving the attention of
theoreticians, movements of dissent and even policy analysts in different parts of the world. Only in the last few years a realisation has dawned
on the thinkers on development that in their pre-occupation with socio-
economic issues the traditional concern with human freedom had oddly
been left out. While all the thinking and rethinking was going on in
respect of the relationship between development and socio-economic
goals both among Third World thinkers and their associates in other

parts of the world, most of the Third World societies were being subjected to authoritarian tendencies, in both domestic and international arenas, and much of this in the name of development. To repeat a point made elsewhere in this book, development has emerged as perhaps the most important reason of State.

Interdependence or Forced Integration?

Crucial to understanding this trend towards universalising the development paradigm is the enormous pull of the centre-culture and its artifacts in integrating the whole world in the image of its own particular regional model. The contemporary manifestation of this thrust in the face of new assertions from the peripheries is to be found in the model of 'interdependence'. Couched in a mutualist jargon the new formulation provides a more persuasive basis for progressive homogenisation of the world. But common to them both is the forced integration of various regions and cultures into one common whole. Colonialism and the economic expansion of the West, backed by superior military technology, represented the first major attempt in this direction. Where colonialism left off, development took over—in ways that proved even more pervasive and potent. It has been a mighty juggernaut that has been at work, shaping and reshaping so much of the global landscape and the diverse cultural streams thereof. Where old or newer forms of diversity still persist—and they do—there is an attempt to suppress them, tire them out into surrender or cooptation, or assign them subsidiary and peripheral roles.[20] Even the phenomena of multipolarity at the international level and political competition in local contexts are sought to be turned into instruments of integration and homogenisation.

The large and powerful currents unleashed by technology, militarism, consumerism, the world market and the mass media spawned by the increasingly transnational model of capitalism, the 'universalist' ideology of development, as also the vision of 'catching up' that seems to haunt most of the Third World regimes—all these are gravitating to more and more points of convergence and cooptation into one global whole. These currents, of course, involve fierce competition and conflict around new issues and forces generated by the logic of forced integration into a world market—in respect of access to the control of natural resources, the enormous growth of the 'unorganised' sector of each economy and the new international division of labour entailing permanent mar-

20. There has been a lot of talk of non-governmental organisations (NGOs) these days. For a critical analysis of how these are sought to be coopted see my "NGOs, the State and World Capitalism" in *State Against Democracy, op. cit.*

ginalisation of whole social strata: women, immigrant populations, millions of children in large parts of the world, the rural and the urban poor. And underlying them all are vast and irreversible ecological consequences as an integral aspect of the economistic logic and the techno-economic imperatives inherent in it, colonising not just the diverse cultural and national entities but colonising nature too and as that involves irreversible decisions in the present, colonising the future as well. The technological *putsch*, the global communications blitz and the great draw of consumerist culture spawning the whole globe lie behind this fierce competition among vastly different societies to converge towards one common desire—a lifestyle fashioned after the capitalist West.

Search for Alternatives

It is out of a growing concern at the grim consequences of such a model of integration and homogenisation, and the consequently felt threats to cultural autonomy and individual freedom that a whole series of new responses have of late emerged. These range all the way from local challenges at the grassroots of diverse societies to the wider concerns and movements that are increasingly becoming global both in scope and definition. They represent an effort to redefine both the range of politics and thinking about politics and social change. It is an effort to open up new spaces in both the arena of the State—and the States system—and in several other spheres of civil society outside this arena.

This is in many ways a new kind of effort, one that is based on new spurts in consciousness—beyond economism, beyond confined definitions of the political process, beyond the facile (and false) dichotomy of State *versus* Market, discovering new indigenous roots as well as other authentic sources of sustenance and strength, based not so much on either the fractured Old or a mediocre and insipid New as on genuine possibilities of alternatives that can in fact work.

It is from such a convergence of alternative *politics* and alternative thinking that new definitions of the scope and range of human interventions are surfacing and around these redefinitions new social movements are emerging. The environment, the rights and the role of women, health, food and nutrition, education, shelter and housing, dispensation of justice, communications, information, culture and lifestyles—none of these were considered subject matter for politics, at any rate not for domestic politics, not for mass politics in which ordinary people were involved. All this has now changed.

The basic axiom of the modern approach on development is that societies are constructs, and that, being the products of human will, they can accordingly be structured as desired—and the idea is to structure each society along a 'rational' path. To begin with, the basic principle of such structuring was essentially seen as being economic. In the fifties a new society meant, as noted above, capital formation, rising GNP, infrastructure and industry. In the sixties, when the impact of these endeavours began to be felt in terms of new social relations, the formation of new pressure-groups and new distribution of power within communities, developmentalists turned their attention to political science and sociology. The seventies saw the emergence of the environment and pollution as major concerns and ecology stepped in. But each of these were still perceived as dimensions to be incorporated, new specialisations to be pursued for achieving the original aim better.

However, the dislocations of development, the perception that the various hard and soft inputs were not working with the expected linear predictability, led to the growing conviction that society was not a mere aggregate of outputs and that social elements, intrinsically, had autonomous significance. This gained anthropology an increasing importance—not as an exotic ethnology but as a study of the structural constants of various societies and their implications for modern society. Hence the importance of social anthropology. In such a perspective, society is not seen as a mechanical fabrication by inputs but rather as a relational system whose logic is primary in determining the way in which the inputs are used. Social phenomena are no longer epiphenomena of the sub-stratum of material conditions. Rather, the ordering of social elements is seen as a function of the valuational significance of these elements themselves. In brief, it calls for holistic analysis. Holism and values now come to the fore in the unfolding dynamic of development.

Holism thus understood would seem to be opposed to the homogenisation forced by the concepts and methods of modern knowledge and would instead seek to represent organic, integrated and yet particularistic entities. It would as much emphasise the diversity in which a given unity is located as the global and planetary relationships through which the diversities would realise their discrete identities.

We do not subscribe to any universal theory of human behaviour or to globalism based on such a universalist view. It is rather the *structure of interrelationships and linkages* that has permeated the social condition that interests us and needs to be taken cognizance of in our thinking about the human predicament and ways of dealing with it. It is this that we have tried to map and conceptualise in this essay. We are convinced that it is from such a perspective that the close intertwining of the prospects for peace, development and global transformation will emerge.

9

Development Viewed Internationally

Perspective

This paper is based on a Symposium, which was held at the initiative of the Director-General for Development and International Economic Cooperation, organised by the International Foundation for Development Alternatives (IFDA), hosted by the Netherlands government and attended by concerned representatives of the governmental, intergovernmental and extra-governmental sectors. It had before it a critical and timely, even if difficult and ambitious, task. Frankly admitting that the national and international development strategies pursued in the first two United Nations Development Decades had led to an 'absence of development and the prevalence of maldevelopment in many parts of the world', the agenda notes prepared by the Symposium secretariat recognised that:

the present political context is very different from that of ten years ago. Traditional options for action are foreclosed by failures of the past; the attitudes of Governments and other actors have hardened, and it is now much more difficult to mobilise political forces in favour of development. This situation calls for much greater responsibility and for more statesmanship on the part of the world community. It calls for bolder solutions in terms of both substance and political process, if we truly wish to avoid the now obvious road to more gloom, misery and wastage—the road to an unprecedented global crisis that may take its cruel toll in all parts of the world.

Discussion at the Symposium confirmed this perspective. It underscored the point that the search for a new development strategy for the

1980s and beyond—both national and international, both for the South and for the North—had to be pursued against the background of a drastically altered world situation and a new global human *problematique*. This *problematique* is rooted in a number of interrelated phenomena. Among these are:

(1) The pervasive dualism of the world along the North-South axis;

(2) A fundamental disequilibrium in the world economy arising out of underlying structural maladjustments and affecting all regions of the world;

(3) A state of instability in the world political process arising from continuing asymmetry between the world's regions, together with a growing challenge from less privileged regions to the centres of economic and political power and intensifying pressures for a new international order;

(4) Enveloping all other sources of conflict, the conflict over resources and lifestyles, with the North wanting to preserve and even enhance its standard of living, and the South wanting to achieve minimum living standards for which it would need access to resources and institutions—many of which are located in the South—over which the North has acquired control and hegemony;

(5) Penetration into the Third World of the alien lifestyles of the industrially advanced societies and their concomitant structures of production and technology, producing in its wake a structural crisis, growing disenchantment among the people with their elites and new sources of conflict within and between Third World countries;

(6) New dimensions in the increasing militarisation of the world political process with (i) some countries of the North responding to the perceived threat from the South to their economic and political power and their lifestyles with new doctrines of military hegemony and pre-emptive warfare against the Third World, and (ii) the elites in many countries of the South making up for their economic and political failure by resorting to military aggrandisement which, incidentally, can also be used for repressive measures at home—the two aspects together making for an endemic state of insecurity at all levels, and a complete distortion of the development process;

(7) As a result of these various phenomena, a growing confrontation waged in defence of the global *status quo*, at both national and international levels, but essentially triggered by policies pursued by major Northern powers against the South through protectionism, resource diplomacy, doctrines of 'defence' against the Third World, and attempts to sow the seeds of fragmentation in the Third World through the aggressive salesmanship of military hardware, technology and models

of lifestyle and development;

(8) Fragmentation and turmoil in the Third World arising out of mass awakening and frequent shifts and turnover of elites.

The Symposium considered the formulation of a new international development strategy against this broad historical and geo-political context. It was realised that this was not an easy task; for such a strategy has to reckon with the reality of a deeply divided world and the threat of an inimical confrontation born out of the despair that is likely to emerge from the failure of the western paradigm, the disequilibrium in the world economy and the general defensiveness of the global establishment. Seen in this light, the strategy that is called for, if it has to have any chance of success, cannot follow the lines defined (mostly by economists) during the last 20 or 25 years; it must be an essentially political mechanism, involving a major intervention in the historical process to halt and reverse the trends under way on the basis of a completely new approach to the development process.

Alongside a feeling of disillusionment at the past record, there was recognition of an impasse in North-South negotiations and also widely felt scepticism about the present capacity of the United Nations system, and of a United Nations 'strategy' conceived in the conventional framework, to deliver the goods.

This sentiment was expressed at two levels of consideration:

(1) The actual western stance of resistance to any major proposal for change in the present structure of North-South arrangements, the preoccupation of the socialist segment of the North with short-term conflicts bearing on East-West rivalry and its tendency to disclaim responsibility for major sources of inequity and disparities in the world are largely unchallenged at the present time and thus vitiate the effectiveness of the United Nations as a negotiating instrument.

(2) It may in any case be unrealistic to expect the United Nations system to carry the whole burden of the agenda facing humanity, asking it to undertake tasks that ought first to be undertaken within individual societies in the North and in the South, by the Third World countries working collectively and enhancing their effectiveness at regional and global levels—seizing control of their own destinies at the international levels as they had done in the past at the national level—and by the forces of change everywhere engaging in structural transformation and promoting local, national and collective self-reliance. Lacking such transformation and its outward reach to the international order through determined intervention in the global political process, it is futile to expect to make the strategy an instrument of structural change and reconstruction.

Goals and Objectives: Redefining Development

The strategy for the United Nations Development Decades has failed not only as regards the implementation of its targets and policy measures and its lack of operational coherence and power to compel compliance from the various actors; it also suffers from conceptual inadequacies in its basic premises. This point was stressed by Ken Dadzie, the then Director-General for Development and International Cooperation of the United Nations, who said that, underlying that strategy, there had been an unrealistic conception of the world economy according to which growth in the industrialised countries was more or less automatically transmitted to Third World countries through the mechanisms of trade, technology transfer and development finance. Most Third World countries themselves seem to have paid less than adequate attention to the need for qualitative and structural changes in their societies, preferring to rely on the logic of the gross national product (GNP) model whereby a certain course of growth and expansion would necessarily raise production and hence also living standards. In point of fact, the very pursuit of such strategies has increased imbalances, disparities and absolute as well as relative poverty in the world.

There was general recognition, too, that just as the strategy itself had not worked, so had there been little progress in restructuring the existing international order. The present rules of the game—particularly in the trade, financial and monetary systems—continue to maintain the historical pattern of Northern command over the resources of the Third World and ensure a disproportionately large consumption of the world's resources by the industrialised countries.

Indeed, in the absence of restructuring, the Development Strategy has failed to bring about the stipulated qualitative and structural changes in the society which were expected to accompany economic growth and, conversely, because the Strategy lacked a clear conceptual guidance in respect of qualitative and structural change, it has failed to bring about the necessary redistribution of economic and political power and consequent changes in the international order. It is not surprising, therefore, that international discussion over the past few years (certainly since the events of 1973) has focused on the need to restructure the international order, as embodied in the concept of the New International Economic Order. There was broad agreement that this concept encompasses both economic and political dimensions and that it implies a redefinition of the development process.

The Symposium dwelt at some length on this matter of redefining the concept of development and reassessing the development *problematique*. Aside from stressing the need to move away from aggregate

growth as an end in itself and to reject the assumption of some automatic transmission of growth and expansion to all regions of the world
and all classes of people, four other aspects were emphasised as necessary ingredients of a new development strategy.

The Political Process

Stress was laid on the need to explicity recognise the interlinkage
between development and the political process. The current notion of
'interdependence' in fact entails highly asymmetric relationships
between the South and the North, corresponding to the imbalances in
relative influence and bargaining power. This underscores the prior
necessity of restructuring the international political and decision-making
system as an end in itself, but more particularly as a means to a more
equitable and just development process. The same necessity applies to
restructuring the domestic social and political orders. Without decentralisation and participation of large sections of the people and of the
suppressed and exploited regions of the world, it is not going to be possible, merely through directives and exhortations from above, to restructure the socio-economic order; this is basically a political task.

Demilitarisation

Closely related to this political aspect is the military-strategic dimension. Most of the discussion on development, or even on science and
technology, has on the whole avoided the issue of militarisation. Militarisation has become not just a drag on the development process but,
in a very basic way, an instrument for the maintenance of dependen-
ce/dominance relationships, and a means of co-opting new secondary
centres of power and involving them in a wider submilitarisation process to which Third World elites have tended to succumb. This process
is eating into the very fabric of development and, unless demilitarisation is perceived as a development objective and built into the body
of the development strategy, the achievement either of medium-term
development targets or of the larger goal of restructuring the international order will prove very difficult.

Culture

No less important is the cultural context of the development process.
Development is not merely an economic and political concept; it is more
fundamentally a process of culture and civilisation. This insight has
dawned on development thinkers and planners in recent years, especially in the Third World. The search for modernisation and a homo-

geneous process of development over the last several decades has been
accompanied by an erosion of cultural identities—a process which is
in some ways much more corrosive of political integrity and independence, as well as of confidence and self-regard, than either political colonialism or economic neo-colonialism. However, this is not just a
question of a confrontation of values between the North and the South;
it is rather that the world needs cultural alternatives to the dominant
western paradigm of development. This need has acquired added force
from the incipient erosion of the cultural backdrop and integrity of the
North itself. The sweep and momentum generated by a highly technocratic and technology-oriented model of development is undermining the individual, undermining group identities, and undermining the
wholeness of self-definition of entire civilisations—hence the reassertion of the religious, spiritual and aesthetic components of being, in all
parts of the world, and the widely felt need for providing the concept
of development with new and different cultural roots by drawing upon
alternative civilisational models.

Sustainability

Related to the cultural context are those aspects of development usually described as environmental or ecological, but which lie at the very
heart of human survival and are best considered in terms of the notion
of a sustained and sustainable development process. Current mechanisms of development are not only impairing the harmony between man
and nature, but are undermining the productive process itself. As was
mentioned repeatedly, there are tendencies at work which are likely to
erode the balance between man, nature and technology, and in turn
make it impossible to maintain a process of development that could be
sustainable over time. Even in the North—in the so-called food baskets
of the world—there are indications that imprudent recourse to technological inputs, unless reversed, will greatly contribute by the end of
the century to a major erosion of soil, leading to diminishing the already
marginal productivity of land and reducing production capacities. The
tropical regions of the world face even greater danger given their much
greater vulnerability. Technology-induced development, therefore, has
to be replaced by an alternative process of development based on sus-
tainability and restraint—a process that is planned less by experts than
by the people themselves, drawing upon their local environment and
their diverse and almost infinite possibilities. Such a model of development is better adapted to deal with problems of poverty and maldevelopment and inequities all around the world. As regards the
prospects of growth and productivity, there was no pessimism at the

Symposium; rather, there was a recognition of the need for turning away from the dominant western model of development based on rapacious technology to one that drew continued sustenance and power from various ecosystems and the laws of nature, both in the North and in the South.

Thrust of the New Strategy

The basic thrust of the new approach came from an alternative conception of development which gives due regard to political and cultural factors as well as to alternative attitudes and values. It was stressed, for instance, that there can be no real autonomy or self-reliance without a measure of self-control; and unless there is restraint on the degree of competition, acquisitiveness and greed accompanying development, societies will always be subject to external forces. Similarly, unless some notion of restraint and even sacrifice is built into the thinking on development, the objective of collective self-reliance among Third World countries that are at different vantage points in their command over resources and skills will never be realised.

As regards the countries of the North which are materially better off than those of the South, it should be remembered that this difference is to no small extent due to the process of colonialism and exploitation. In a fundamental sense, however, the exploiters themselves are no less victims of the process than the exploited, because they are the encapsulated prisoners of a pervasive culture giving rise to acute maldevelopment.

This maldevelopment is characterised by waste of resources, degradation of the environment, institutionalised consumerism, total dependence on external sources of life support, growing unemployment and recession, persistence of substantial pockets of poverty and a deep crisis of values and cultural identity. This is a structural phenomenon, rooted in the processes of industrialisation and social organisation which have been pursued in the North. Its eradication calls for structural remedies; it must be recognised in the North that a policy of 'more of the same' cannot lead the way out of an impasse.

A Global Strategy Against a Global Crisis

There is thus a crisis in the North, which is no less basic than that in the South. Therefore the new development strategy should be a global strategy which is addressed to the South, the North and the institutions and processes that relate the two. The strategy should encompass what is basically wrong with the North, as with the South, as well as the relationship between the maldevelopment in the North and the inadequate,

unjust and unbalanced development patterns in the South—phenomena
which incidentally provide the context for the both incipient and often
manifest revolt of the younger generation and its alienation, cutting
across both North and South. The new development strategy must relate
itself to this larger global context of structural and cultural change.

As regards the relationship of commitments to be undertaken in the
context of the new strategy by Third World and industrialised countries, respectively, policy prescriptions must be addressed to both industrialised and Third World countries. Such prescriptions could relate
to a variety of desiderata and could include, in particular, measures to
ensure a continuing improvement in the well-being of the entire population. This approach would not require that the commitments of industrialised and Third World countries should be conditional upon each
other; one can achieve balance without symmetry. Still less would it
mean that the goals and objectives of the strategy should be anything
other than the shared goals and shared objectives of the entire international community, consistent with the spirit of the United Nations
Charter itself.

The Strategic Objectives

The Symposium deliberately focused on the larger historical perspective and on the goals and objectives of development that should inspire
a new international development strategy. It was felt that this focus has
been generally lacking in deliberations on the strategy and on specific
policy measures. And yet, without clarity on these basic matters, a 'strategy' would either remain a pious declaration of intent or get distorted
in the course of its implementation, or both. This is precisely what has
happened in the past. On the other hand, such an approach and method
as were advanced in the Symposium would not only highlight the basic
thrust of the strategy but also define its policy content.

Thus, in summary, there emerged from the Symposium a succinct
formulation, radically different from previous ones, of the goals and
objectives of a new international development strategy: the primary
objective, according to this formulation, is to manifest the firm commitment of all the members of the international community to promote
genuine sustainable, equity enhancing and people-oriented development of Third World countries and arrest the maldevelopment of both
Third World and industrialised countries. In order to remove the obstacles to the attainment of this objective, structural changes must be pursued at both national and international levels, the latter within the broad
framework of the new international economic order and the negotiating processes aimed at its advancement, on the basis of the collective

self-reliance of the Third World and the creation of an international environment conducive to alternative processes of development in both the North and the South.

Framework for Policy

The discussion at the Symposium brought forth the basic policy implications of such a strategy.

Collective Global Responsibility

A strategy for development along these lines has to be global in scope, that is to say, it would be simultaneously pursued at domestic (local and national), regional and international levels, in both the South and the North. The development strategy must be conceived as a collective responsibility of the entire international community and as involving a constantly interactive relationship between the industrialised and Third World countries, i.e., between national (including local) development policies pursued by each set of actors, and their international impacts and implications. The development of Third World countries will remain an unfulfilled goal if they remain unable to secure a share of resources commensurate with their development needs due to unfair competition from industrialised countries. Conversely, western lifestyles and their demonstration effect on the South must be restrained if maldevelopment is not to become totally globalised.

Accountability

This follows directly from the first: there is need for a system of international accountability of each State for the impact of its national development, or maldevelopment, on the development of other nations. This again is especially relevant to the rich and powerful countries having disproportionate access to, and use of, world resources and pursuing a lifestyle and technology that produces the bulk of environmental hazards for the world. Such a concept of accountability is no less relevant to the richer classes within societies.

Removal of International Stumbling Blocks

There emerged from this ethical perspective for development an appreciation of the international obstacles to an alternative development strategy. These obstacles are largely institutional in respect of financial transactions, trade barriers, technology transfers and control of communication and information channels. In each of these areas the responsibility and accountability of the industrialised countries must be stressed.

Confrontation/Negotiation Dialectic

Implicit in this emphasis on undoing the effects of maldevelopment, reversing policies that promote global disparities and dependencies and creating conditions for collective self-reliance among Third World countries is the question of process: how does one get there? The formulation that emerged in this context was one of a dialectic between confrontation and negotiation. As already indicated, major elements of the North have moved along the path of confrontation by resorting to protectionism, resource diplomacy and doctrines of defensive warfare against the South, as well as through attempts to fragment the South through its submilitarisation. In response, the South is left with no option but to match this confrontation by internationalising collective self-reliance, engaging in its own version of resource diplomacy and trying to work out new global coalitions of interest that derive strength from divergences of interest within the North and its incipient fragmentation.

Approach to Negotiations and Time-Frame

Within this overall context of confrontation, and indeed as an instrument of global structural transformation (which should in fact be the aim of the confrontation), it should also be possible to enter into negotiations with the North. The principal aim of these negotiations should be to change the rules governing international flows of trade, money, finance and technology. The effective functioning of international institutions dealing with economic transactions should also be demonstrated, and collective self-reliance should emerge as a forceful determinant of the new development strategy. In short, the principal *raison d'etre* of a new international development strategy should be the creation of a new international economic and political order.

Bearing in mind that such a strategy may not embody a settlement of all outstanding issues, particularly those relative to the restructuring of the existing international economic order, it should provide for negotiations on such issues, set out principles to guide these negotiations and establish deadlines for their completion. Such negotiations should be global and integrated in character and be closely meshed with other ongoing negotiations; they should concentrate on a range of carefully selected key issues of the North-South dialogue, including energy, and should have a scope which would be so defined as to maximise the impact of the leverage of the Third World and afford mutually advantageous opportunities for trade-offs.

The implementation of key targets as operational components of the new strategy—and hence also of the process of negotiation—may be conceived in the time-frame of a decade but only in the form of a dynamic process, with different time-frames for different components, and with an in-built and effective mechanism for review and reappraisal, leading to adjustments and correctives whenever the strategy is seen to deflect from the goals and objectives of development for which it was devised. It should be in the form not of a 'plan of action' document, devised and adopted at the start of the decade, but rather of a manifesto, which provides the framework of a sustained commitment to, and implementation of, development goals and their operational components, and embodies institutional mechanisms for continuous negotiation, monitoring, appraisal, criticism and modification.

Key Policy and Negotiating Targets

The new international development strategy and its framework of negotiations should aim at a few key issues and adopt them as its priority policy and negotiating targets.

It should above all aim at two key elements of national *self-reliance* in the Third World and eradicate the obstacles facing them: sustainable production of domestic food supplies and endogenous capacities of developing, acquiring and adapting technology.

It should provide the concept of development with new and different *cultural roots* by drawing upon alternative modes of civilisation; in particular, it should push forward the eradication of marginalisation based on forced illiteracy and racism, and should move towards a fully worked-out code of conduct on control of international mass media and information networks.

It should incorporate *demilitarisation* as a development objective and should initiate moves towards a step-wise and time-bound programme of disarmament and demilitarisation, for without progress on this front progress on economic and political aspects of development, the environment, the achievement of collective self-reliance and transformation towards the new international economic order will always remain problematic.

It should pay much greater attention to the present waste and maldistribution of development *resources*—especially food, technology and energy—and should aim at effective means to increase the command of Third World countries over such resources.

It should aim at full participation by the Third World in the management of all *global commons* which are outside the scope of national sovereignty over resources, all of them to be dealt with under the comprehensive framework of the 'common heritage of mankind' at the present historical juncture.

Within the context of the policy priorities outlined above, the strategy should promote negotiations—made meaningful by the increased collective countervailing power of the Third World to complete the unfinished agenda of UNCTAD and other international forums: namely, to establish a restructured international framework for *trade, monetary and financial co-operation* which should accommodate the different economic and social systems and patterns of development prevalent in the world community and which would be based on institutionalised democratic processes of consultation and decision-making. This framework should include:

(1) International measures to regulate the activities of *transnational corporations* in the fields of trade, money, finance and technology, including effective codes of conduct, backed up by comprehensive national legislation in both home and host countries;

(2) A *trading* system which makes room for the changing economic potential of the Third World and which also provides a sound base for the world commodity economy;

(3) A *monetary* system which ensures greater stability, helps to control inflation, provides for better and more equitable methods of creating and distributing reserves and of adjusting to both deficits and surpluses, and promotes resource flows to the Third World;

(4) A system of *financial transfers* for development based increasingly on *automaticity* and operating according to widely acceptable and socially responsible criteria, as is the case within nations;

(5) As part of the latter, a system of *international taxation*, which should be universal, progressive and start at low rates, and which could be initially applied to the use of the global commons and also levied on internationally undesirable activities e.g., arms expenditure or trade, pollution, accumulation of destabilising exchange reserves.

Means for Action

There is, finally, the key question: how does one ensure effective action to implement the new strategy, and the goals and objectives which it is designed to serve? And how can an international development strategy be 'new' while the political context of the world and the various relationships between regions, in international institutions, within nations, and in respect of goal-serving by governments continue to be 'old'? Nothing by way of fundamental change by and for the people of all countries can be expected without struggle, without a bold application of levers of power and collective bargaining, and without setting bold targets and going after them within the stipulated time.

Collectively, the Third World is capable of applying such levers and setting such targets which, even if they seem unrealistic today, can be made effective and indeed inevitable by the end of the century—if only the necessary commitment and resilience were forthcoming in particular from the leaders of the Third World, informed by the courage of conviction and a vision of the future, and liberated from conventional thinking on development.

Moreover, this leverage and pressure can be complemented by building relevant linkages between foci of interest and power that could engage others outside the Third World in the collective effort for global change. The more powerful actors in the North interested in preserving the *status quo* have for some time now been talking of a process of 'differentiation' in the South and making it a basis for impairing the solidarity of the South and for co-opting important Third World centres into the global power structure. In reality, however, the real differentiation that is taking place is in the North, largely under the impact of Third World pressures but also independently thereof, and often on the basis of genuine ethical considerations. The conciliatory negotiating posture of the 'like-minded' countries towards the South, the growing conflict of interest within the 'trilateral club' itself, the increasing pressure on some of the western governments from domestic intellectual and political movements in their regions (anti-nuclear, anti-military, secessionist), and the growing salience of various grassroots movements aiming at alternative patterns of development and lifestyles in the context of the growing maldevelopment crisis and the 'energy crunch' show the vitality of forces of change in the North, while also providing elements of differentiation from which new North-South coalitions can emerge.

The potentially strongest allies of the Third World in the confrontation with the international structures of Northern economic power are the Northern working classes and their labour unions. But most of these are presently conservative and immobilised by fears of declining employment. Although it has been demonstrated in several industrialised countries that increased trade with the Third World has been creating jobs at home, imports from the Third World, as well as immigration, loom large—even if irrationally—in these fears. These could be allayed through democratically planned industrial adjustment.

Moreover, if the labour unions of the North were to relax their defensive postures, they could explore the vast possibilities of common action together with Third World unions, for example, within the transnational corporate system. Whereas at present individual corporations are able to play off against each other the interests of unions in their different host countries and in their home country, a common front among all these could reverse the balance of power and benefit the workers in all the countries involved.

The need was expressed for mass political conscientisation at the national level, both in the North and the South, to generate increased awareness of maldevelopment and to stimulate positive action. The new strategy itself should become an important instrument of such political education.

Finally, in the struggle for global structural change, a number of allies could eventualy emerge even among the more powerful actors of the North themselves, who may finally understand that genuine and accelerated development of the Third World could indeed be in their own interest. For instance, proposals of massive transfer of development resources from the North to the South (which have been discussed from time to time) could—if launched and implemented prudently so as to avoid the pitfalls of maldevelopment—make the South into a healthy and indispensable engine of growth for the world economy, on which the prosperity of many powerful countries in the North depends so much.

How could the 'North-South dialogue' be led into a new, more productive and truly co-operative phase? The major effort for change in international co-operation will have to come from the countries seeking change, that is essentially from the Third World. Collectively, the Third World is capable of overcoming the current weakness of the United Nations system by making it part of a renewed approach to negotiations from positions of strength. However, the negotiating positions of the Third World have in the past been weakened by persisting divisions within the South and by doubts about the objectives of many negotiations. Effective South-South negotiations should therefore be initiated as necessary preparations for stronger Third World participation in negotiations with the industrialised countries. A useful complementary step would be the creation of a Third World supporting team for policy analysis and preparation of effective negotiations.

Collective strength in negotiations is dependent on the commitment to them of individual governments. In order to carry full conviction, Third World governments must recognise multilateral diplomacy as a genuinely important part of their overall development effort—perhaps signalling this by appointing a cabinet minister for multilateral affairs—and inject their international concerns into their domestic political processes, so that the impact of the international order on people's daily lives and welfare may be understood by all and the efforts to change it will attract the support of the masses.

The renewed strength of the Third World may bring about positive changes in negotiating styles and performance; above all, it could convince the international community that there is indeed a shared need, which must be met, among the people of both industrialised and Third World countries for structural changes in the present international order.

Third World countries, acting collectively, can exercise 'negative' leverage by withholding access to their resources, their markets, their finance and their labour. In other words, they can use the strike weapon against the North (or parts of it). The present international economic crisis may provide them with opportunities to do so. For instance, until they are reasonably satisfied that progress is being made at the negotiating table, Third World countries could withhold payments, including the servicing of debts, walk out of the International Monetary Fund (IMF), respond with their own counter-measures to Northern protectionism, and withhold support for transport and tourism. In the exercise of 'positive' leverage, they could organise purchasing consortia (rather than undergo bilateral Northern salesmanship); they could buy their way into private corporations, both national and transnational, to establish control of key sectors directly affecting their own economic interests (including banking, engineering, commodity trading and transport).

All these elements provide a scenario of considerable potential for all-round mobilisation for structural change at both domestic and international levels. It is a scenario of coalition-building between progressive governments and progressive movements in both the North and the South, as well as elements in the United Nations system, which are convinced of both the necessity and the inevitability of structural change in the international order. As the Symposium drew to a close, the conviction had clearly emerged in the minds of a large number of participants that without building such leverages and new coalitions of collective power, and without bringing grassroots and intellectual pressures to bear upon the prevailing order, the development strategy for the 1980s and beyond would fail to make any significant dent in the present international order—a necessary prerequisite for a new era of development and for any hope for a humane and just world, indeed for survival itself.

10

Development Theory and
the Third World

The recent spurt of scholarly interest in the rise of new 'States' and 'nations' has activated a vigorous historical inquiry into similar phenomena in the older States on the one hand, and a considerable effort at formulating general theories and models meant to provide guidelines for an understanding of these phenomena in the new States, on the other. By and large the initiative for these efforts has come from North American and European scholars. More recently, scholars from the developing nations have challenged some of the western formulations. The different backgrounds of historical experience and the diverse socio-cultural contexts of the two sets of scholars have raised questions regarding (i) the *relevance* of prevailing conceptual frameworks to an explanation of variations in the behaviour of social and political phenomena, (ii) the *empirical validity* of these frameworks in different historical settings, (iii) the *methodological assumptions* implicit in the strenuous quest for a general theory, and (iv) the basic issues of teleology and directionality, determinacy and choice in comparative theory. It is an effort to expose the existing theories and models of State and nation-building for their inadequacy when it comes to the concrete and diverse experiences of a variety of countries and regions, to examine the empirical validity of these theories and, if possible, to suggest ways of moving towards a more satisfactory model of comparative research. Judging from the debate that has ensued, discontent with the existing theoretical formulations would appear to be widespread. While there have been attempts at codifying the agreements arising from the current theoretical formulations, especially among the

western scholars,[1] no similar agreements on alternative perspectives
have yet emerged. What I propose to do in this paper is to raise certain
unsettled issues pertinent to State and nation-building, issues that reflect
the growing debate in the literature. My attempt here is not to collate
a 'report' but to draw meaning from a whole lot of papers and discussions in order to provoke a further consideration of the problems and
controversies that have emerged.

Alternative Theoretical Models

Although a clear and systematically articulated confrontation between
opposing theoretical standpoints has yet to take place, a variety of alternative models and critiques have emerged. The systems theory stand-
point continues to be defended by expanding it from its original
'structural-functional' premises while still offering an extended rationale for the latter,[2] but the organised methodological-empirical critique
that has been attempted,[3] plus the fact that no coherent rebuttal of this
critique has been forthcoming, appears to bury the too often flogged
and licked hobby horse of structural functionalism.

Social Mobilisation

A little more sympathetic attention has been received from social scientists, including from the Third World, by the social mobilisation theory
as propounded by Karl Deutsch and subsequently developed by a
number of other authors. Stein Rokkan had taken notice of it at some
length as part of his more inclusive concept of centre-periphery linkages
and in his phasing of the European nation-building experience. Gabriel
Almond also tried to accommodate this perspective in his approach to
a synthesis of a variety of theories of 'political development'.[4] Charles
Tilly[5] took up the same theme in his attempt to dimensionalise the
nation-building process in Europe on two major (and relatively inde-

---

1. Stein Rokkan, "Models and Methods in the Comparative Study of Nation-Building",
Acta Sociologica, XII,2,1969; "Variations in Nation-Building and State-Formation: Impli-
cations for Theory Building and for Comparative Research", in S.N. Eisenstadt and Stein
Rokkan (eds.), *Building States and Nations*, Beverley Hills, Sage Publications, 1973.

2. Gabriel Almond, "Approaches to Developmental Causation", Introduction to Gabriel
A. Almond and Scott Flanagan (eds.), *Developmental Episodes*, Boston, Little Brown & Co.,
1973.

3. "Application of Comparative Political Analysis to the Study of Nation-Building: Some
Issues in Theory and Methodology" in Rajni Kothari (ed.), *State and Nation Building: A
Third World Perspective*, New Delhi, Allied Publishers, 1976.

4. See Notes 1 and 2.

5. "Notes on Western European Statemaking since 1500" in Eisenstadt and Rokkan (eds.),
op. cit.

pendent) dimensions, viz., the acquisition of 'stateness' and the 'pattern of mobilisation'.[6]

While the theory of social mobilisation has been very influential in social science circles, serious doubts have been raised about the viability of this theory as an explanatory model. Jose A. Silva Michelena[7] has shown how the package of social mobilisation (urbanisation, education, industrialisation, mass media exposure, etc.), participation, growth of democratic rights and demands, and the legitimacy of the political order broke down in the case of Latin America, partly because it ignored the empirical relationship between agricultural development and land reforms on the one hand and the urbanisation-industrialisation complex on the other, and partly because it wholly sidetracked the international context of economic dominance and the linkage of the developing political systems to this pattern of dominance-dependence. Thus, in Latin America new opportunities for participation increased *in spite of* the prevailing political system. As a result, new loyalties emerged, almost wholesale, in favour of the political parties and leaders and not of the system, or else remained absent, making for anomic participation by the urban masses in riots, demonstrations, marches, etc., that were not politically goal-directed.[8] Recent work on the relationship between social mobilisation and politicisation in the context of India[9] also suggests that the Lerner-Deutsch package of modernisation and social mobilisation does not bear scrutiny, either as a homogeneous interrelated web of indicators or as a sequence of developments. The tacit assumption by most of the western theory that the critical developments and 'inputs' come from society to which the State responds with 'outputs' is also disproved by evidence from the new States where the major thrust of development consists in the permeation of the social structure by one or more political centres. It shows that the major differentia in the process of development pertain not just to the degrees of urbanisation and industrialisation, etc., which lead 'from tradition to modernity', but to the relationship between changes in the traditional society comprehending the network of agriculture, the rural countryside, the community organisation, and the territorial distribution of pop-

---

6. Tilly talks of a third dimension too in his paper, *viz*, the acquisition of political rights as claims made on the State, and resulting from an interaction between the 'degree of stateness 'and the pattern of mobilisation'.

7. Jose Augustine Silva Michelena, "State-Formation and Nation-Building in Latin America" in Kothari (ed.), *op. cit.*

8. *ibid.*

9. Rajini Kothari and Bashiruddin Ahmed, "Social Mobilisation and Politicisation: India's Pattern of Interactions", Centre for the Study of Developing Societies, 1969, Mimeo. The paper is based on a detailed investigation of a cross-section of the Indian population.

ulation on the one hand, and the growth of a mobile and educated middle class on the other.

The extent to which a political system can answer the needs and demands of its populace depends crucially upon the fit between the size of its urban middle class and the opportunities made available by economic development, and this in turn depends on the rate and character of agricultural development. Agricultural development and land reforms can, of course, also be incorporated in the theory of modernisation. But once this is done, not only the emphasis on a necessary sequence and on 'prerequisites' of modernisation falls apart, but also the still strong and pervasive dichotomy informing the theory of modernisation breaks down. Perhaps far more useful leads can be found in the work of Barrington Moore, Jr.,[10] and in some of the more sophisticated variants of Marxist theory. But these, in turn, suffer from a presumption of socio-economic determination of the political process and leave out the dynamic role of political and intellectual interventions in social transformation.

Centre and Periphery

Much more relevant to a comparative study of nation-building and State-formation is the centre-periphery model of political development, though generally it has received scant systematic attention among the theorists of political development, partly because of its accent on the primacy of the political order over any simple notion of social or economic determinism or 'interest aggregation'. The most lucid general statement of this concept is to be found in the writings of Edward Shils.[11] But the recent work of Rokkan who has consciously adopted the centre-periphery model in his analysis of European development, the general formulations of S.N. Eisenstadt who seems to extend and exemplify the early leads of Shils,[12] the comparative theoretical work of Bendix on nation-building,[13] and the social class analysis of Barrington Moore can all be usefully interpreted within a common conceptual framework of (i) centre formation (either through a leading territory or dynasty or a dominant social class), (ii) the process of infringement of

10. *Social Origins of Dictatorship and Democracy: Lord and Peasant in the Modern World*, Boston, Beacon Press, 1966.

11. Edward Shils, "Centre and Periphery" in *The Logic of Personal Knowledge: Essays Presented to Michael Polanyi on His Seventieth Birthday*, London, 1961.

12. S.N. Eisenstadt, *Modernisation: Protest and Change*, Englewood Cliffs, Prentice-Hall, 1966.

13. Reinhard Bendix, *Nation-Building and Citizenships : Studies of Our Changing Social Order*, New York, Wiley, 1964.

the periphery by the centre (through the play of power and the process of policy-making), and (iii) the encroachment of the periphery on the centre (through demands on the machinery of the State). My own early work on India views political development as interaction between the penetration by the centre and the response of the periphery to it, supervened by intermediate structures and traditions.[14]

Although there is somewhat wider acceptance of the centre-periphery model than of some other models, there is no clear agreement on its usefulness as an explanatory theory. At best it is seen as an important descriptive and heuristic device. A number of specific questions have been raised. What are the territorial implications of the model? If the 'centre' is a territorial concept, is there a single centre or could there be more than one? If there are more than one, in what conceptual interrelationship do they stand? How do these definitions vary with the size of the State? What is the degree of social and cultural homogeneity requisite for a 'centre' to be accepted as a legitimate locus of authority and loyalty? To the extent that such homogeneity is absent or there is resistance to the dominant centre from the regional centres which may imagine themselves as competitors or as 'counter-centres', is the former still to be conceived as a 'centre'? Examples cited include Canada (English *versus* French), Belgium (Walloons *versus* Flemings), Spain (Castillians *versus* others), and some of the Latin American countries with a binary or polarised situation in respect of authoritative or legitimate centres. At a somewhat lower key, there is the question of a special kind of differentiation comprising a political centre and an economic centre: what if these were not in the same place? the issue becomes serious when one of these centres, say the economic one, lies outside the territory of the State, and its command of resources and network of effective power and influence are such that it becomes far more powerful than the formally 'independent' political centre. In such cases, as is frequently the case in Latin America and Africa, and parts of Asia, where did the 'centre' lie?

Another set of questions have warned against any presumption of stability or continuity in the centre-periphery analysis as western theorists using this framework usually do. (They have done so with almost every conceptual framework though this may not be inherent in the framework). R. Mukherjee[15] refers at length to the need to take into account the changing class characteristics of the ruling elites in any comparative study of nation-building; N. Pasic in the same vein discusses

14. See Rajni Kothari, *Politics in India*, New Delhi, Orient Longmans Ltd., and Boston, Little, Brown & Co., 1970.

15. Ramkrishna Mukherjee, "Nation-Building and State-Formation in the Third World: Problem Method and Data", in Eisenstadt and Rokkan (eds.), *op. cit.*

the case of the Balkans.[16] As Pasic puts it, it is necessary to identify who the actors are, what their social composition is, what their motives are, who sides with whom and for what reason. There is need to discern the position of the elites and classes, their specific characteristics from one region to another, and from one historical phase to another. Besides, implicit in Pasic's comments is a rejection of political positions being determined by reference to class composition, for the same social class may perform wholly different functions. Thus, whereas the bourgeoisie were nation-integrators in France and Germany, they were pitched against integration in Austria-Hungary, and later in Yugoslavia, where it fell to the Communist Party to lead the movement for national liberation. Nowadays there are quite different sources of nation-builders—the intellectual elites, the exploited masses without definite class character, and so forth. In some of the new nations the intellectual elite occupying the 'centre' played a much more autonomous role. In others, however, the local elites were tied in a dependent economic and political relationship with a 'centre' that lay outside the territory. It is necessary, thus, to consider and interpret the problem of centre-peripherey relationship in a dynamic way, with special attention to the changing character of each.

Most of these questions raise the issues of definition, analysis, and interpretation, but they also throw up suggestive hypotheses that must be tested under various conditions and complexes of statehood and nationhood, economic independence, size of territory, and nature of political system—issues so far not systematically explored in the centre-periphery model of nation-building. My attempt to apply the centre-periphery conceptual framework to political development in India several years ago[17] suggested (a) that its large size and cultural heterogeneity necessitated, on the one hand, a dominant 'centre' which was not just territorial but also entailed a political-organisational locus (e.g., through a dominant party) and, on the other hand, impelled this centre to enter into a relationship of bargaining with and accommodating a large number of 'intermediate centres' which, in effect, became the loci of institutional and interest aggregation; (b) that such a network of centres compelled the process of 'national integration' to be conceived not in any centrally linear fashion but in terms of a complicated interplay between the persistent autonomy of the cultural centres and the jealous primacy of the political centre in the new scheme of things; (c) that such a framework of integration required a measure of 'democratic' func-

---

16. "Factors in the Formation of Nations in the Balkans and Among the South Slavs", in Eisenstadt and Rokkan (eds.), *op. cit.*

17. *Politics in India, op. cit.*

tioning, not simply as an ideological choice but also as a pragmatic necessity; and (d) that with such a process of integration advancing, new conceptual formulations evolved in course of time. The concept of 'centre'
moved from a territorial notion to a more strictly political one focusing
on a dominant party, coalition or leadership; the concept of periphery
also changed from the territorial to the social encompassing the
depressed classes, scheduled and backward castes, tribes and so forth;
and the concept of 'nation' itself tended less to depend for its identity
on cultural and linguistic demarcations characteristic of national consciousness in most of Europe than on a transcendent idea of statehood
coinciding with that of nationhood. Accompanying all this, of course,
is the assumption that one is talking of a genuinely independent centre,
independent not only politically but also economically and culturally
To the extent that such independence is missing, as is happening of late
in India, the trascendent centre may lie outside the national territory.
Conceptually, therefore, a far more complex structure is found in which
the territorial 'national' centre has to be distinguished from the political centre (this may be a dominant party, or even a single leader within
the nation, but it may also be a colonial metropolis, or a continental
centre outside the nation), while the territorial notion of 'periphery'
needs to be supplemented with a societal or social class notion of periphery, and hence viewed dynamically over time. Furthermore, empirically speaking, there is in all States and nations (except in the most
primitive ones) likely to be a whole series of centres and peripheries,
with a vertical structure of both centrality and peripherality. And yet,
at the same time, for the series of centres to be meaningful, one has to
conceptualise something like the 'most central of all centres', which is,
in effect, the notion of a transcendental centre, the acceptance of whose
authority determines its centreness.

All this notwithstanding, precisely because of the meaningful controversy and the dialogue it has generated, the centre-periphery framework of the theory of nation-building appears to offer a good way of
distinguishing between the varieties of nation and State building experience, ranging from the typical European experiments to those going
on right now in the Third World. For one thing, it draws attention to
the role in nation-building of the political and intellectual actors as autonomous and dynamic agents and not simply as mechanisms responding to some basic 'inputs' from the other segments. Also, it enables us
to study a whole lot of policy and ideological issues without rendering
the conceptual framework itself value-loaded; the problem of peripherality can be conceived as much in terms of social as national integration, depending upon the problem under study; the issues of

governmental performance can be studied as much with respect to equity, distribution, and social justice (along the centre-periphery continuum) as with respect to political stability and coalition-making among various centres and various peripheries. Above all, this is a framework that is amenable to a variety of methodologies ranging from the descriptive typologies and paradigms, to analytical 'aids to understanding' via an identification of salient parameters of nation-building, to the generation of correlational, sequential, and causal hypotheses that distinguish between different empirical sets of temporal and contextual relationships.

The centre-periphery model is, of course, no more than an additional conceptual apparatus among the many that already exist; there is also no doubt that the way it has been developed so far, it raises more questions than it answers. There is little hope of its becoming a unified theory, which is perhaps just as well. All the same, it seems to offer a useful vantage point from which to study development processes in politics, and more especially the processes of State and nation-building. Its major attraction is that it emphasises the more typically *political* variables of political change and stability rather than merely seeking explanations from the 'independent variables' that lie beyond the political sphere, as is the case with a lot of other theories, both of the liberal and of the Marxist vintage.

But in order to turn what is yet no more than a mental diagram into an empirically sensitive instrument, the centre-periphery theories will have a lot more homework to do for some time.

Variations in State and Nation-Building

Apart from the debate on various alternative conceptual schemes for analysing State and nation-building there is the whole issue of the wide variations in State and nation-building experiences. Here too, serious divergences of viewpoints and perspectives have surfaced. These relate to (a) the revelance of general theories based largely on the European and North American experience to an understanding of the course of political development and modernisation among the new nations, (b) the theoretical assumptions underlying the recent interest in deductive model building as an aid to the comparative theory that sought to encompass a wide variety of political entities, and (c) the application of methodological assumptions implicit in the theories of political development and modernisation to a study of concrete historical phenomena such as State-formation and nation-building taking place in specific contexts of time and space. The most clear and explicit divergence in viewpoints that has emerged is between the intellectuals from Europe and North America and those from the new nations (including Latin America), although the methodologically specific and middle range specialists from the western countries appear better to appreciate the empirical perspectives of the non-western experts. It is not possible to present or interpret the whole controversy here. What I shall attempt to do, instead, is to highlight certain themes recurring in the critical discussion that has now begun in the literature of political science.

There appear to be striking contrasts between the European historical experience in State and nation-building and the contemporary experience in a large part of the developing world. The dimensions of these contrasts are many—the initial condition and cultural contexts, the timing and sequences, the impingement by the international system and the role of ideology and, above all, the arenas of decision-making and government-populace relationships. Without doubt there are many important differences among the different European countries too, as has been emphasised, among others, by Hans Daalder,[18] just as they exist among the new States of the contemporary world, as between Latin American and Asian countries, or within each of these continents and, indeed, within even single countries. But the overriding contrast that has emerged is between the historical experiences and context of the West and the contemporary ones of the non-West. The fact that some among the former 'failed', as we have been constantly reminded by the eloquent Juan Linz in regard to Spain and Portugal,[19] or that some among the latter have probably 'succeeded' better than the others, does not yet minimise the overall contrast in conditions, sequences, and social contexts between the early arrivals and the latecomers to independent State and nationhood.

On this there is some measure of agreement, although the committed comparative theorists continue to stretch the relevance and usefulness of the European experience for the contemporary nation-builders. Conditions that facilitated European State and nation-building, such as relatively small size of populations, cultural homogeneity, flexibility coming from the dynastic wars and international balance of power, a vast peasant base for resource mobilisation, ample time for a sequential treatment of developmental crises, and a gradual politicisation of the periphery, are specified by both the western and the non-western scholars. The controversy that arises—and remains mostly unsettled

18. See his paper "On Building Consociational Nations: The Cases of the Netherlands and Switzerland" in Eisenstadt and Rokkan, (eds.), *op. cit.*

19. See Juan Linz, "Early State-Building and Late Peripheral Nationalisms Against the State: The Cast of Spain", paper presented at the Cerisy meeting and published in Eisenstadt and Rokkan (eds.), op. cit.

—concerns not so much the particular statements of differential conditions but rather the scope of prevailing general theories that seek to encompass both the historical European and the contemporary non-European experiences.

The issues have been squarely posed by a large number of scholars from the Third World. Ramkrishna Mukherjee has expressed serious doubts about the utility of deductive models for explaining anything, least of all the variations between specific experiences guided by specific contexts; there was need to return to the long-neglected and often maligned inductive tradition in the social sciences. He has illustrated his point with his work on radio listeners and on the relationship between income and satisfaction and the contrast between the conclusions of his empirical investigations and the aggregate ranking presented in the *World Handbook on Social Indicators*.

Yash Tandon from Uganda had long ago questioned the basic assumptions and definitions implied in the European notion of a centralised State or in the contrary conception of 'consociational democracy'; these conceptual formulations were of little consequence to the nation-builders of Africa who were trying to forge political authority out of multi-tribal societies and reconcile whatever authority they could manage to derive with the compelling and concurrent mandates of a mass democracy and a socialist State.

J.A. Silva Michelena from Venezuela has questioned the whole theory of modernisation which formed the mainstay and theoretical rationale of a lot of specific formulations in the literature. These include the theories of nation identity (Pye, Rustow), rationalisation of authority (Silvert), structural differentiation and social mobilisation (Deutsch), political participation (Almond and Verba), the development of political capacity (Eisenstadt), and centre-formation and coalition-making (Rokkan, Bendix, Moore). Whereas all these formulations have helped us in understanding analytically some of the interrelationships between society and politics (for instance, through a typology of crises), none of them provides an explanatory theory, not to speak of causal theory with predictive power. But the more important point is that these limitations of specific theories derive from a basic lack in the more general theory of 'modernisation' or 'political development', which shows these to be empty concepts, empty of socio-economic content, not informed with any historical points of reference, and always underplaying the structural constraints operating on the political process—social class structure, agrarian and industrial relationships and, above all, the international structure of dominance and dependence. Lacking a clear idea of the relationship between the operating political and economic structures and the developmental causation for specific national and international constellations, the modernisation paradigm fails to provide an adequate general or even comparative theory.

These points become more vivid when one considers the writings of Condido Mendes of Brazil.[20] Commenting on the experience of the southern countries of Latin America, he elucidated the general critique of modernisation theory, as posed by Michelena, by showing how different historical conditions made even some of the most prevalent concepts change their meaning when applied to particular configurations. Thus, for instance, concepts like 'people', 'elite', and a common 'civic' culture, as used in social mobilisation, participation, and centre-periphery theories, do not really apply in Latin America due to a very special kind of cultural and political context. The assumptions that there is an elite and a mass, that there is a reciprocal flow of primary and secondary messages leading to a national consensus, and a common awareness and identity, is not very relevant to a historical condition which lacks a reciprocity of perspectives and a basic 'duality', inhibiting a sense of political community. The prevailing theory of elite hardly applies to a situation where an indigenous entrepreneurial elite did not emerge, where there is a basic structural ambivalence stemming from the frustration of economic dependence and, hence, the absence of a genuine national bourgeoisie, and where the middle classes are driven to find their self-esteem and identity by forging a special relationship with the military and merging themselves in the glare and giganticism of their super-cities with their real point of reference—the 'centre'—being outside the country. The emerging civic pantheon is thus extremely equivocal, without a clearcut cultural anchor, and in which the national elites themselves perform no clearcut roles. Development has thus to be necessarily conceived in discontinuous forms, as rupture lurks in all that went before. In such cultural conditions it is difficult to see how the existing models of development can furnish any meaningful explanatory leads.[21]

The Latin American experiences of late have attracted a great deal of attention, both in the comparative literature and in the general theoretical discussions. Of interest in this regard are the typical 'explanations' advanced by scholars from the northern hemisphere. According to Juan Linz, who is familiar with the Spanish-Portuguese literature (and has done a good deal of work on nearly similar tendencies in Spain and Portugal as well)[22]. intellectual discussion in Latin America highlights

20. See his paper "Nation-Building in Southern Latin America", in Eisenstadt and Rokkan (eds.), *op. cit.*
21. On all this see Kothari (ed.), *op. cit.*
22. Linz, *op. cit.*

abstract and symbolic categories rather than the usual categories of interests, linkages, their articulation and representation. The stress, instead, is on the collective representation of the wholes. To use Durkheim's terms, there is greater concern with the issues of mechanical solidarity than those of organic solidarity. There being no clear congruence between the symbolic categories and the social reality, the ideas of intellectuals—who seem to dominate the political discourse in these countries—bear little relationship with the interests of specific social groups. A constant concern with the legitimacy of regimes leads to a questioning of the cultural inheritances and national identities. The problem facing Latin American societies concerns not so much the goals before them as the frustration with governmental performance, political efficacy, and so forth. A rejection of the 'politics of interest' impels recourse to symbolic battles. 'Social mobilisation' is not conceived in a participatory and representational idiom but in terms of overall identities and ideologies. Here is a basic difference in the middle class culture: instead of mobilising and organising the rural-ethnic peripheries, there is emphasis on incorporation, identity, and such other themes. Probably all this is because of the basic lack of authentic and original culture (unlike in the great Asian and African civilisations), too strong a dependence on the European heritage and, as Mendes has pointed out, the failure to provide the original inhabitants of the continent—the Indians—a clear role and position alongside the western immigrants in the forging of a national identity.

There is some merit in this 'psychological' analysis of the Latin American situation; Mendes and Linz are no doubt struggling to come to grips with a baffling cultural phenomenon. At the same time, however, they manage to ignore and bypass the more crucial problems of dominance and dependence—economic, intellectual, and ultimately, cultural and political—raised by Michelena and other scholars belonging to the *dependencia* schools. As I see it, the problem of authenticity of culture is closely related to the problem of authority of wrong theories—the theories of national integration and national identity, of interest aggregation, of functional interrelationships and linkages in the framework of a stable aggregate, and of a necessary transition from the absence of such an aggregate to its realisation. The style of expressing the two ends of this transition has been generally dichotomous (in spite of universal protestations to the contrary)—from traditionality to modernity, from the 'communal' to 'associational' forms, from the 'mechanical' to 'organic' solidarity, and from *gemeinschaft* to *gesselschaft*. There is the further assumption that the end-product of each of these transitions is teleologically determined and would be realised in the same ways as in the industrially advanced countries.

These two aspects of intellectual importation—a positivist-rationalist theory of structural integration and a philosophical-methodological assumption of teleological progression towards pre-determined outcomes—and their normative persistence through pedagogic traditions that are unrelated to the actual configuration of problem situations—account for the ambivalence and equivocation pinpointed with such feeling by Mendes. The crisis of universalist aspirations found in many of the underdeveloped areas arises precisely from their inability to resist being sucked in the intellectual mainstream of the dominant nations. The problems that arise are a consequence of psychological pressures emanating from the alien and half-baked intellectual traditions on the one hand, and the objective conditions of economic and technological dependence on the other. Hence the *somewhat* better situation found in India or China not just for their being ancient civilisations, which is no doubt true, but also because these nations are too distant and too big to be easily permeated and 'colonised' in any total way as is the case with large parts of Latin America, and Africa, as well as parts of Southeast Asia.[23] Hence also the great symbolic appeal of Castro in Latin America, Nyerere in Black Africa (lately diminishing), and of Mao in the whole underdeveloped world. Ali Mazrui has highlighted the peculiar style of Nyerere asserting his country's political autonomy by an ideological idiom that was at one and the same time expressive of both the real or mythical continuity of local traditions and affirmative of its independence from the dominant norms and traditions of the West.[24] Gandhi had time and again asserted India's autonomy, by employing the devices of both a reinterpretation of tradition and a positive assertion of a futuristic present.

The Indian case has been discussed by both the western and the non-western scholars. I have already mentioned several points above—the role of the intermediate and horizontal 'aggregation' and 'mobilisation' rather than vertical and total ones, the great importance of demographic (rural-urban) proportions in nationbuilding under conditions of acute scarcity of economic resources and opportunities, the dissociation between the cultural and political wholes, the different meanings attached to the concepts of nationhood and national integration, and the great role of intranational diversities and autonomies in the process of integration. D.L. Sheth has taken the discussion to a new pitch by

---

23. In a different context, the same issues are brought out in respect of the Japanese dominance in East and Southeast Asia in the paper by Joji Watanuki, "State-Formation and Nation-Building in East Asia" in Eisenstadt and Rokkan (eds.), *op. cit.*

24. "Social Cleavage and Nation-Building in East Africa" in Eisenstadt and Rokkan (eds.), *op. cit.*

addressing himself to the whole issue of teleology and asking if we are
to presume a common future for all, or there are to be different direc-
tions along which nations would move despite a common and, no doubt,
comparable heritage of ideas, technologies, and even formal structures
of government.[25] The essential tasks in moving from the deductive
generalisations to empirically sensitive theory, according to him, are two-
fold: to demarcate the area of choice from the area of determinacy at
given points in time and situational context—the essential problem of
leadership—and to build into a comparative theory the role of normative and value components as against some simple reference to institutionalised structures and functions—the essential problem of ideology.
Here the endeavour of social science has to be different from that of
the physical sciences (from which social scientists continue to draw their
analogies), for it dealt with the constant intervention of human agents
in the process of history. A theory that is not sensitive to this dynamic
and constantly differentiating element in social and political situations,
would either, in the telling phrase of Mendes, 'condemn' the nations
to a state of permanent atrophy or make such theory irrelevant to the
real actors who are making or unmaking the nations. When at a
UNESCO meeting that took place in August 1970[26] Gabriel Almond
responding to the criticism by Michelena and others of the prevailing
theory of modernisation argued that the principal components of modernisation were now a part of the world culture and hence were universal, Sheth asked if the institutional accomplishments of the European
civilisation between the sixteenth and eighteenth centuries were to be
taken as fixations for all that was to come ever after, or were we going
to allow the present and future generations some leeway for innovation and creativity? The dangers of a historical determination in any
attempt at 'general theory' (as against a more creative use of history
in reorganising human experience for fulfilling new ends) became mar-
kedly evident as the issue was lustily joined at this meeting.

Concluding Observations

Many of these criticisms are now well known. But they need to be
raised continually, particularly given the ruling paradigm in the social
sciences according to which theoretical concepts drawn from the European historical experience can be applied to new historical phenomena, now and in the future, in a large majority of the late twentieth
century world. Actually, these issues and controversies, if properly fol-

---

25. Sheth, *op. cit.*

26. UNESCO Meeting of Experts on the Problems of State Formation and Nation building held at Cerisy-la-Salle in France, 7 to 14 August 1970.

lowed up, could open a whole vista of theoretical and empirical investigation. To mention a few insights that need to be pursued, it seems
that underlying the so-called gap between theory and data—a continuing problem of all knowledge—one may discern important divergences in theoretical perspectives arising out of the different
backgrounds of experience, learning, and ideology. It is necessary to
explicate these divergences systematically and build them into comparative analysis. Second, it will do us all much good if we consciously
recognise that the theories of modernisation and development have so
far, from necessity and the accident of their origin, been informed by
one major prototype, namely, the European modernisation experience.
As new experiences emerge, there is need for new theoretical prespec-
tives. It is necessary to recognise this reality and devise theoretical and
methodological ways of dealing with it for, otherwise, both the defensive affirmation of a 'world culture' and the charge of 'ethnocentrism'
will cause a psychological hiatus that will be difficult to bridge. Third,
as we recognise ths reality of confrontation between alternative theoretical perspectives, we must move a significant step forward towards
translating our models into sets of testable hypotheses and testing them
on the basis of data from a variety of space and time contexts. Let us
humbly recognise that we have not done this in any systematic way so
far, nor have we subjected what little has been done to tests of significance and validity. Theorising is a legitimate activity, provided it follows certain rules of the game. At present the field is replete with
irresponsibility and casualness in theorising without much respect for
empirical validity and intellectual relevance. The need is to move to
a more responsible theoretical and methodological approach. Once that
happens, a lot of existing theories and models that continue to rule the
roost in the social sciences will stand exposed.

11

Development and Freedom in Asia

To write on Asia is to deal with a subject that is so vast that it is difficult to do justice to it. Not only is Asia the largest region of the world, representing more than half its population, but it is also a region that encompasses some of the richest countries in the world, like Japan and Singapore, as well as some of the very poorest, and one in which very divergent development strategies have been followed. It is a region that straddles the North-South divide and envelops all the major ideological currents known to mankind—capitalism, socialism, totalitarianism, as well as indigenous alternatives in the form of Gandhism, Buddhist socialism and Islamic fundamentalism. So that, whereas it is true that 'Asia is one' as the great Japanese thinker Tenshin Okakura and the great poet from India Rabindranath Tagore both said, it is also divided today along many lines. In a basic sense it is one, but it is one that encompasses a lot of diversity. Asia also embraces all the world's major religions as well as many of its non-theological spiritual traditions.

Global Relevance

The only reason to direct attention to this vast Continent is precisely that it encompasses so much and is going to provide a testing ground for so much that is at stake in this fast changing world of ours. It is a region that, during the coming years, is likely to become vulnerable to all the traumas of the international power game. As Marek Thee has stated so vividly, it is already extending "from West to East, along the borders of the USSR and China, and in sensitive strategic areas lying athwart the great power divide, which includes the United States and Western interests... With the main world energy resources located in Asia; with the strategic lifelines of all the great powers running across the continent and along the rims of Asia; with the USSR and China seeing each other eye to eye across their lengthy common border; with so many nations in Asia in the wake of anticolonial revolutions now only in the early stage of modern nation-building and confronted with numerous unsolved social, ethical, religious and national problems; with such manifold issues susceptible to great power manipulation and interventions: the center of gravity of world conflict is decidedly moving toward Asia".

In the Asian region, development strategies have long been the product of international forces and especially of western domination—or reactions thereto.

This is true of Japan, perhaps the most advanced of the industrial nations of the world, deeply influenced by the West and now showing itself capable of competing with the West on its own terms (though it is also demonstrating the major weak points of such a model of industrialisation and modernisation).

It is true of the People's Republic of China, which for a good 30 years refused to accept the dominant development strategy preached by the westerners but now finds itself in the middle of such a radical about-face that it is in danger of losing its unique identity and becoming prey to the global struggle for power and for the human mind.

It is true of Vietnam, which became an immense battlefield between imperialism and nationalism, but which has since become a battlefield in another kind of war, namely the one within the world communist movement, which of course reflects the titanic struggle for power between China and the USSR.

It is true of the Middle East, which was once seen as the source of the greatest economic challenge to western hegemony, the OPEC offensive since 1973, and which since then presented an even more fundamental challenge to the West, this time to its entire *Weltanschauung*—the great Iranian Revolution, the full implications of which have yet to be worked out, even though it might now appear to be in the throes of much confusion and a lot of violence and anarchy.

It is true of the whole complex of ASEAN countries, in which global corporate capitalism seems to be finding client states keen on economic development at all costs, thus giving rise to a new genre of development strategy known as 'repressive-bureaucratic developmentalism'. This system, though it exhibits several shades of authoritarianism, includes some of the most cynical repressive regimes found anywhere in the world. South Korea could be included in this category.

It is true of Sri Lanka, which chose a moderate path of welfare-type developmentalism by means of which it managed for a long time to promote a minimal level of welfare for the mass of the people without resorting to authoritarian measures, but which now finds itself deeply in trouble, with respect to both economic solvency and political viability, and is desperately seeking external support to bail itself out of problems of its own creation.

It is true of some extreme manifestations of withdrawal from the world political process—Burma, Kampuchea and, in a way, North Korea.

It is true of Pakistan and Bangladesh, split asunder and ruled, as the result of coups, by military regimes in alliance with technocrats and external forces. These countries manifest deep pathologies of inward-looking nation-building with the greatest cost being paid by the mass of the people both in terms of their freedom and in terms of their development.

Above all, it is true of India, an enigma in many ways, beset by some of the worst manifestations of poverty and inequality on a massive, in fact continental, scale and yet somehow struggling both to retain democratic forms and to make important strides in economic self-reliance. Nonetheless, like China and in a different way Japan, it is likely to experience growing convulsions and major reverses under the impact of both internal and external forces in the struggle for both these objectives.

This then is the vast terrain of our subject matter. I am deliberately omitting such areas as the Asian republics of the USSR, most of which are Islamic; Mongolia and the tiny states and principalisties in the Himalayas—Bhutan, Nepal, Tibet; the vast range of border states on the northeast of India in each of which a protracted guerilla struggle is going on; and above all Afghanistan, home of a proud mountain people living under the shadow of intense superpower rivalry. But even without these, the picture of development as concerns both the strategy of economic areas and the character of political and cultural development is so diverse that one is in danger of getting bogged down in descriptive and classificatory exercises which only bewilder and do not leave one any wiser for all the analysis.

Dialectic of Development

And yet this need not be so, for we are addressing the topic of development strategies at a time when not just Asia but the whole world is entering an age of diminishing options and is experiencing a loss of confidence and a decline in the capacity to manage change and provide workable, if imperfect, governing structures. There is emerging a deep sense that we have gone wrong somewhere in our whole way of thinking about development, and that there is need for fundamental reconsideration of the whole development problem. To that extent there is a certain unity of the human condition that transcends the great diver-

sity that I spoke of earlier. The diversity we face in Asia combined with
the fact that all these various entities face serious problems illustrates
this situation of common destiny, and this problem of declining capacities when it comes to responding to new forces of change. What is more,
there are global forces at work, both at the base of societies and in the
international arena, which seem to focus more on the basic characteristics of this problem than on regional or comparative analysis. We have
to consider the problems of Asia in the context of the social transformation that appears to be so far-reaching and so full of dangers to human
survival as well as opportunities for building a creative alternative to
the present system. We are still struggling to get an intellectual grip
on this context, and, I am afraid, not too successfully. A certain dialectic of world history is unfolding before us, arising from the collapse of
the western era, and an as yet unarticulated and ambiguous response
to it. I have dealt with this dialectic of world history elsewhere in the
context of its global manifestations. Here I would like to focus on just
one aspect of it, namely the situation arising out of the erosion of the
doctrine of development that held sway for so long and is now in crisis.
Most of what I have to say has relevance outside of Asia as well but
nonetheless pertains especially to the Asian region.

Let me list a few obvious factors first. We have lived through a period
not just of massive increase in populations but also of highly imbalanced
increases in terms of their distribution by nation, region, social and ethnic
group and resource endowments. The result has been highly unequal
economic, technological and socio-political burdens. We have also been
witness to very large movements of people across political and cultural
frontiers. This has given rise to massive dislocations, unprecedented
human suffering and rather serious ethnic and racial tensions. But loom-
ing above everything else is one major factor which, if we fail to handle
it with care and discrimination on the basis of an ethic of human solidarity (restraint and self-control by all), will in all likelihood make the
human enterprise unworkable and so conflict-ridden as to become
unmanageable. In large parts of Asia, there is taking place a serious scarcity of resources in a world that is getting increasingly competitive and
crowded. The sudden disappearance of the presumption of continuous
availability of resources in the Asian region has given rise to major pressures and conflicts to gain access to them. At the same time the ethic
of consumerism has taken hold of all classes and all nations and is leading to the relentless destruction of natural resources—forest lands, river
beds, coastal terrain, reserves of soil and water and jungle. This process
is seriously reducing productive capacities and making technological
progress—which is acquiring a momentum of its own—an enemy of
the poor.

All over the world, there is a slowing down of growth rates, a crisis in economic relations between States, emanating from the world capitalist centres and spreading to both the developing world and the socialist world, where it is in turn amplified by the inherent weaknesses of these two spheres. It affects most severely the poorer parts of mankind, both regionally and socially, and provides the basis for very considerable violence arising both from the restlessness of the poor and the backlash of an elite intent on preserving its privileges, living standards and lifestyle. No issue is going to be more important than this struggle to preserve living standards on the one hand, and the struggle of the poor and the dispossessed to make it in this world, on the other.

More basic than all this is the psychological factor: a growing sense of insecurity at all levels. At the top, governments everywhere are becoming unstable propositions. The most powerful among States, *viz.* the superpowers, are reeling from a sense of insecurity both *vis-a-vis* each other and *vis-a-vis* the rest of the turbulent world that is beginning to assert itself and will no longer accept a passive role. At the other extreme, at the bottom of society, the poor and the oppressed feel insecure because their plight, mainly their economic plight, is getting worse and because the environment around them is crumbling. There is nothing to hang on to, and the political authorities and symbols they have relied on are failing them, leaving them in the lurch.

Then there is the growing spectre of world militarisation. The point about insecurity that I made is not found in just psychological and attitudinal forms. It is found in the behaviour of States, in their brutalisation, in their increasing reliance on force, both internally and externally. Seriously contributing to this is the world power structure, which, partly because it cannot any longer 'manage' the world according to the old *status quo* and partly because of the inherent logic of this stage of world capitalism, which causes an increasing reliance on the production and sale of armaments, is leading to a global arms race from which no one is free and for the sake of which local sources of conflict are exacerbated and a world market created for arms, particularly those of the most modern type.

In sum, we are moving into a period of the growing vulnerability of States and the increasing deprivation of the needy and the deprived. The traditional institutions of a modern State, as the modern State was conceived in Europe and adopted everywhere else, are unable to cope with this situation. This is creating pressures on the elite to hand over power to technocrats and experts who are likewise unable to deal with a crisis that is fundamentally political. This then produces the need for overriding institutions and creates a role for personality and charisma in politics, the only result of which is long-term instability and uncertainty. Internationally, it is a period of growing pressures from the world power structure, politically and economically, strategically and technologically. There has been a striking decline over the last several years in the autonomy and self-reliance of developing countries, although there is some evidence of an opposite tendency, especially in Latin America, though that evidence is still far from conclusive. There is a growing temptation to seek remedies for domestic problems through international co-optation of one kind or another. India provides a striking example of this but it is true of other countries, too. 'Interdependence' is being turned into a process of recolonisation.

This then is the scenario of the human condition. It is a scenario that would dishearten, depress and disorient most people. However, it is precisely a scenario that must not be accepted fatalistically, for that would be the main precondition for the fulfilment of our worst fears. It is a scenario that must be taken up as a challenge, as a gauntlet thrown by dishonest and corrupt interests. We have to pick up that gauntlet and respond to it in a creative, constructive and critical spirit. We have in other words to meet the challenge head-on.

Challenge and Response

I, for one, am convinced that there is room for counteraction against the dominant tendencies of our time; for precisely during this period of growing conflict over resources, increasing hegemony of the world capitalist system, and declining autonomy in various societies, we have also seen some major assertions and reassertions of the human spirit in the form of a challenge to western dominance. For instance, I consider the secular assertion of Islamic power as manifested by the OPEC challenge of 1973 and the Iranian revolution as fundamental challenges to western hegemony. The issue is how does one manage the transition from an initial revolutionary upsurge through the rabble reaction to it (like the Jacobin reaction to the French revolution) to the ultimate victory of the cause. The issue is how to join the various civilisational challenges mounted by the powerful thrust of Afro-Asia and Latin America into a major counterforce against the growing backlash of a declining civilisation, that of the West, and how to involve the middle-sized powers of the world in the same process.

The issue is also how to develop a set of alternatives that take us beyond the managerial limits of both world capitalism and State socialism, how to repair the weaknesses of the socialist option that have already developed, and how to recreate an authentic alternative to the corrosive competitiveness and individualism of the modern worldview.

It is a challenge that must be faced, mediated and managed, but it must be done in a manner that responds to the turbulence and transformation at the bottom of our societies.

We have to recognise quite clearly that we are moving into a fundamentally new age, an age of the people and an age of populist leaders. These are two contradictory forces, one highly democratic and egalitarian to the core and the other highly elitist and authoritarian to the core. The new age is thus also deeply deceptive and cunning. It is a strange combination but very real nonetheless. The very process of democratisation also creates the conditions for institutional erosion and heightened expectations from individual personalities. The whole problem of 'charisma' is a problem of taking a shortcut to solving political questions by identifying a whole society with a person. Both people and leaders resort to it out of a sense of insecurity.

It is necessary to mediate in this critical situation and to provide alternatives to the people so that their democratic aspirations may find new channels for crystallisation and fulfilment. The very forces that at present seem to succumb to criminality and corruption—the large lumpen element in our cities, the youth, the rural middle classes, the educated unemployed—can be mobilised from the bottom for a constructive crystallisation process, rather than succumbing to cooptation from the top.

I cannot emphasise this point too much. The story of most of our societies is a story of lost opportunities and missed challenges, of a professional elite that has degenerated into an exploiting, domineering and parasitic stratum because it has lost the capacity to feel inspired by any challenge or avocation and is thus unable to steer society in a positive direction. But this situation can still be reversed and I have no doubt it will be. When and by whom are open questions, but history does not foreclose new possibilities. Indeed, it always throws up surprises.

The Issue of Freedom

Let me draw the various threads of this paper together by dealing with what seems to me to be the basic problem of all human development, namely, the problem of freedom in human affairs and of democracy and the institutions that sustain it. It is a problem of fundamental significance to the Asian region, especially to countries of South and Southeast Asia, and of course to Japan. But I have in mind particularly pluralistic and multi-ethnic societies where the management of power demands an institutional framework that supports both diversity and nation-building.

There is as yet no adequate theory of democracy for multicultural societies. The closer democracy gets to the grassroots, the more the operating elite is found unable to handle multiple polarities and heightened demands from below. As this happens the system takes recourse to authoritarian shortcuts and, since they do not work, the politics of sheer survival.

A series of questions arise. Is it inevitable that in pluralistic societies membership in the effective political community is restricted to the dominant groups? How is it possible to respond to the demands of the lower classes in a liberal polity that has no access to external colonies? How does the class factor operate in a multi-ethnic society? Then there is the question of poverty and economic development. According to the dominant theory of development based on liberal internationalism, poor societies lacking adequate production of surplus must rely on foreign aid, preferential trade and technology transfers. But, in fact, these resource transfers have only reinforced the structure of internal disparities and inequities. There is, further, the whole issue of ethnicity and class. Cultural and ethnic pluralism is not a serious problem for a liberal democracy so long as membership in the political community is limited to the upper and middle strata and so long as democracy means the politics of accommodation and cooperation. It is only when politics moves into the mass age, when, in short, ethnic differences take on a class or quasi-class character, that the problem becomes serious. It is against this background that the parallel phenomena of radicalisation at the bottom and authoritarianism at the top, with the left and 'radical' parties either losing ground or becoming part of the dominant structure, have to be perceived.

Faced by these myriad cultural expressions of the political process, the political elite resorts to populist and plebiscitary politics, leading to a gradual undermining of institutional intermediates and the federal structure of government and communication. After that, all that remains is charisma and its direct appeal to the masses, so that mass society becomes the purveyor of an authoritarian polity and a captive State structure. Such a resort to populist politics and a commensurate operating style on the part of the top elite (and their local dependents) also escalates tensions in other fields—in minority politics especially but also in such areas as the politics of language and regionalism. In the course of time, all these processes of tension-generation and the decline in the mediating role of politics sow seeds of disaffection, parochial separatism and ultimately disintegration, which can only be stopped by resorting to even more repression by transforming issues of social management into problems of law and order and 'security'. All this takes place against a background of heightened consciousness and politicisation of the lower strata and peripheral communities.

On the other hand, such a system, based as it is on an ideology of justice without institutionalisation thereof, generates pressures from the educated and semi-educated class, and from the relatives of various influential people, to expand the State apparatus far beyond the normal bounds of efficiency, leading to a large 'lumpen bureaucracy' that then becomes a drag on the exchequer. Thus arise the parasitism of the urban middle classes.

In institutional terms, the theory of development has given rise to a growing faith in centralised institutions. In different ways, both the liberal doctrine of a free society and the communist doctrine of a classless society have endorsed the role of a centralised bureaucracy for achieving social ends. During the very decades when participation has become the dominant value with people everywhere, it has come to mean even less in actual practice. The capacity of citizens to actively intervene in the social process that the doctrine of participation requires has been severely circumscribed because of the high degree of centralisation in most institutions resulting from the growth of the technocratic State. To sum up, the sources of the decline of democracy are to be found in the transformation in the nature of the modern State under the impact of 'developmentalism'. The post-1945 era of State and nation building in diverse historical contexts, based on a common struggle for political autonomy and human dignity encompassing vast regions of the world, represented a major new era in human history. What is threatening the creative orientation of the State is the developmental creed and its attempt to turn the State into an economic instrument—an agency for exploitation, control and subjugation—nationally and internationally. The crisis of the State arises from a totalitarian vision of State power as a result of the homogenising thrust of developmentalism which is undermining its role as a civilising agent and as an instrument for the promotion of human values. Herein lies the intellectual and political challenge of our times.

There is   need to return to some of these basic issues, for they are among the central questions of our time. They were very much part of intellectual reflection, study and discourse a few decades ago. This has since been discounted due to preoccupation with the so-called 'scientific' study of politics at a time when the ground has been slipping from under most societies, the traditional limitations on the exercise of power are disappearing, and cultural and ethnic identities are being rapidly eroded. There are some indications that out of the present struggle between the centralised and increasingly repressive State that has taken shape in large parts of Asia under the impact of modern forces, on the one hand, and various movements of protest and defiance based on local organisations of the poor, ethnic minorities, and the peasants, on the other, there may emerge an alternative formation that will prove more sensitive to indigenous cultures, their great diversity and essentially decentralised character, their tenacity against the homogenising thrust of modernisation, and their in-built restraints on the exercise of power.

This confrontation between centralising and decentralising thrusts, which is already going on and is being waged in various regions as well as nationally (and, in respect to the larger forces at work, internationally) is at this moment of time generating a massive backlash from powerful interests, both in the economy and the polity, in the countryside and in the metropolitan areas, against the forces of change. But it appears that the issue has been joined and the basic forces at work cannot be kept down for long.

I am convinced that this task is fundamentally ethical and intellectual, arising out of the fact that old models have become useless as necessary new visions and perspectives are beginning to arise. We face the challenge of providing a conceptual and moral perspective that goes beyond modern capitalism and modern socialism and humanises the State, puts human beings once again at the centre, and at the same time calls upon modern man to control his desires and appetites and live in greater harmony with nature and technology, to redirect technology toward building the sustenance for both the biological and cosmic aspects of the human collectivity. On all this there is much to learn from the wisdom that prevails in large arts of Asia.

However, these issues relate as much to the problem of freedom and spirituality as to the problem of power and the organisation of the State. While the crisis that we face is fundamentally a crisis of human freedom, it is also a crisis of the State. In saying this I am no more than restating the basic predicament of man: how to achieve freedom while being a member of a civil society, a State. There can be no freedom until the State itself, and with it the economy and the technology under whose impact it is being pulverised, becomes a condition of freedom instead of becoming an impediment to it. Fundamentally, therefore, we face the task of humanising the human enterprise called the State. Let us hope that we in Asia can work together to achieve this, despite the highly contradictory impulses that seem to be at work.

BEYOND ALTERNATIVE DEVELOPMENT

12

Ethnicity

A new 'spectre' is haunting the power elites of our time. It is the spectre of *ethnicity*, variously expressed as assertion of cultures, communal upsurges, revival of religions, voices and 'movements' of marginalised peoples, regions and nationalities. It represents the affirmation of diversity, of indigenous identity, of organic as against televised or museumised cultures—or classicised cultures as found in ancient texts. But it takes other and quite opposite forms too. In its defiance of the modern nation-state and western technology it too takes on homogenised and monotheistic forms, destroys diverse boundaries and identities that come in the way of its messianic sweep, gets militarised, and stresses revenge and martyrdom in the cause of 'victory' rather than sublimation and transcendence of the immediate. In doing so it undermines the finer qualities of the sacred and the mystical and emphasises hard and 'fundamentalist' notions of religiosity, culture and ethnicity.

At the present juncture of world history ethnicity takes on both centralising and decentralising, dominating and liberating forms. Its more humane version respects plurality and 'includes' other identities. Its more angry and defiant version is monotheistic and 'excludes' others. What is more, the two are found to be caught in a strange partnership against the more secular and 'scientific' drives of the modern State and modern capitalism. So long as this happens to be the case, the future of ethnicity as a mode of shaping human prospects will remain unclear. Equally unclear is how ferocious and aggrandising or temperate and compassionate it will turn out to be.

Much else is unclear too. Whether, for instance, the search and drive for identity and dignity will undermine prevailing unities (both political and civilisational) or provide a more enduring basis for a new and more creative unity. Whether under its sweep 'people' will come into their own and provide the basis for democratic transformation or new forms of hegemonies and even fascist control will take shape. Whether in their new political incarnation Shiite, Sinhala, Malay, Melanasian and Hindu ethnicities will bolster statist and militarist regimes or regain genuinely religious and cultural roots. If the former, what will happen to the various 'minorities'? If the latter, will they be willing to move away from the present tendencies towards majority chauvinism in these regions? Both possibilities exist on all these questions. The precise outcomes are by no means clear.

In order for them to be clear the leaders and intellectuals of various ethnic movements will need to deal with basic theoretical issues, in turn based on somewhat detailed analyses of trends that have already crystallised and the emerging prognosis for the future. This essay is an effort in that direction.

Understanding Ethnicity

No matter how uncertain the future unfoldment of the upsurge of ethnicity will be, the sources of the upsurge—the reasons for it—are fairly comprehensible (even if subject to finer points of debate).

Response to Homogenisation

Ethnicity is a response—including reaction—to the excesses of the modern project of shaping the whole of humanity (and its natural resource base) around the three pivots of world capitalism, the State system and a 'world culture' based on modern technology, a pervasive communications and information order and a 'universalising' educational system. The project of modernity entails a new mode of homogenising and straitjacketing the whole world.

There have been many other modes of homogenisation too throughout history—through custom, through authoritative hierarchy, through a theology and a meaning system interpreted by an assigned clergy for lay populations inhabiting diverse spaces. Modernity is not the first 'universalising' credo. There have been others before it. In fact the notion of the universal appeared in other civilisations—the Indian, the Chinese, the Egyptian and the ancient Greek—long before the universalising claims of the modern Occident. What is new and distinctive about the modern western conception of universalisation—and homogenisation based thereon—is a three-fold claim. To begin with, it is the first effort to project a particular into a universal, expecting the rest of the world to accept the worldview and organising principles of that particular. Second, it is the first effort to universalise from a secular and

temporal space; all earlier efforts at universalisation were of a transcendent nature, the quality of the universal being a state of communion between the individual and the ultimate. Third, the modernist
perspective on universalisation and homogenisation is *colonising*, necessarily rejecting all other universals and castigating them as ahistorical and anachronistic or at best historical antecedents to this more
'scientific' and 'rational' and hence superior universal. It is a mode of
homogenisation that takes upon itself the task of fragmenting and splint-
ering all other social and ethical cohesions, undermining all other unities and imposing its globalising will and power on all others. It is the
first claim to universality that leaves no one out of its domain. Every
other entity or belief system is by definition illegitimate. There is only
one legitimate structure of power, morality and truth. All others are invalid.

Ethnicity represents a powerful rebuttal to this paranoid drive of the
modern project of fashioning the world after the *idea of a world* as eman-
ated from the Occident following which it has almost succeeded in subjugating the immense diversity and richness of human experience. It
is an affirmation of all 'the others' who were sought to be brought under,
colonised and in course of time excluded and dispensed with. This is
why, culturally and regionally speaking, there is more ethnicity in the
South than in the North (though of course there is a lot of diversity in
the North too and there is affirmation of it, in both the West and the East).

This then is one and perhaps the most potent source of ethnicity and
its basic location in the historical process. But there is a second source,
closely related to the first, but located by and large *within* the South.
It is a response to the North within the South. To the homogenising
thrusts of capitalism, the nation-state and technology. To regimes that
are engaged in integrating diverse social formations into a global marketplace. To the claims of secular authority to superiority over, and
legitimate exclusion of, other entities and worldviews, similar to the
claims of the Occidental project. Most societies of the South, prior to
their achieving independent statehood, were described as 'ethnic patch-
works' that, they were told, needed to be replaced by homogeneous and
centralised nation-states that would undertake to 'integrate' all diversities and cultures into one common mould. This too, like the global
project, was carried to excess and undermined the fine balance of antec-
edent civilisations. Ethnicity represents a revolt against this. It is an
affirmation of the hitherto subdued and excluded, reflecting deep stirrings of consciousness as well as emerging capacities of challenging hegemonies, engaging in a recovery of both civic and sacred spaces that
are sought to be overtaken in the ruthless march of modern econom-

ism, modern statehood and modern technology. And in many instances it is an affirmation of the local, the regional and the 'ethnic' against the internal colonisation that has often accompanied the more pervasive and corrosive forms of the nationalism of the nation-state.

Ethnicity in the past, particularly in Europe during the nineteenth century, became a basis for new and emergent nationalism, struggling to be born out of heterogeneous imperial States. The more recent assertions of ethnicity are, however, pitched against existing nation-states and the hegemony of the national centres. They may themselves at times be expressions of new 'nationalities' and may even strive to become new nation-states (carved out of larger ones) but even then they represent assertions of diversity and plurality as against the homogenisation and colonisation represented by existing nation-states which are, in turn, willing to be intergrated into a 'world order'. The new expressions of ethnicity are a challenge to both these homogenising thrusts—of the nation-state and world order. And it is by no means clear that the new social and political formations that will emerge out of the ethnic upsurge will necessarily prefer to take the same old form of nation-state. Not only is the international system based on nation-states in crisis; the experience of individual nation-states too has been highly disappointing, particularly for cultures under attack. The nationalism of these nation-states is found to be oppressive and paranoid.

Response to Majoritarianism

In fact, a third source of ethnicity lies precisely in the *problematique* of this paranoia—of the nation-state and, in its name, of the national 'majority'. Among the many negative 'transfers' from the West to post-colonial polities in the Third World are the notions of majority and minority and the idea that both legality and legitimacy are based on 'majority rule'. These notions have been particularly harmful for plural societies. These societies had for centuries survived without these concepts. They had survived on two main grounds: respect for various diversities and notions of multiple identities, co-existence and togetherness. These were by no means always easy grounds to live with. Outbreaks of social tension and even group violence were not infrequent. There were also many structural inadequacies and many forms of domination of, and exploitation by, the more powerful and the more clever and deceitful. But the latter were not necessarily more numerous; more often than not they were small groups, often single families or clans. In any case there was no attempt to foist the will of a 'majority' on the society as a whole. Nor did the poorer or oppressed strata suffer from any 'minority complex'.

Even today the claims to being in 'majority' and the 'rights of a majority' are hardly ever pressed by large masses of the people belonging to the so-called 'majority community'. It is invoked by a small number of people, speaking 'on behalf of' the larger numbers, seeking their sanction from imported ideas of majority and minority. The so often invoked sentiment of a 'threat to the unity of the country' is brandished by a small section of upper class and upper caste people who speak of the threat coming from minority communities, of the minorities having been given too much license or having done better economically and of the 'majority' having been at the receiving end because they had so far remained disunited and unmindful of their 'natural' rights. Majoritarianism has emerged as the creed of some paranoid individuals who then try to poison the minds of entire communities who happen to be diverse and differentiated (castes, occupational groups, linguistic groups, even groups having diverse religious symbols and community-based godheads) but who are asked to 'stand together' as one large and numerous mass and face the 'threat' from the 'minorities'. The large mass of these people do not want this, their sense of identity is diverse and multiple, and the idea of their being a 'majority' is a synthetic product of the self-proclaimed defenders of the 'unity' of a given faith or religion which had in fact all along encompassed a series of diverse entities. Thus the Hindus, or the Malays or the Sinhalese (or the Sikhs in Punjab), have always been large umbrella concepts encompassing a wide spectrum of distinct social and cultural—and even religious —identities. Often, as in the case of the Hindus, the concept itself is not indigenous but given to them by visiting (or invading) outsiders. It is only with the advent of a synthetic (as against eclectic or agglomerative) ideology of 'unity' and the modern concept of an arithmetic plurality, both reinforced in reaction to 'the others', that majoritarianism has made its way in the mass mind.

In turn the paranoia of the 'majority' is matched by the paranoia of the 'minorities'. Pushed to the wall by the growing accent on numbers in a 'democracy', feeling betrayed by the State that had, to begin with, provided a sense of security to the 'minorities' who had in turn remained loyal to the government and the dominant party in control of the State, and feeling discriminated against and pushed around, there develops that curious psychic state called the 'minority complex'. A sense of inferiority envelops this psychic state, fear and insecurity grips the mass mind and there soon develops a deep sense of alienation from the 'system', the State and the 'nation'. This in turn produces fanatics and fundamentalists who take on an aggressive stance, also call for a closing of ranks (the minorities too are not monoliths, nor is that the view of the large masses among them as they encompass a great deal of diversity and differentiation) and sow seeds of a separatist psychology: we're not needed here, so let's get the hell out of here! The small groups that continue to struggle against such a tendency (and 'dare to belong' in Baljit Malik's ringing assertion after the November 1984 carnage of the Sikhs in India)[1] soon get branded as timid and compromiing the integrity and honour of the community.

Yet, on the opposite end of this aggressive stance there also grows an even more frightening tendency (frightening from the point of view of democratic ethics)—of 'falling in line', simply to survive! There develops a psyche of the defeated and the helpless, of being embarrassed to oppose dominant tendencies, of straining to be 'fair' to those in power and, on the contrary, to be indifferent to the plight of the oppressed and the discriminated—in the process accepting marginalisation of the self and the community by default and as a *fait accompli*! This tendency gets greatly reinforced in periods of stress and insecurity, of violence and vendetta: the insecurity gets internalised by individuals, groups and entire social strata. Such a state of mind then plays into fear psychosis on the one hand and narrow opportunism on the other, 'playing safe' being the most pervasive form of opportunism, producing the phenomenon of so many 'sell-outs' who are hated from within and held in contempt (even while being used) by the dominant 'majority'.

The same state of mind, however, foments deep alienation and discomfort with those belonging to the 'majority', communication channels get choked up and increasingly each side gets distant and estranged from the other. With this the fundamentalist appeal grows and the call for 'standing together' finds fertile ground. It is in this context of a growing sense of alienation from 'the other' that all calls for 'unity' in effect become calls for disunity with respect to the larger nation or the State.

Such a paranoia of the 'minorities', in yet another chain reaction, reinforces the paranoia of the majority, now generating a strange tendency of adopting the style and stance of the insecure 'minorities'. The result is an insecure 'majority' that somehow feels beleaguered by 'minorities' that are seen as having more clout (economic prosperity, access to arms, foreign support, constitutional guarantees, what have you). This gives rise to not just the majoritarian chauvinism that is everywhere in evidence but a new kind of fundamentalism of the 'majority'. It is fundamentalism that breeds on, and takes its cue from, the fundamentalism of the 'minorities'. Communities that are more numerous are

---

1. See *Lokayan Bulletin*, Special Number on the November carnage called *Voices From a Scarred City*, Vol. 3, No. 3.

everywhere more diffuse, internally plural and tolerant of a lot of ambiguity. This is now sought to be reversed. The Hindus, for instance, are called upon to close ranks, adopt a unified theology and one common doctrine, a clergy that is ordained and a common 'book'—in short, they are being asked to 'semitise' themselves. Which is a far cry from the highly plural and decentralised landscape of traditional Hinduism. Somewhat similar tendencies are at work among the Sinhala Buddhists and the Islamic Malays and Indonesians.

Negative Ethnicity

With all this the regenerative and holistic dimensions of 'ethnicity' or 'community' get transformd into negative and exclusive ones, giving rise to the virus of *communalism* as the term has been used in recent decades in South Asian and nearby countries.

Communalism can have two meanings. In a positive sense it means consciousness of the common identity of a group of people based on their cultural heritage (language, religion, caste, region, etc.). In plural societies, such ethnic identities have always existed. They have been positively experienced and expressed. Positive consciousness of communal identities in culturally diverse contexts has, by and large, been associated with two other characteristics: (a) a mutual respect for other identities, and (b) a possibility of living and celebrating diversity organically, as parts of a whole. This is what 'unity' has meant, a unity of diverse parts of society. The possibility of diversity in the context of positively felt identity has been the basis of stability and security for people—in our mixed villages, *mohallas*, and inner cities.

Communalism

As against this there is the negative sense of communalism which is based on an exclusive identity that denies respect for other identities and thinks of unity as something to be achieved not organically but by subjugating the others.

Similarly, secularism too has had two opposite meanings, a typically Asian one (Indian or the original Ceylonese) with which we began and a typically western one to which we seem to be moving. According to the former, there was no rejection of religious or cultural identities but equal respect for them all. While the State itself adopted no religion, thus denying any official sanction to a particular identity, it guaranteed protection to all religions and belief systems (including atheistic belief systems). According to the latter, more homogenising and all-prevading meaning, religion and culture are to be pushed out of the domain of the State, and civil society is to find its unity by surrendering its diverse cultural terrain to the modern State with its 'modernising mission. The latter version of 'secularism' as a project of the modern State has been aimed at removing these diversities and undermining allegiances based on religion, language or culture. Similarly, 'development' and 'modernisation' of the socio-economic structure are to be viewed as creating conditions for 'modernising the minds of the people', making them move into a post-ethnic consciousness.

The paradox of modernisation has been that instead of helping religious, linguistic and cultural identities 'wither away', it has actually hardened them and provoked ethnic conflict and communal violence. But much worse, it has transformed positively experienced identity and diversity into negative identities. It has given a negative meaning to communalism in which self-identity is perceived and defined as the negation of the other and *vice versa*. The two characteristics of a culturally diverse society, of living with other identities and feeling a unity with them, are no longer possible. Identities have not withered away—what have withered away are the conditions under which diverse identities can together share a social space. Identity has thus been rendered negative, it has been reduced to a negation of the 'other'. Cultural survival has been reduced to meaning the removal of the other, the exclusion of the other, the death of the other. Outbreaks of communal violence are not expressions of a feeling of religious identity *per se*. They are expressions of the perversion of positive and diverse identities into negative and fractured ones. This transformation of cultural identity is most severe where the all encompassing thrust of modernisation has been most accelerated and pervasive, e.g. in Punjab, the land of the Green Revolution, and in Gujarat, the land of the White Revolution. The same tendency has been reported from the Philippines where too these two 'revolutions' were pushed through.

The convergence of the growth of modernisation and the rise of communalism as a destructive force can be explained at two levels. First, it is in these pockets of rapid economic growth that the positive roots of culture have been destroyed as part of the homogenising thrust of undermining cultural identities. Second, it is in these pockets that real or perceived shrinkage of social space has taken place. People perceive change, and assume that opportunities should have increased with modernisation. But such rapid change, guided by the market, not by human concerns, involves massive dislocation and displacement of people from traditional means of livelihood. The new opportunities have a narrower social base. Thus just as what is known as computer illiteracy in the West will be higher than the illiteracy in the three R's, the introduction of western style education in non-western societies has reduced access to learning instead of expanding it. The process of competition for scarce privileges and livelihoods aggravates the feeling of threat from the 'other' precisely while it undermines any positive identity of the self.

The culturally homogenising, socially fragmenting and atomising processes of modernisation, induced largely through State intervention, thus create conditions of social and economic vulnerability and insecurity in which the State takes on the role of manager of those vulnerabilities and insecurities. In a period of apparent growth (benefitting a minority) but real shrinkage (which displaces millions from their homes and livelihoods), people compete for scarce resources and benefits, and to do this they must organise. 'Ethnic' groupings have been one way of bargaining with the State. When equality is a proclaimed social ideal, and inequality is the reality of what development and modernisation results in, each individual and group interprets its loss as someone else's gain, and interprets the other's gain as a result of its being well organised as a group—linguistic, religious, caste or regional.

Economic survival is preconceived by all as the issue—for the upper class doctors and lawyers in Gujarat fighting reservations for educational seats for the depressed castes and tribes, as well as for the marginalised and poorer strata of the Hindus, or the Malays resenting the upward mobility of the Chinese in Malaysia. Because electoral politics and government interventions respond to ethnic groupings, these economic issues are transformed into issues of cultural survival. If 'they' get jobs, 'we' will be unemployed. If 'they' prosper, 'we' will be deprived. And this struggle for economic survival, which merges into a struggle for cultural survival, is experienced by *all* communities, not just the minorities, not just the marginalised. In India the Hindus see Muslims and backward classes being pampered for votes. The Muslims see Hindus as excluding them in new ways, and see the State as encouraging such exclusion. The same is the case with the Sinhala and the Tamils in Sri Lanka. It is this overarching disease of cultural decay, of growing inequalities, of ethnicity as an exclusive basis for ensuring gains and protection from new vulnerabilities, that accounts for communal feelings turning violent and causing social breakdown. This is what explains why communal violence is taking the form of an epidemic.

Diversity itself is not a cause for communal hatred. Different religions and linguistic groups have inhabited these lands for centuries, defining their self-identity in terms of their manifold diversities. What is new are the processes which have made cultural identity incompatible with diversity and have made affirmation of ethnic identity a means to economic advantage over others. In this new complexity, when

Hindus or Sinhalas fight Muslims or Tamils, or upper castes fight backward classes, they do not fight them because their *faith* is in danger. The
engineered violence of a 'rath yatra' (a procession led by a chariot) or
other religious festivals does not explain how daily, in every house, conversations about communalism are conversations about who got jobs
and who did not, who got economic privileges and who did not. It does
not explain how the manipulators of public sentiments are finding ready
ground for sowing seeds of communal hatred. It does not explain why
phenomena which used to be localised in space and time spread over
large areas and last for weeks and months.

Role of the State

The role of the State in creating conditions of vulnerability and in then
stepping in to manage these vulnerabilities has yet another offshoot.
When each community or caste or religious group interprets its insecurity as a result of the privileges of a competing group gained through
'favours' and 'patronage' from the State, the resulting communal conflict and violence does not aim at fighting another community but rather
fighting the State which is presumed to be dominated by or be preferential to the other community. The other community is perceived as
a surrogate State. What is narrowly seen as communal violence could
thus, in a broader perspective, reflect deeper conflicts between a fragmented civil society and the State. Each community does not merely
see the other as the excluding 'other', but further sees the other as an
instrument of the State for excluding it in economic and political affairs.
The State creates these vulnerabilities. And each time it steps in to create
'security', new insecurities are generated in people's minds, new fears
that the State is biased *against* them—and *for* a contending faction or
group. The shrinkage of people's space, of the space for civil society,
are the causes of the symptoms of communalism (as also of other maladies like terrorism and fundamentalism). Communal ideology allows
the perception of this shrinkage not as a process which all communities
are victims of, but as a process relative to the gains 'other' communities enjoy.

Divide and Rule

Emergent communalism thus becomes a complex but effective expression of the divide and rule policy. 'Unity' takes on the perverted meaning of consolidating fragmentation whereas 'security' takes on the
perverted meaning of deepening insecurity. And at each stage and level
of the breakdown of unity and security in civil society, the State inter-
venes in ways that accelerates the breakdown. *Ethnocide* engulfs larger

and larger parts of our region. The annihilation of the Tamils in Sri Lanka, the Sikhs in North India, the Muslims in Gujarat and Meerut, the Chakmas in Bangladesh are just the beginnings.

Where will it all end? In the recovery of the conditions of diversity as the condition of survival for all, or in the annihilation of all? That survival is only possible in diversity should be more than evident from the logic of self-destructiveness built into the destruction of diversity. It ncessarily gives rise to concepts of separation, exclusion and isolation. Those Hindus and those Muslims who think that religious uniformity is a condition for peace need only remember the Karachi riots, where, in spite of a common religion and an Islamic State, the Mohajirs fight the Pathans and Punjabis. If we do not divide ourselves up by religion, we will do it by language, or by caste, or by race. Divisiveness and fragmentation is an infinite regress. For every Hindu who thinks that the Indian Muslims should be sent to Pakistan, there is a Punjabi in Pakistan who thinks that the Mohajirs should be sent back to India. And for every Indian who thinks that the Tamil refugees from Sri lanka should be sent back, there is a Sinhalese who thinks that all the Tamils should be asked to go to India. We seem to be trapped in our cultural diversities.

Negativism

This outbreak of negative identities is proceeding at a pace that heralds not just a fast growing erosion of State authority but something even more basic—social breakdown. The deeper social conflicts that the State had 'successfully' mediated for so long appear to burst forth unmediated and unchecked whereas elements that are supposed to be part of the State structure are themselves found to 'join the fray' and engage in reckless manoeuvres. Each time this has happened, the poorer classes of all communities have borne the brunt of the 'breakdown' of the law that follows.

The result is an upsurge of communal violence in which all kinds of unscrupulous elements are found to get busy and engage in the most gruesome acts while the bearers of State power are found to 'stand by' and allow the marauding mobs and hoodlums, professional and otherwise, to take over. The government of the day, already rendered impotent by personal insecurities and squabbles at the higher echelons, simply collapses and hands over charge to the police, paramilitary and the army who have no understanding of the real issues underlying the latest breakdown and treat them all in the same way. Everywhere it is the same: imposing curfews, rounding up hundreds of people (most of them innocent), issuing orders to 'shoot at sight', engaging in flag marches and allowing the lower constabulary to jump the gun at the slightest provocation, in the process killing a lot of innocent people and deepening the sense of hurt and ill-feeling among the affected segments of the public, thus making it impossible to mend matters in a normal way.

Worse still, there is reason to believe that at least a fair chunk, if not too many, of those who have been entrusted the task of imposing order on a situation seething with violence, arson, loot and rape are themselves found to exploit the situation. And one notices that the 'higher ups' in the system, from Cabinet Ministers to senior civil servants to Commissioners of Police, have little control over the local power structure (consisting of mafia politicians, professional gangsters, peddlers in liquor and drugs and what can be called lumpen policemen).

Vacuum

What one notices is a growing combination of two rather serious trends, both of which point to an incipient breakdown of the State—a collapse of political authority at the lower reaches of society consequent upon its increasing centralisation and tendency to look outward, and the filling in of the consequent vacuum created by a new genre of 'politics' that combines communal crimes, fundamentalist slogans and pure terrorism that is not any longer extremist in any ideological sense but simply aimed to kill, knife, rape and loot. Violence becomes an end in itself, a source of profit and livelihood, a new profession that is not bound by any external rules. As this happens the police too become helpless, can shoot and 'round up', but have no clear sense of who is being shot or rounded up and, as the risks of engagement grow, both give up and give in. They give in not to those with a better grip on the situation, but to those with greater fire power than themselves—to battalions from outside the region, to the army and, in the meanwhile, to those wielding guns and knives and various new devices of setting fire to individuals and homes and shops, a whole new 'technology of terror'.[2] Thus in Meerut in North India (a scene of continuous communal skirmishes) the Provincial Armed Constabulary (PAC), which itself egaged in heinous acts of atrocities against innocent people, when asked to comb the place for arms, asked for army protection. It is this combination of terror on others and fear for themselves that is becoming a prominent feature of police behaviour in strife-ridden situations.

---

2. See my "The How and the Why of it", *Illustrated Weekly of India*, January 5, 1985. *India*, January 5, 1985.

Lumpenisation

No wonder, the people turn increasingly to local lumpens who may themselves be engaging in terror but who also happen to be the only source of protection of a slum or a resettlement colony. Ultimately when a semblance of peace returns, it is not because of the claims made on behalf of the police or district administration but because of a temporary truce between rival bands of the lumpens belonging to rival factions of the ruling party's underworld.

The situation has become so serious that a senior civil liberties activist in India (who has spent most of his life working in the slums and among poor and migrant labourers in Delhi) told me recently, after spending several days in the walled city in Delhi during a serious outbreak of communal violence, that we should engage in a dialogue with the lumpens, listen to their complaints against the police and the Congress party politicians and win them over for restoring peace and tranquility. They may in fact be better placed to restore order than the police and the administration who can be dictated to by mafia politicians before whom they feel powerless.[3]

Whether one agrees with this view or not, what is becoming clear is that the more the agents of the State and party leaders withdraw from the scenes of carnage and rioting, the more the writ of the lumpens and the bullies is going to expand. This is particularly becoming the case in what is known as the 'old city' in all metropolitan areas. These are all walled cities, with fortress-like structures, from behind which both the lay citizenry and their 'protectors' operate, in which the police may patrol but dread to move around except at the sufferance of the new mafia style bosses (the old style party bosses disappeared long ago), and where, in almost all cases of increased tension and violence, the army has to be called in to restore order temporarily, but where long-term accords can only be achieved as a result of deals among the rival strongmen of the area.

What is emerging in the various walled cities is the almost total autonomy of whichever 'power structure' that has emerged consisting of wholly local figures who owe no loyalty to anyone higher up and who for their own reasons have come to the conclusion that government, party and the like cannot be relied upon any more to provide either justice or peace and they must fall back upon their own resources—organisational, financial and lethal.

---

3. This is Inder Mohan, for long President of the Delhi unit of the People's Union of Civil Liberties (PUCL) and a prominent trade unionist and social worker among the slums and resettlement colonies in and around Delhi.

Terrorism

Unfortunately such a picture of who wields power in densely populated and communally mixed areas is too static. It does not bring out the true character of the malady afflicting the cities and their rural peripheries. It only provides the anatomy of power in these areas, not the emergent physiology and chemistry of *terror* that is found to accompany each successive episode of communal violence. To understand that one has to bring in two additional factors—the growth of terrorism and the increasing appeal of fundamentalist and chauvinist slogans. Terrorism is raising its head among those (the Sinhalas in Sri Lanka and the Hindus in India) who claim to be a 'majority' that has been wronged by public policy (which is supposed to 'favour' and 'pamper' the minorities) and among the minorities like the Tamils or the Muslims and the Sikhs. Given the rapid decline in the authority of secular power, the constantly deteriorating state of the law and order machinery to whom the leaders of government and political parties have entrusted the whole job of maintaining peace, and the growing spurt of communal feelings among the middle and lower middle classes which are exploited by politicians for narrow gains, there has taken place a mushroom growth of those who specialise in terror. It is a situation of ideological vacuum accompanied by a rise of a 'pragmatic' younger generation that is no longer driven by dreams of the future but by concern with the here and now. Under pressure of declining economic opportunities and the growing appeal of safeguarding communal and caste interests, pragmatism takes on more and more banal forms. The result is terrorism. Hence the growth of not just lumpens—which is an old story—[4]but of terrorist squads patrolling these areas.

A large part of the rising spectre of terrorism—on the part of the agents of the State engaging in reckless shooting and of mafia politicians, and on the part of armed gangs of a communal type—is amoral and non-ideological. It is carried out as a vocation, for sheer profit. But what makes it truly venomous and deadly is its tie-up with fundamentalist and chauvinist organisations and leaders. Ideological vacuum of a socio-economic and party political kind is being increasingly filled in by doctrines and slogans based on sheer hatred of this or that community.

---

4. I had laid it out in quite some detail in my long article "Where Are We Heading?" in the *Indian Express* which has since been republished in a more expanded version, "Democracy and Fascism in India" in the first volume in this series of books, *State Against Democracy: In Search of Humane Governance*, 1988

Alienation

There is taking place an increasing alienation of diverse local communities from the State which is in some respects a more far-reaching development than even the growth of violence and terrorism, which of course thrive on such alienation. For it signals the incipient breakdown of civil society in the absence of determined effort on the part of all concerned to prevent it. It is part of a much larger phenomenon. This is the slow but growing withdrawal of the ordinary citizen from the constitutional apparatus called the State, as well as from the larger organic entity enveloping all smaller affiliations and identities called the nation. Whoever one talks to in the general public gives the feeling of increasing indifference, apathy and alienation from, if not antipathy and rejection of, the State. There is an equal if not greater withdrawal from 'nationalist' commitments. With a few exceptions all the talk of threats from abroad seems to make no dent on the general public. Similarly, while people do get upset and even disgusted at the hoary tales of terrorist killings, this does not make them feel any closer to the government or any of the other organs of the State—with which in fact many of them feel equally disgusted. The awe and respect for the army has also precipitously declined in these countries. What has grown instead is one's identity with one's own caste or linguistic or religious community and often a withdrawal into still narrower shells of primary and secondary loyalties—of peer groups and family—and often into just one's own lonely and miserable self. It is a frightening situation and accounts for growing rates of violence and anomie directed against both the self and the other.

Communalism thrives on this larger canvas of societal breakdown. Of destruction and decay of institutions. Of erosion of legitimate authority. Of the decline of civil society. And of the collapse of the democratic State that had for so long given cohesion to civil society without undermining its diversity and plurality.

Defence of Privilege

Having laid out this emerging scenario of negative, exclusive and insecure forms of ethnicity and communalism, there is need to return to a point made earlier which bears repetition because in it may also lie the clues to future intervention. It is that, while the 'poison' of communalism spreads under the pressure of widely felt insecurities and the power of chauvinist and fundamentalist doctrines, it is the doing of a small minority in all communities. Thus in so-called majority communities what has taken place is a small minority's interpretation of a 'dominant' or 'hegemonical' culture that is proclaimed to be dominant or hegemonical and backed by the demand that the State should accept it as such and the 'minorities' should be forced to accede to that formulation. With this the majoritarianism of the 'majority' community is forced on the State which is asked to confer a special and privileged status on those belonging to it and a secondary or inferior status on the others. In point of fact, of course, such privileges get conferred on a small group of people who in any case happen to be privileged and have access to the resources and opportunities provided by a modernising State and a corporate capitalist economy.

Predictably, the reaction this produces in the 'minority' communities also plays into the hands of small, privileged groups. Thus in the state of Kerala in India, known for long for amicable co-existence among diverse communities of Hindus, Muslims and Christians (each found to be numerically large and each encompassing a diverse spectrum of communities), the communal virus has been spreading and affecting each of them, thanks largely to the political compulsion of narrowly conceived electoral calculations. The result is Hindu communalism exploited by the privileged among the dominant castes, Muslim communalism exploited by the rich and privileged strata known as the 'timber mafia' that has benefitted from the Gulf money (against which in fact the Hindu communalists are directing their ire),[5] and Christian communalism in which the Catholic clergy with massive Church and other institutional resources are found to play a major role. Recently when the two Communist parties (and their allies) took a principled stand and refused to have any dealings with the communal parties (e.g., the two factions of the Muslim League with one of which they were once in alliance), it was found that while the mass of the people responded positively to it, the communalists among the Hindus also chose to support it as against the Congress-led alliance which had included the Muslim parties. As Justice Krishna Iyer, a leading independent figure in the Kerala Left, commented, "secularism has now become the haven of Hindu communalists".

Privilege and Violence

The point at issue, of course, is that whether it is communalism of the electoral variety or communalism of street violence, it is always a small group of highly placed and politically influential people who see in communalism an instrument of perpetuating their power and priv-

---

5. In point of fact, there are large numbers of Hindus and Christians from Kerala in the Gulf (especially in Saudi Arabia), perhaps as large as, if not exceeding, the Muslims (of Kerala) in absolute numbers.

ilege. As socio-economic issues get sidetracked by an elite that is unwilling to face mass pressures for justice and equity, and as communalism appears to be the most handy instrument for this, there takes place a marriage between privilege, violence and corruption. Defence of achieved standards of living and accumulated wealth and privilege is everywhere taking recourse to instruments of violence. In the international arena it takes the form of defence of ostentatious living standards, packaged as the 'American way of life', by recourse to strategic doctrines directed against the Third World.[6] In the domestic arena it is defence of the same living standards of the rich, packaged as preservation of 'merit' and 'quality' in the social and economic sphere and of 'national security' in the political sphere, put forward by and large by the same social groups (with the richer and privileged strata from the 'minorities' coopted into the power structure).

Wages of Secularism

What is important to gauge here is perhaps the most crucial theoretical point in our understanding of the exclusivist and divisive conception of communalism. It is that there is far more of a secular than a religious basis to it. It is more a struggle for survival and retention of secular (political and economic) power and control over secular vantage points (in the State and in the economy) than for religious values or even religious advantage or ascendance. True, religious symbols are utilised in this process but they are addressed more to goals of power than of piety. The more the use of fundamentalist and chauvinist symbols in the desperation for preserving or denying secular spaces, the more the areas of religiosity, mysticism and spiritual transcendence are found to recede. This is the most important paradox of 'religious revivalism' in societies striving to become 'secular'.

Many factors have contributed to this situation over a period of time. There has taken place everywhere an erosion of major institutions in which the people could participate at local levels and growing centralisation of power in a narrow coterie alongside a wilful discrediting of politics as such. With this the regard for diversity and the mediating role of politics have weakened. The replacement of political managers by just managers has produced far greater centralisation than ever before and a considerable decline in the capacity to engage the nation's diversities into a common framework. Meanwhile the accent on modernisation has emphasised values of efficiency and 'merit' which has

---

6. For documentation on this, see my "Disarmament and World Order" in the second volume in this series, *Transformation and Survival: In Search of Humane World Order*, 1988.

alienated the upper classes from those lower down. Hence the growing demand for undoing special entitlements provided to the latter in the form of reservations and the like. To the upswing of communal passions across religious divides has got added new communal divides across castes and ethnic divisions.[7] With this the concept of 'secularism' has undergone a dramatic shift from a conception based on respect for all diversities to one based on State power and technology steamrolling through social diversity and imposing a homogenising ethos on it.

'Revivalism'

It is against this basic change of ethos in the political sphere that one has to understand the role of religious revivalism and so-called 'fundamentalism' which are usually held responsible for the upsurge in communal violence in recent times. In point of fact there is nothing religious in the revival of religious symbols and appeals and there is nothing fundamental that those who are called fundamentalists are raising. These are not even truly pious people. Not even the so-called *sadhus* and *maulvis* and *bikhus*. They are people determined to exploit the institutional vacuum that is at large and move into it with both lethal ideas and lethal weapons.

But it is not these individuals and organisations that have created the situation we face; it is the situation that was created for them by the leadership that is mainly responsible for their heightened role in the current scene. In fact the goings on of these people are an indirect tribute to the larger ethos created by the new secular elite—of homogenising diversity, imposing a synthetic culture through modern communications and creating an increasingly tight-knit elite that will, they believe, produce a strong and powerful State. The appeal of the new religions—both of the majority and of the minorities—is based on doing to religion what the national elite is doing to secular affairs. The fundamental feature of any religion is individual piety and regard for different ways in which piety is achieved. What the new religions are trying to do is to homogenise the religious impulse, first by basing it on the deep anxiety and insecurity of 'the other' and second by 'marketing' it (like marketing any other commodity).

Look at what is happening to religious festivals. Each of these is turning into not a sacred but a secular affair, taken out of the immense diver-

7. See D.L. Sheth's M.N. Roy Memorial Lecture on Reservations, delivered in March 1986 and published in *The Radical Humanist*, April 1986. For a more detailed analysis by him, see his article on the same theme in the *Economic and Political Weekly*, November 14, 1987.

sity of family and community ceremonies in which they used to be observed and wholly divorced from deeper religious beliefs. With this religion is brought into the marketplace, propagated through blaring loudspeakers often going on for days and even weeks. Strong-armed men and sometimes women are found spearheading 'yatras', 'jaluses' and 'raths' that are meant to create trouble.[8]

The so-called 'revivalism' of religion is thus wholly rootless, appropriating cultural symbols and metaphors that can be invoked in a period of growing insecurity all round. With this goes the whole space that was preserved for the sacred and the revered and the mythical. Instead it becomes a take-religion-to-the-streets affair. When this happens, it is sheer madness. The police and even the Army remain tame spectators before these marauding mobs.

It is in the context of this perversion of both secular and religious space that the substitution of democratic by communal politics and the decline in respect for diversity have to be understood. Where politics itself gets discredited there can be no respect for diversity. Moreover where the affairs of the State are handed over to a managerial elite the accent is bound to be on homogenisation not on diversity, on order not on consensus, on repression not on accommodation. And this then creates a climate in which chauvinist forces and a threatened upper class combine to mount a backlash against the poor and the deprived that is clothed in communal terms.

With this what used to be the doings of mafia gangs and hired professionals—as happened in the 1983 massacre in Jaffna or the November 1984 carnage in Delhi—spreads downwards and poisons the psyche of entire communities. This is yet to happen in full measure but the process has begun. As it spreads religion becomes the main playground for diverse *secular* forces, provides easy escape routes to an elite that is facing growing pressures of an economic or political kind and prepares the way for imposing a centralised and authoritarian regime in the name of restorting order and 'unity'.

Chauvinism

It is this growing convergence between a secular and technocratic vision of the State and the search for a chauvinist ideology that provides the new setting of communalism and of the more exclusivist and negative thrust of ethnicity. It is a thrust that is drawing its inspiration from wholly new and unsuspected sources. From the State which is sup-

---

8. On this see my "Communalism: The New Face of Indian Democracy" in the first volume in this series, *State Against Democracy, op. cit.*

posed to be secular. From the modernist national elite that is supposed to provide correctives to parochial tendencies. From the security establishment which is supposed to provide protection to all communities. From the educated middle class which is supposed to be committed to democratic values. From the science and technology elite which is supposed to nurture a 'scientific temper'. From the votaries of 'high culture' who are supposed to be the custodians of humanism, compassion and catholicity. The negativist thrust is drawing on new insecurities and vulnerabilities of the owning classes and privileged social strata, the upper and middle classes being found to be far more communal than the poorer and 'lower' classes. The 'higher up' one goes the more the appeal of chauvinist tendencies. Thus one finds that among the professionals engaged in scientific and technological establishments there is widespread frustration and disenchantment arising out of a highly competitive and hierarchical organisational milieu, inducing cynicism on the one hand and social conservatism on the other. Meanwhile the accent on a technocratic and futurist perspective looks down on the inevitable pluralities and bargaining culture of democratic politics and its universalist credo undermines respect for diversity. The combined result of such insecurities and the ascendant norms of 'high tech' is a highly distorted perception of nationalism and national interest. It is a new and peculiar model of ethnicity that is induced by modernity (as against ethnicity that is a reaction to the excesses of modernity)—chauvinist, defensive, reckless, steamrolling and straitjacketing all that comes in the way, in the end ruthless and fascist.

End of Politics

Underlying this new convergence of technocratic and chauvinist tendencies has been a basic turnaround in national priorities: from the primacy of the socio-political dimension to the primacy of the communal and chauvinist dimension, leading to a gross neglect of pressing economic issues, of growing disparities, deprivation, discrimination and destitution. This is accompanied by another turnabout which is in some respects even more basic: from a system that was based on the centrality of the political process to one that denigrates the values of politics and seeks to replace it by a reign of experts and technocrats, and through them of the corporate sector, the import sector and the transnationals. The latter have always insisted that the State was too politicised, too open, too tolerant of the 'rights' of trade unions and slumdwellers and tribals and other presumed roadblocks to progress that can only be achieved through large-scale investments in modern technology, telecommunications, agribusiness and the rest. There was need to clean it all up and prepare the way for catching up with the 'advanced' nations.

In this thinking, the very understanding of social change has been turned around: from one in which democratic politics provides the motive force to one in which technology provides the prime spur to national power, greatness and unity. The only element of politics that was necessary for this was continuation of the same regime in power through any means and if for this the religious and ethnic minorities, the national peripheries and various kinds of popular movements have to be fixed or bought over, this should of course be done.

This new convergence of a technocratic model of the State and a communal model of the nation has been the striking feature of the last few years. Normally, one thinks of technocrats and managers as being modern, secular and all that. This is an illusion. As they have no politics, they have no real stake—except profit and power. An apolitical approach, lacking as it is an overarching frame of values, necessarily ends up being amoral.

I have dealt elsewhere with the implications of the dominion of the technocratic over the political in the new alignment of forces.[9] Here I want to deal mainly with the more basic turnabout mentioned above—from the socio-political to the communal. Whereas all kinds of projects continue to be inaugurated, new plans and policies keep getting announced and both the electronic media and ad agencies as well as new modules of mass persuasion keep stressing 'development', the fact of the matter is that so far as the State is concerned, none of this is of any consequence. More and more attention is given to the communal dimension—both by the rulers and all the others who influence affairs: the political parties, the press, the the judiciary, the caucus of 'advisors' and the few journalists and publicists who may have access to power and decision-making.

Increasingly, the people too—except, of course, for the really poor and underprivileged—seem to be drawn more and more to think of society in essentially communal terms, or in terms of the perennial anxiety about threats to national unity from extremists, terrorists, etc. This also gives precedence to the communal issue over pressing socio-economic problems like growing unemployment and marginalisation of vast sections of the people, or even over such urgent matters as increasing incidence of droughts and ecological disasters. It also gets precedence over important political problems that account for so much discontent and instability in the system—federal relations, electoral reforms, reform of the

---

9. See the chapters "On Humane Governance", "Decline of the Moderate State", "Democracy in the Third World" and "The Phenomenon of Two Indias" in *State Against Democracy, op. cit.* and "Choices Facing a Divided World" and "Bridging Two Worlds" in *Transformation and Survival, op. cit.*

law and order apparatus at the grassroots of society, autonomy for the media following the massive diffusion of modern communications, etc. Each of these issues—economic and political—received a great deal of public attention in the years gone by, even if the government of the day failed to measure up to expectations. Today all of them seem to have receded into the background.

Rise of Technocracy

These issues have receded in the background because of the displacement of a model of politics that was addressed to the people to one that is addressed to the upper strata of society, to the various elites. Few people realised that inherent in this withdrawal from a populist to a managerial style of conducting national affairs was a turnabout from 'secular' to 'communal' politics. Many thought that things like liberalisation of the economy, greater opening up to private foreign investment and the International Monetary Fund/World Banks constellation and getting rid of elderly party stalwarts committed to 'slow' processes of politics and replacing them by a younger lot, heralded a new pragmatic and 'dynamic' phase. Little did they realise that the process of depoliticisation that was inherent in this shift would soon produce a yawning vacuum that would then be filled by all manner of adventurers, both dilettantish and devilish, and provide a playground for unending conflicts and violence, feeding on pent-up frustrations and paranoid tendencies.

It is in this spectrum of events, spurred as well as superimposed by a leadership that had lost confidence in its own earlier 'secular' and 'socialist' credo, that the turnaround towards the communalisation of the State is to be found. It has made major inroads into the framework of distributive justice, opened up the economy—and the ecology—to efforts to privatise all resources and initiatives. By providing greater play to vested interests and to new 'power brokers' at the grassroots and intermediate levels, it has further opened the field to local mafias and professionals in violence—at the cost of the poor in all communities. Ill-euipped to perceive the nature of the deteriorating social scene and disdainful of 'politics', the new elite seems to have decided to turn its back on the masses and pin its faith on the new emerging ideology the world over—technological modernisation. This necessarily involves focussing on the advance guard of society that is available for such transformation, leaving the rearguard to its fate, in effect dispossessing it and if need be, dispensing with it.

It is not as if this is some kind of a master plan. It is rather that a managerial mind tends to treat issues of power and authority with misplaced confidence, verging on arrogance and aggressiveness. It encourages hawkish tendencies and feels good at being smart and decisive instead of negotiating one's way through various parameters and levels.

Forced Ethnicity

The impact of such thinking has been the most severe for the truly 'ethnic' communities living in the hinterlands of these societies. These are increasingly being forced to cave in and think in terms of mere retention of the extremely limited opportunities that the system offers and are prevented from joining larger movements for social justice and transformation. For the tribal people and the inhabitants of forest ranges where capitalism and colonial style exploitation (made presentable as development projects) have eroded their resource base, forced them to move out of their traditional homelands and threatened their cultural identity and economic stability and self-reliance, the political system is increasingly treating them either in law and order terms or as ethnics and aliens with whom some kind of territorial arrangement must be worked out. Financial temptations and largesse are offered in return for their suspending their demands for greater autonomy and managing their own affairs according to their own traditions and lifestyles. This is forcing the tribals and the forest people to think of their genuine aspirations along narrow communal and sectarian lines which make them run to the Centre for 'concessions'. And the more they accept being treated in this manner, the more they open themselves up to metropolitan and international pressures for economic exploitation and the mining away of their rich natural resources. The greater the communal orientation, the less their capacity of self-conservation and sustained livelihood.

To come back to the main point of this long essay, the shift in the attention of the State from basic economic and political tasks to communal and religious appeals, as well as the growing tendency towards taking major sources of conflict and confrontation out of the political arena, are forcing one segment after another of these plural societies to fall back on their primordial resources and think of their struggle for survival along essentially communal lines.

In order to comprehend this more fully, there is need to conceptually clarify the contradictions inherent in the 'modern project', epitomised in recent decades as 'development', with its institutional location in the modern nation-State, and to see how in the process of clarifying and facing up to these contradictions, ethnicity can be made into a positive and liberating rather than a negative and excluding process.

Development and Ethnicity

A common assumption of 'developmentalism' as a modernising project and ideology has been that ethnicity is destined to wither away as an anachronism, to give way to a totally secular social order where identities of colour, creed, and language will not impede full social participation. This assumption of a post-ethnic consciousness in the developmental paradigm sees ethnic distinctions as losing force either to a working class consciousness (as in Marxism) or to an emphasis on 'nation-building' as a norm in which the State and the Market come to replace older ethnic identities (as in bourgeois Liberalism).

Yet history does not seem to be following this developmental path to secular identities. The more rapid the development of a region, the more modernised its infrastructure, the ethnic identities seem to deepen, and ethnic conflicts seem to intensify. The usual explanation for ethnic conflicts is to trace them to historical differences that breed conflicts, and to go into the history of religious, linguistic and regional clashes and communal tensions in the past. Thus scholars in Sri Lanka study Tamil-Sinhala differences, and scholars in India study Hindu-Muslim or Hindu-Sikh tensions as carryovers from the past. But these histories do not provide any explanation for the paradoxical deepening of ethnic identity and conflict with the acceleration of the process of modernisation. The issue of ethnicity is more complex than the developmental view suggests. On the contrary, ethnicity becomes a ground for reassessing the cultural, economic and political impacts of developmentalism. These related and complex impacts are found to create new vulnerabilities and new responses which feed into the rise of ethnic consciousness and new ethnic assertions. Instead of disappearing, ethnic identities harden as a combination/convergence of three trends.

1. Developmentalism, as culture, creates a uniform spread of commercial values and conspicuous consumption based on western lifestyles and in particular on the hegemony of the 'Market'. There is an implied 'universality' in this culture which is assumed to work for all societies. We have already examined this particular model of universality as opposed to the universalism of earlier more philosophical systems of thought. Here I want to simply say that, unlike other models of universality in past civilisations, this particular model is so arrogant and ethnocentric that it has no built-in mechanisms of self-correction in it. Ethnicity and recovery of ethnic spaces become the only correctives. Diverse communities respond to this 'universal' culture of developmentalism (and the Market) by turning to their religions and cultures as a corrective source of values. Thus Buddhist revivalism in Sri Lanka was a response to cultural destruction in Sri Lanka during colonialism.

Post-independence ethnic consciousness has similarly been fuelled by a response to the culture of development. The Punjab conflicts too have at one level a genuine cultural upsurge as a corrective to the commercial culture spread by the Green Revolution. The Green Revolution, and the spread of capitalist agriculture, created new inequalities, disrupted community ties, dislocated old forms of life and fractured the moral and ethical fabric that had provided social norms. Alcoholism, smoking, drug addiction spread as more money circulated in the villages. Religious revivalism became a moral corrective to these trends. In the early phase, when Bhindranwale preached from this ground, his most ardent followers were women and children because they suffered most with a drunken or drug addicted father/brother/husband in the family. During this phase, Bhindranwale made no anti-Hindu statements. He was popular because he was seen as transforming society into a 'good' society. Even today, rural people in Punjab remember him only in his capacity as a preacher and a social and religious reformer

'Revivalism' is thus often a corrective response to the homogenising and commercialising force of modernisation and development. That in Sri Lanka it turned into Sinhala chauvinism and in Punjab Bhindranwale later became the inspiration for terrorist violence is part of the complexity of ethnicity. This ambivalent nature of ethnic and cultural upsurges can make us more alert to the complex but real ways in which the modernist world and modernist consciousness are falling apart. We need to recognise these ambivalences and ambiguities, and learn how to cherish beneficial tendencies towards diversity while struggling against the conditions which create the possibility of these diverse stirrings themselves becoming homogenising, violent and excluding.

The hegemonical theories of the homogeneous culture of the market as created by development assume the destruction of other cultures which can provide human values outside the market. In the recreation of a transcendent ethical order which is a source of lasting human values, of first principles of human conduct, earlier systems of culture are being revived because these values cannot come from the market and its narrow economistic ends of profits, consumerism and commoditisation.

The recovery of diverse positive identities as diverse yet ethical approaches to the 'good' life cannot thus be simply dismissed as the growth of religious fundamentalism, though given the tendencies of elites to 'communalise' politics and society in that negative sense, the danger of these positive resurgences being transformed into exclusivist and even annihilatory usages always exists. For instance, the concept of 'Ram Rajya' which had been a non-hegemonical democratic concept in India, say under Mahatma Gandhi, has degenerated into a crude communal concept as found in the attempt to gain control over *Ram Janma Bhoomi*. If 'development' itself has become a problem, and has sowed the seeds of discontent and ethnic conflict, a corrective to development can only come from other worldviews, other visions. The recovery of these subjugated 'others' becomes a difficult, touchy, yet essential task. There are inherent dangers in such a recovery, but also opportunities which we cannot afford to miss.

2. Developmentalism, as economism, has become a source of new economic vulnerabilities, and new inequalities. In multi-ethnic societies, where overlaps have existed between religious and regional identities and economic functions, issues of economic insecurity and class contradictions are very conveniently transformed by the elites into ethnic, caste and religious issues.

The best illustration of how easy it is to see an ethnic factor in primarily economic and class issues are the Deccan riots that took place in 1875 in Ahmednagar and Poona districts which had been brought under large scale cotton cultivation to provide raw material to the British textile industry during the cotton famine caused by the American civil war. Cash crop cultivation as part of colonial policy drew money lenders from Gujarat and Mewar to the Deccan, and new land tenure arrangements meant to suit high and uniform revenue generation eroded the security of landownership of the peasant and transferred ownership through debts to the small class of money lenders. The money lender, traditionally a part of the *jajmani* system of village interdependence, now became a powerful investment in the colonial policy of commercialisation of land and land use. When the American civil war ended, and cotton supplies from America were resumed, the prices of cotton fell in the Deccan, and peasants were instantly indebted and dispossessed of these lands. Their lands and houses passed into the hands of money lenders. Enraged, the peasants of Poona and Ahmednagar attacked the money lenders to recover these lands. For the peasant, the reality of exploitation was experienced through the money lenders. An outcome of economic vulnerabilities induced by global integration thus became a local economic conflict between peasants and money lenders, and since the peasants were Maratha and the money lenders were Gujarati and Marwari, the conflict also got an ethnic colour.

The recent communalisation of the Punjab problem seems to have a similar basis. The Green Revolution, a 'development' strategy for linking Third World agriculture into the global markets of fertilizers, pesticides and seeds, has generated severe economic vulnerabilities for both small and rich farmers in Punjab. The farming community in Punjab also happens to be Jat Sikh, and economic tension between the Centre

(Delhi) and Punjab farmers, and between farmers and traders has been ethnicised easily, first by the Centre, and later by the people of Punjab.

In May 1984, the farmers' agitation was at its height in Punjab. For a week, farmers *gheraoed* the Punjab Raj Bhawan—from May 10 to 18. By conservative estimates at any time more than 15-20 thousand farmers were present in Chandigarh during the *gherao*. Earlier, from May 1 to 7, the farmers had decided to boycott the grain markets to register their protest against the central government procurement policy. On 23rd May, 1984, Harchand Singh Longowal, the Akali Dal president, announced that the next phase of the agitation would include attempts to stop the sale of food grain to the Food Corporation of India. Since Punjab provides the bulk of the reserves of grain, which are used to sustain the government distribution system and thus keep prices down, a successful grain blockade implied a serious national crisis and would have given to Punjab a powerful bargaining tool for its demands for greater state autonomy. On 3rd June, Mrs Gandhi called out the army in Punjab and on 5th June the Golden Temple was attacked, which was for the Sikhs an attack on the Sikh faith and Sikh dignity and honour. After Operation BlueStar the Sikhs as a farming community has been forgotten; only Sikhs as a religious community remain in national consciousness. Nothing after that could be read without the 'communal' stamp on it. Thus in the resolution passed at the *Sarbat Khalsa* in April 1986, the Sikh extremists talked of the need to "defeat the communal *Brahmin-Bania* combine that controls the Delhi *Darbar*. This, according to the extremists, was the only way of "establishing hegemony of Sikhism in this country".

What began as economic demands and a recovery of ethical order was thus transformed in Punjab into a war between two hegemonic tendencies—one of the State, the other of the extremists. What began as a recovery for diversity, a search for economic security and cultural identity, has been forced to turn into ethnic chauvinism, embroiling ever lager numbers, ever larger regions into violence.

3. The third tendency by which development ethnicises and communalises conflicts is the role of the electoral politics in dividing up the development cake. Since ethnic groups have a collective nature that is valued by political parties interested in group support, ethnicity is made a pawn in electoral politics.[10] Since development has in general taken decision-making away from local communities into state and national capitals, communities became willing pawns as part of their survival strategy in the context of the centralisation of power that

---

10. See my "Communalism : The New Face of Democracy", op. cit. What follows here has been in large part drawn from the analysis in that paper.

accompanies the development process. The distancing of decisions from the people, the role of representational politics in offering a premise to cover that distancing, and the need to turn that premise into delivery of votes, combine together to fragment society and divide it along the boundaries of new and emergent identities.

With this the notion of party as an instrument of mass transformation gives place to one of party as a mechanical contrivance which keeps you in power. Once this happens, the idea of pluralism in democracy gets perverted into communalism by emphasising the numerical power of majorities *versus* minorities. In this sense those who argue that communalism is a direct child of secular politics are right. It is secular politics reduced of all normative content (which is how secularism is often conceived). Elections become ends in themselves, instruments of the *status quo* and of self-perpetuation rather than of change. In a number of Third World countries elections do take place but they take place essentially for perpetuating whosoever happens to be in power. In a sense this has also happened in the West, above all in the US and the UK. In all in these countries, elections have become a legitimising process for highly authoritarian politics. And in all of them what you are really getting, without always noticing it, is the substitution of a political process based on competition for programmes and policies, and a debate on those policies, by a mere numbers game.

Of course, the communal implications of the numbers game in a plural society are not immediately apparent. One still thinks of numbers in terms of caste, regions and so forth. And yet if you examine the matter carefully, the numbers game does seem to have given rise to an ethnic calculus and ultimately to communal politics. When you go to the constituency level, and you want to basically play this game, then everybody begins to say, if you want to win in this constituency you must solicit the support of this caste or that community. This is almost inevitable. Once competition based on issues of ideological consideration is eschewed, the numbers game essentially becomes an ethnic game.

Such an ethnic orientation of the numbers game has two prominent features. One is the rise of new political organisations that are sometimes blatantly and sometimes not so blatantly communal. This happens at the local level or starts at that level and then moves up. (In India, the Shiv Sena is a good example of this.) Secondly, there takes place a capture of specifically political organisations like parties by cultural and sectarian organisations. What started as non-political organisations take on a political role. Such organisations declare that they have nothing to do with politics but they go on spreading their tentacles. So that in course of time political organisations like parties and trade unions and professional associations like those of students and teachers become increasingly dependent on sectarian and communal organisations which are not supposed to be political.

This particular brand of communal politics has far-reaching consequences. For it begins to affect the hitherto unaffected areas, e.g., the working class, the students, the youth generally. We know from the reports of various communal 'riots' that a lot of participants in these riots tend to be rather young, people who have had no experience of earlier divides, e.g., the partition of India in 1947, and of the kind of prejudices or hurt feelings that their parents nursed. It is participation that is largely apolitical. And it spreads in both time and space. These riots go on for weeks and sometimes for months, they recur after having stopped and they stop only to regroup and start again. Unlike in earlier times they begin to permeate the rural areas. They affect the press and the larger climate of opinion. And they affect the law and order establishment—the police and the paramilitary forces. As all this happens the State itself gets ready to coopt the ethnic upsurge and forces the latter into new polarities and hostilities which it makes full use of. What started as a challenge to the State and its modernist project gets absorbed by it, and the promise of its creative and regenerative potential gets destroyed.

Ethnicity as a Movement

This is a good point to return to where I started, viz., a consideration of the ambivalent nature of the concept of ethnicity, in particular under conditions where both the modern nation-state and its project of 'development' are ceasing to provide a framework for social transformation and instead are being used by narrow interests to distort priorities and definitions of collective goals. Three different strains can be identified in the evolution of ethnicity as both a political and an intellectual movement. There is, first, the more genuine assertion of human diversity against the homogenising thrust of the modern State, modern capitalism and modern technology—together conceptualised earlier in this paper as the 'modern project'. This takes the form both of countering recent tendencies and of recovering lost spaces before their powerful onslaughts, as well as freshly conceiving human arrangements and their cultural, ecological and gender underpinnings.

There is, second, the opposite tendency among the opponents of the 'modern project', of a monotheistic, militarist and messianic type. This is found, for instance, in the effort of Ayatollah Khomeini and his 'Iranian Revolution' to glorify the Shiite version of Islam and with it of both the Iranian State and the *Imam* himself. Or in Pakistan's version of the

Islamic State and the effort to endow religious significance to hegemonical concepts of a secular variety emanating from Saudi Arabia and
some other Gulf countries—such as the Islamic bomb, the Islamic
Summit and the Islamic mission of world conquest. But it is also found
in a number of other seemingly religious projects of a hegemonical and
militarist kind that are in reality essentially secular and statist—in the
dominant conceptions of Hindu militants, Sinhala nationalists and the
Bhoomiputrist Malays.

There is, third, an even more clearly 'secular' distortion and exploitation of ethnic and 'communal' identities by governments, dominant
political parties and ascendant new formations of a party kind. These are
out to capture or retain State power by moving away from socio-
economic and political issues and focussing public attention and emo-
tions on communal claims and counter-claims, fomenting a scenario of
conflict and violence and thinking of both the collective 'self' and the
collective 'other' in exclusivist and antagonistic terms.

The crucial test of ethnicity as a civilisational process, as providing
a creative basis for organising civil society and bringing into its arena
the real stirrings of the human spirit, lies in affirming the vision underlying the first of these tendencies at the exclusion of the other two.

There is a further test. So far this more enduring and ennobling, as
well as more imaginative and historically more significant, tendency
has been limited to micro spaces—often quite large but still micro and
local and limited. How to expand these towards more macro crystal-
lisations? How to at least instil in the present macro structures the new
perspectives gained from experiences in alternative institution-building
at the grassroots and in the new social movements for a more truly
democratic political culture that was at once indigenous and inclusive
of various diversities? How, above all, to inform prevailing States and
the State system with the new agenda of preserving diversities, sus-
taining life support systems and building complementarities, mutual
nurturance and holistic vision?

The future of ethnicity as an effort at reconstructing the human endeavour towards both a more just and a more humane order will depend
on meeting these two crucial tests.

The Restructuring of Civil Society

Ethnicity, when negativised, is at the root of much of the contemporary social violence which in extreme cases turns into ethnocide. But
ethnicity as a creative and regenerative force is also the opening to a
humane future. As a response to the universalising and atomising view
of nature and society that the project of modernisation is based on, eth-

nicity opens new spaces, in thought and in practice, for diversity and community as a basis for organisation.

In one way or another, the insecurities that underlie the many dimensions of ethnic conflict arise from the breakdown of the social order and of community. The State, the market, the development process, are all instruments of reducing identities to isolated 'selfs' in competition with others. The individual is made the centre of social space. There is no conception of the collective as a whole except as a collection of individuals. The erosion of security that this collapse of community leads to is now being expressed everywhere through ethnic and communal regroupings, oftentimes expressed in negativised, other-annihilating forms, but sometimes also expressed as sources of both recovery of a lost sense of community and assertion of new and revitalised forms, in which the individual's position and dignity in social space is defined by a creative intervention in community affairs. The regeneration of community, not as a collection of isolated individuals but as interactive structures both internally and *vis-a-vis* each other, can become an important source of transformation by becoming the basis of collective reconstruction of the 'whole'. It can become the source of alternative people's security, where people derive protection not from a militarised State but through the creation of structures of mutual nurturance and protection within and across community spaces. Self-interest can then be perceived to lie in the larger social interest, in the welfare of a relational complex. Redefining the individual's roles and positions in community spaces can provide alternative sources of security and democratic participation in which the individual good derives its authenticity from a common good, and individual freedom is seen as freedom for all, not freedom at the cost of others.

The European concepts of society, State, and democracy conceptualise the self as autonomous, individualistic, self-interested, egoistic, fundamentally isolated from others and threatened by these others unless the others are dominated and subjugated by the self—or by a transcendent entity like a centralised State that is then dominated by a few selves in the name of all. In this personal security involves generating insecurity in others. Freedom and democracy for the self involves violation of the freedom and democratic rights of others. Ethnicity can provide, together with social movements and citizens' actions, a different ground for security and democracy which through the new collectivities of civil society are able to translate into real security and democracy for all, including the most excluded, oppressed and marginalised. It is only through a clear and coherent identification with the new social consciousness being thrown up by social movements that ethnicity can regenerate and recover spaces in civil society. Without such a new thrust of common identity, even the new consciousness of an ethnic variety will generate new universalising and militaristic tendencies which, by insisting on excluding others, will destroy civil society even as they fight the existing State system. Fundamentalism and terrorism are modelled too much on the systems they fight to be real challenges to them—the former through its excessive universalisation of particular cultures and the resultant threat to other cultures, the latter through its excessive dependence on the culture of violence.

The second reason why ethnicity needs to be linked to other movements—the human rights movements, the survival movements, the movements based on identities of class and gender, the ecology movement, the literary and spiritual movements for self-respect and self-determination of subjugated peoples, the peace movements—is that without such links it faces the danger of itself becoming negativised by implicitly accepting the 'otherness' of the subjugated self and reinforcing the excluding paradigm that has been so useful in projects of domination. It will also fail to take realistic account of certain new situations (some of which are irreversible) that have already occurred under the impacts of the age of modern science and technology and the modern secular State and thus speak and act from a dead or disappearing ground of options.

On the other hand, social movements that address themselves to issues of equity and justice also need to be informed by ethnicity. This is because without locating themselves in the struggle for collective identities and the search for community, these movements can themselves become new sources of fragmentation and erosion of security. Movements of human rights, for instance, often adopt the atomising tendencies of the modern western worldview and reduce rights and responsibilities to the individual level, thus inadvertently eroding the social moorings and security of the weak and the already marginalised strata of society. Without ethnicity, social movements fail to address themselves to the issue of rebuilding the community as a basic political instrument for curbing the power and greed of dominant groups and individuals. The positive promise of ethnicity lies not in a 'return to the tribe' or the mere 'revival' of a particular culture. That, quite clearly, is not even possible. It lies, instead, in the building of a social order which celebrates diversity and organic unity, and is organised around principles of equity, justice, peace and dignity as the new social movements are redefining these concepts in a new framework of social context and intellectual search.

The basic search in all this is to open up civil space for the 'citizen' who happens to be living in a plural society but whose basic identities of a primary and secondary kind are in danger of being at once swamped and done away with. They are being swamped by the demands of an all-encroaching State, of a Market that reduces all needs to standarised 'commodities' and an information order that superimposes a 'universal' culture over diverse national and sub-national cultures. They are being done away with by the permeation of modern technology into not just economic but also broader social spaces and modes of communications, interpersonal interactions and even intimate arenas of friendship, love and conviviality. In the public sphere the technocratic State both dominates and abrogates the democratic process by reducing and delegitimising the arena of politics; its basic design is to close rather than open up civil spaces. This is then responded to by negativist identities of a 'communal' kind that exclude others and in their own way insist on new homogenisations and monotheistic drives, and further close up spaces for the ordinary citizen. In turn, as we have already seen, such communal appeals are utilised and exploited by the technocratic elite that turns chauvinist and militarist.

Genuine ethnicity if it is to be humane and rooted in the richness of human diversity must be seen as an answer to all these tendencies. It is to be seen as an answer to the centralising State, to the techno-managerial model of the economy, to the hegemony of the Market and to the inane vulgarity of the mass media and the ad agencies. It is to be seen as countering the continuous contractions, negations and closings in that the technocratic vision of the modern State and market necessarily involves. And it is to do this by positing the opposite of this—a continuous expansion, affirmation and opening up of civil spaces. Finally, it is to do this by not counterposing culture and community against the State, as has so often happened in the negativist and reactive expressions of ethnicity. Rather, it must call for transcending narrow communal and exclusivist modes, exercising self-control and civilised restraints on oneself and one's kith and kin and, on the basis of such understanding, transforming the full scale and scope of the State by making it a mechanism of democratic and decentralised participation. Once this happens, we will be able to transmute the whole sphere of public discourse and process of resolving conflicts with a new spirit and framework of goverance. Of humane governance in which everyone is involved and through which a new coherence and a new togetherness is sought to be achieved in and through the very diversities and multiple identities that give to each and every one a sense of pride, dignity and belonging.

Celebration of Diversity

I shall conclude this essay by conceiving ethnicity as a call for celebrating diversity instead of either undermining it under some abstract 'universalist' logic or using it for fomenting negativist reactions to existing hegemonies which can only engender new forms of homogenisation and exclusion. Diversity is not to be seen as a 'problem' to be managed but a resource to build upon, a basic resource emanating from the very nature of both human and natural orders. Diversity happens to be the essential 'nature of nature'; it also happens to be the essential characteristic of culture throughout human history. The same is the case with any lasting and self-sustaining polity: hence the worldwide preference—and movements—for decentralisation of political systems. These movements for decentralisation have gradually been moving out of mere devolution of powers and authorities from national centres lower down within the governmental apparatus into arrangements in which myriad spaces within the social order are opened up and various communities provided scope for self-governance, identity and a pride of place within the larger human setting. Such a striving is aimed at achieving two simultaneous goals, as Gandhi continuously stressed: restoration of dignity to the individual and development of resilience to the social process. The two are closely interrelated: there can be no dignity for the individual if social resilience breaks down or gives way to a permanent state of tension and alienation. The western conceptions of freedom and dignity are based on a competitive and atomising ethos; it necessarily undermines diversity and emphasises 'freedom from' external constraints rather than 'freedom to' achieve one's own realisation in communion with that of others.

Conceived in this manner, diversity becomes an enduring and creative basis of unity and coherence in a world undergoing massive transformation as well as a world seeking peace and 'order' that are neither imposed nor passive but are rooted in justice and equity and the authenticity of diverse cultures and lifestyles.

Such a conception of unity and coherence is inherently democratic. It can sustain a process of change that does not lead to alienation, a system of justice that does not necessitate polarisation, a form of order that is non-oppressive and a framework of peace that becomes a condition of self-affirmation of both individuals and communities. It is in and through such a celebration of diversity that human conflicts— which will continue to exist so long as life exists—can become catalysts of democratic transformation.

Index

230

Rethinking Development

Liberation movements, 168
Lifestyle, 9
American, 110-11
Basic issues of, 54-55
Concept of alternative, 38
Conflicts over, 148
Quality of, 46
Linear Model of Growth, 78
Linton, Ralph, 81
Linz, Juan, 171, 173-74
Lohia, Ram Manohar, 86
Longowal, Harcharan Singh, 217
Lynd, 81

Mahbub-ul-Haq, 115
Malay, 192
Malik, Baljit, 196
Malthusianism, 112
Mao, 63, 139, 175
Political philosophy of, 63
Marx, Karl, 24, 63, 124, 134
Marxist revolution, 35
Marxist theology, 107, 121, 122,
127, 166
Mazrui, Ali, 175
Mead, Margaret, 81
Melanasian, 192
Mendez, Condido, 173-76
Michelena, Jose A. Silva, 165,
172, 173, 174, 176
Middle East, 180
Militarisation, 69, 104, 143, 148,
183
Military
Allies, 116
Establishments, 97
Technology, 143
Minimum Wage, 19, 88
Minorities, 195
Fundamentalism of, 196
Oppressed & discriminated,
196
Paranoia of, 195-96
Threat from, 195

Mitra, Ashok, 86
Modernisation, 88, 139, 148
Doctrine of, 48, 49, 166,
172-73, 176-77
Model of, 19
Modernity, 50
From tradition to, 121, 174
Monetarism, 66, 112
Moore, Barrington, Jr. 166, 172
Moynihan, Daniel Patrick, 110,
116
Mukherjee, Ramkrishna, 172
Multinational Corporations, 128
Activities of, 158
Rise of, 128-29
Myrdal, Gunnar, 124

Naoroji, Dadabhai, 125
Narveson, Jan, 116
National Income, 89
National integration, 78, 89, 175
Nation-building, 76
Theories of, 164, 166
Variation in State and, 170-76
European historical experience
in, 171-72, 176
Natural resources
Destruction of, 58
Pillage of, 67
Conflict over, 148
Equitable distribution of, 108,
109, 111, 114, 117
Non-renewable, 59
Pressure on, 115
Redistribution of, 38
Renewable, 59
Transfer of, 73, 132, 160
(See also Ecology, Environment)
Nature, approach to, 62-63
Nepal, 109
Non-alignment, 72
Non-violence, 19, 85, 88
North, Developed economy of,
4, 159